The Philosophical Traditions of India

An Appraisal

Raffaele Torella

INDICA

Original title: *Il pensiero dell'India. Un'introduzione.*
Roma, Carocci Editore, 2008.

Translated from Italian by Kenneth Frederick Hurry

Published in 2011 by
Indica Books
D 40 / 18 Godowlia
Varanasi - 221 001 (U.P.)
India
email: indicabooks@satyam.net.in
www.indicabooks.com

ISBN: 81-86569-96-0

Printed in India by First Impression, Noida (U.P.), India
09811224048, 09899578245

Contents

Part Two
Opponents of Brahmanic Culture: The Materialism of the Lokāyatas, Jainism and Buddhism

Foreword

At the end of last century, when the Istituto dell'Enciclopedia Italiana requested me to take on the scientific direction of the section devoted to India in their great *Storia della Scienza* — all ten of its splendid volumes now having been published, one after the other —, what helped me overcome my perplexity at such a heavy commitment was above all the idea of getting cultivated readers to know an India that was different from the usual *mystical* India, and so forth, to which they were accustomed.[1] On that occasion, I was also asked to write my own contribution on Indian thought, which, in line with the work itself, would primarily concern theories on reality, epistemology and logic. The challenge of presenting the thought of India — perhaps for the first time — abstracting as far as possible the religious and soteriological dimension — was far too exciting not to be accepted. This book is the result of that initial contribution, albeit of wider scope and more in depth.

The West's love story with India (in actual fact, reciprocated in a rather tepid manner) is over two thousand years old, fascination with India having started well before the campaigns of Alexander the Great. Since then the West has always made much of Indian 'wisdom', but has taken great care not to grant it even the smallest space in its histories of philosophy. Although 'most wise', Indians have never been admitted to the great halls of western philosophy, not even as auditors. Wise, ascetic, impersonal, deniers of the world, despisers of passions and emotions, Indians have enjoyed undoubted prestige in the imagination of the West[2] which, however, wholly

[1] On similar lines is the recent book *Passioni d'Oriente: Eros ed emozioni in India e in Tibet*, Torino, Einaudi 2007, edited by G. Boccali and the present author, aimed at refuting another mythical vision, that of an ataraxic and disembodied India.

[2] Equally schematic is another vision of India, oneirically parallel and antithetic, a land of boundless riches and lasciviousness, the India, that is, of mahārājas and the *Kāmasūtra*.

preoccupied in utilising them as a foil to its own identity, seems to have set aside quite early on any desire for real investigation of the meanders of this grand and enormously complex civilisation.

The aim of this work is to help readers approach the thought of India from inside, seeking to outline, first and foremost, the cultural parameters within which it arose and developed and within which it should be read, with the final aim of answering the crucial question as to whether India is entitled to belong to the general history of philosophy (the answer is clearly affirmative). It is not a manual, even though it does its best to present the greatest possible quantity of data. It also contains a not negligible dose of arbitrariness, shown for example in granting certain schools less space than they have traditionally enjoyed (e.g. Vedānta) and more space to others, or even including for the first time schools wrongly deemed marginal, such as the Pratyabhijñā. This, however, is not merely the personal taste of the author, matured over decades of frontier work exploring the manuscript tradition and philological-philosophical interpretation of the texts, but also reflects the desire to present to the reader what he/she particularly and presumably knows least: for example, the naturalism of the Vaiśeṣika system, or the linguistic and epistemological thought of Buddhism, rather than what is to be found in actual manuals (the Upaniṣads for example are barely mentioned, their relevance from any properly 'philosophic' perspective being fairly limited).

The size of the book itself has forced me to leave out both ethics and aesthetics. Although — all things considered — excluding the former was fairly easy, for the latter it was much more painful. The extraordinary level of India's poetic and aesthetic thought needs a separate volume — as would also its linguistic thought, to whose importance and originality I have however repeatedly made reference in this volume.

I shall conclude in Indian fashion, recalling with deep gratitude my forerunners in these studies: Raniero Gnoli, my *guru* and predecessor in the Chair of Sanskrit at Rome's 'Sapienza' University, and his own *guru* Giuseppe Tucci, a '*guru* of *gurus*'.

Rocca Priora, October 2010

neutri M.

An Indian Philosophy?

Is there any such thing as an Indian 'philosophy'? The various ways in which this question has been put over the centuries and the answers to it should, first and foremost, be seen as belonging to a variety of historic-cultural options. At the extremes we find assertions, on one side, of the radical difference between western and Indian civilisation (the latter often identified *tout court* with 'oriental' civilisation) and, on the other, of the substantial uniformity peculiar to the single, unvarying human nature that underlies merely superficially diversified forms of manifestation and speaks a timeless language to those who know how to question it. Significantly diverse, too, are the answers given in the western and Indian worlds respectively (historically, the question itself has, however, always been formulated in a western context).

In the main, western answers have been negative, marked in particular by the influential pronouncements of Hegel and Husserl, often directly or indirectly repeated. In apparent contradiction, this is accompanied by a generalised appreciation of Indian 'wisdom', widespread since the pre-Hellenistic period (cf. Karttunen 1989) and never since eclipsed in western culture and imagination. In his opening to *Lives and Opinions of Famous Philosophers*, Diogenes Laërtius states that even translating the term 'philosophy' into other (barbarian) languages is impossible.[1]

In outlining the requisites that philosophy must possess to be such, Husserl refers strictly to the Greek model, since in his opinion only the Greeks managed to develop pure theory. Philosophy (we read in *The Crisis of European Sciences and Transcendental Phenomenology*; cf. Mohanty 1992: 298) must be freed from practical

[1] I.4 "Thus, philosophy is a creation of the Greeks: its very name has nothing in common with a barbaric denomination."

interests and the philosopher must not be involved in mundane activities; it must be distinguished by its awareness of the hiatus that exists between the external world and its representation; it must seek universal truth; not be subject to any pre-established belief and must subject everything to critical examination. This Husserlian view of philosophy as pure theory is thus like Christianity's pure contemplation, as well as the purity of the physical sciences.

Prior to Husserl, Hegel had already reproached Indian thought for being unduly and inextricably mixed with practice, albeit in its most lofty dimension of seeking spiritual transformation and liberation. To this, he added other critical considerations, destined to have a long-lasting impact on western thought: Indian philosophies and religions deal with unity and substance and are incapable of appreciating the individual as a concrete being, whereas philosophy is interested in the content of unity, in the concreteness of the Absolute, in the subjectivity of substance, and in the actuality of autonomy. India is the land of 'dawns', but both 'auroral' and 'primordial' are for Hegel synonyms for 'unripe' and 'imperfect'. The spirit of the world goes from East to West and, in this fateful passage, the past (the East) is not to be contemplated-admired, but merely preserved-surpassed (Halbfass 1973: 109). Hegel's opinion changed considerably starting with his 1825-26 *Lectures*, when the first news and translations of Sāṃkhya and Nyāya texts began to circulate in Europe, due particularly to the pioneering work of Colebrooke, but the resonance of his partial change of attitude was not as strong as his earlier slating.

These presumed deficiencies, however, are proudly assumed to be the peculiar merits of Indian culture as a whole by the most significant and influential of Indian answers to our opening question. Followers of Neo-Hinduism state that the Indian equivalent of 'philosophy' is *darśana* (literally 'view'). The vast semantic field covered by this word contains, on the one hand, a strong emphasis on direct, personal experience — the antithesis of the abstract, if not bookish nature of western 'philosophy'. This is accompanied by a total involvement of the thinker, who here is not limited to playing with more or less elegant and congruous constructions, but seeks to identify the route of his/ her entire adventure in the world, including it in the context — not only cognitive, but above all transformative — of the Absolute. In actual fact, however, such a reference should be taken with caution. While it is true that all the thought and religious experience of India insistently predicate the absolute necessity of direct experience, just as frequent are warnings aimed at solitary seekers and at 'wild' mysticism. The adept's experience, albeit essential, must follow a defined course, delimited by revealed scripture and his master's mediation. Direct vision and spiritual realisation are the prerogatives of primordial sages, such as the Vedic *ṛṣi*s.[2] They are the ones who have 'directly experienced' *dharma*,[3] and later traditional teaching draws its incontestable validity, or even its right to exist, solely from this direct primordial vision.[4] Controlling experience is one of the principal tasks of tradition, which, however, as allowed by Abhinavagupta in the *Tantrāloka* ('Light of the Tantras'; IV.40cd-42ab, XIII.134cd), does not deny the possibility of a 'spontaneous' (*sāṃsiddhika*) or autogenous (*svayambhū*) master, capable of entering into unison with the Absolute without the support of — or even against — all traditional teaching. The existence of

---

[2] See below (pp. 96-100) the related question concerning *yogipratyakṣa*, 'perception of the yogin'.

[3] The formula appears for the first time in the *Nirukta* by Yāska (I.6.20): *sākṣātkṛtadharmāṇa ṛṣayo babhūvuḥ*, "the seers (*ṛṣi*s) are those who have had direct experience of *dharma*". To them belongs the task of transmitting the Vedic mantras to others, i.e. to all those that do not possess this gift of direct vision. The *Nirukta* formulation is later repeated and adapted to different contexts (Seyfort Ruegg 1994: 307-308). The meaning of *dharma* in the above phrase has been much debated (see lastly Aklujkar 2009).

[4] Cf., for example, in Appendix II, p. 211 the comment of Abhinavagupta: "the author, precisely because he has personally known what was to be known, deems he is qualified to compose a text for others. If this were not so, such a work [the *Īśvarapratyabhijñā-kārikā*] would be a mere deception". The centrality of this requirement as guarantee of a master's reliability is also affirmed in the commentary of Pakṣilasvāmin on *Nyāyasūtra* I.1.7. More generally speaking, the relationship between *śruti* ('revelation') and *smṛti* ('tradition') may be assimilated to the relationship found in classical Indian epistemology between direct perception and inference: the latter is 'guaranteed' by the former (cf. Pollock 1997: 404-412).

such a 'perfect' man, however, a man whose glance would suffice for instantaneous liberation (*Tantrāloka* III.40), is presented as so exceptional and so improbable as to give the impression of being a mere theoretical possibility, an extreme case conceived as a relief valve to avoid any risk of implosion of the overly-controlled structure of tradition. Moreover, although the *Kiraṇa-tantra* ('Tantra of the Rays') considers that, of the three possible forms of knowledge — deriving respectively from the master, from scriptures, and spontaneously — the last is by far the highest (*vidyāpāda*, IX.14ab),[5] most texts go on to warn against entrusting oneself to a master who embodies this kind of knowledge (i.e. the 'spontaneous' or 'autogenous' master) and, after all, recommend a 'normal' master (cf. *Tantrāloka* XXIII.7-10).

This claim by neo-Hinduism concerning the central role of direct experience in the Indian concept of philosophy, albeit laden with significance as regards its grounds as an answer to normative western claims, is based on a very strained reinterpretation of the term *darśana*, to which are attributed a general prominence and connotations substantially unknown in classical and medieval India. The term recurs in an increasingly regular fashion in classical philosophical historiography — or, rather, doxography — starting from the *Ṣaḍdarśanasamuccaya* ('Summa of the six *darśana*s') by Haribhadra (eighth century C.E.) and culminating in the celebrated *Sarvadarśanasaṃgraha* ('Compendium of all the *darśana*s') by Mādhava-Vidyāraṇya (fourteenth century C.E.), from which the West

[5] The same well-known passage of the *Kiraṇa-tantra* is also invoked at the end of Utpaladeva's *Īśvarapratyabhijñā-vivṛti*, a capital text of Tantric thought, now almost wholly lost (except for a single significant fragment I have recently published and translated: cf. Torella, 2007a, 2007b, 2007c, 2007d), but known to us indirectly through the sub-commentary (*vimarśinī*) by Abhinavagupta. The interpretation of the two great kāśmīri masters (*Īśvarapratyabhijñā-vivṛtivimarśinī*, vol. III, p. 401) is here however completely different from the one given above: *svataḥ* ('spontaneously, independently') does not signify the irresistible emergence of intuition from the depths of individual consciousness, but the progressive articulation and rational demonstration of the truth, beyond any participation of the master's and of revealed scripture.

drew its first systematic notions about Indian thought. Here, *darśana* means 'world view', in other words the coherent presentation of a body of theories mainly concerning the nature of the real and the conditions of knowing it, integrated by concepts of an ethical-religious nature (instructions on ways of liberation, union with God, etc.). These latter concepts, however, occasionally betray the fact that they are a later or artificial addition to a pre-existing corpus, in itself unitary and coherent. At the most, in its meaning of '(philosophic-religious) system' rather than 'philosophy' — moreover with a diffusion largely restricted to doxography — *darśana* cohabits with near synonyms such as *naya* 'principle, method, procedure [partisan, dogmatic]' (especially in a Jain context; see below), *vāda* ('doctrine', 'debate'), *mata* ('opinion, idea, conception'), *dṛṣṭi* ('view, concept'), the last-mentioned occurring frequently in Buddhist texts and almost exclusively with the negative connotation of unilateral and potentially self-contradictory concepts. With the permission of the neo-Hindus, therefore, the Indian equivalent of 'philosophy' is not to be found in the term *darśana*, since, first and foremost, those connotations of the immediacy of personal experience and the all-inclusiveness they wished to attribute are alien to it. On the contrary, one may frequently come across a connotation that is the exact opposite, as when a discussion that does not manage to rise to a wider and more involving level, but stagnates within expected or over-defined parameters, is termed *dārśanika* (the adjective deriving from *darśana*), in which case a more appropriate translation would seem to be 'scholastic'.

As the Indian equivalent of 'philosophy', the term *ānvīkṣikī* has enjoyed a certain popularity, the first to call attention to it being H. Jacobi.[6] The term in question is a feminine adjective — referring to *vidyā* 'science, knowledge' underpinned — with the meaning of 'investigative [science]' from the root *īkṣ-* 'to observe', preceded by the preverb *anu-*. Here, *anu-* may add the connotation of 'posteriority, ulteriority' (as compared to the presentation of an immediate fact),

---

[6] On *ānvīkṣikī*, see Jacobi 1929, Hacker 1958, Halbfass 1990: 273-279, Cardona 2007: 694.

as also of 'prolonged and intense application'. The *locus classicus* is found in the initial section of the *Arthaśāstra* ('Treatise on the Useful') by Kauṭilya (traditionally dated to the fourth-third century B.C.E., but in reality its dating is fairly problematic), which lists the four basic sciences:

> The sciences are: *ānvīkṣikī*, the three Vedas, economic activities (*vārttā*) and good governance (*daṇḍanīti*). [...] A science (*vidyā*) is so-called because thanks to it what is right (*dharma*) and useful (*artha*) is known. *Ānvīkṣikī* is that science that assists mankind in that it investigates, seeking the grounds, what is right or wrong in the Vedas, useful or useless in economic activities, proper or improper in governing and what, generally speaking, is the strength or weakness of these sciences. (pp. 12-13)

"*Ānvīkṣikī*", concludes Kauṭilya (ibid.), "has always been the torch that illuminates all the sciences, the means of all action, the basis of all religious rules". From this and the few other passages in which the term occurs, it is sufficiently clear that, rather than the Western 'philosophy' or any other definite discipline, *ānvīkṣikī* indicates a wider critical and investigative attitude that perennially tests the validity of the rules regulating human activities, extending even to what is taken as the final basis of all rules, i.e. the Veda itself (hence the reservations put forward in the *Rāmāyaṇa*, which warns against its potentially subversive nature vis-à-vis traditional knowledge).[7] The limited diffusion of the term itself [8] is indicative of its lack of general significance, making it incomparable with that of 'philosophy'. *Ānvīkṣikī* soon stops embodying this sort of unlimited yearning for critical examination and continual calling into question and undergoes a double pensioning off: on one side, we see it included in many of the traditional lists of 'loci of knowledge' (*vidyāsthāna*)

---

[7] "Those so-called sages that look at all the existing scriptures of the *dharma* assuming an 'investigative' frame of mind (*buddhim ānvīkṣikīṃ prāpya*) debate pointlessly..." (*Rāmāyaṇa*, II.94.33cd).

[8] Cf. for example *Nyāyabhāṣya* pp. 2-6, *Nyāyamañjarī* vol. I, p. 9.

— such as in the *Kāvyamīmāṃsā* ('Investigation on ornate poetry') by Rājaśekhara (ninth-tenth centuries C.E.), which ranks it beside archery or music —, while on the other it meets one of the traditional *darśana*s, Nyāya, which it will declare its only legitimate heir, transforming it from an ever-reviving critical impulse to an 'orthodox' and highly formalised system. The same can substantially be said of the term *parīkṣaka*, which some have seen as the Indian equivalent of 'philosopher'. *Parīkṣaka* is more properly a 'shrewd investigator' (Wezler 1990), one who questions things instead of accepting them as they seem to be, as does the man-in-the-street (*loka*). In actual fact, a Sanskrit term does exist, which in structure and meaning is very close to our 'philosophy', although up to now scant attention has been paid to it: *tattvajñānaiṣaṇā*, 'the desire to know true reality', a term found only rarely however.[9] *Tattvajñānaiṣaṇā* can be linked to several better-known terms — which may be its hidden matrix — such as *dharmajijñāsā* ('the desire to know *dharma*') or *brahma-jijñāsā* ('the desire to know *brahman*'), which appear respectively at the beginning of the *Mīmāṃsā-sūtra* and the *Vedānta-sūtra*.

To the question we asked to begin with, we can draft a preliminary answer. Although it is effectively true that there is no Indian equivalent for 'philosophy', there are however thousands of authors and texts that over twenty-five centuries have asked questions — in their own way and in their own context — about the nature of the ego and of the universe, about epistemology, language, logic, etc.[10] Rather than imposing a univocal model — inapplicable moreover to western thought itself, taken as a whole — it is best to identify the parameters within which such speculations operate and assess their range, starting with the very elements that have appeared most alien to Western critics.

It is undeniable that 'pure' theory does not exist in Indian thought. No Indian thinker would, with Aristotle, affirm that the impulse to

---

[9] It is used, as far as I know, only by the Buddhist Bhavya (or Bhāviveka) in his *Madhyamakahṛdaya* 'Heart of the Middle Way' (I.5c and III.1d).

[10] J. Bronkhorst sees the birth of systematic philosophy in India in the works of the Buddhist Sarvāstivādins (see below pp. 139-144), possibly under the influence of the Indo-Greeks, who lived side by side with them in Bactria and Gandhara.

know is a primary and universal fact of mankind. In India, this primacy tends to be assigned to the search for pleasure or happiness (*sukha*; see Torella 2007 e, f). When, following common practice, the author provides information for the potential reader or listener at the beginning of a work — first and foremost regarding his own credentials (*adhikāra*) —, he usually also dwells on his *prayojana*, a complex word that expresses both his motivation and his intent. This is followed, as a rule, by a presentation of the *prayojana-prayojana*, the 'motive of the motive', which inevitably includes the thinker's activity in an ethical-religious context: the maintenance of *dharma* or search for final liberation. Recent studies (*in primis* Steinkellner 1989, Eltschinger 2010b) have rightly highlighted this component even in the speculation of the logical-epistemological schools of medieval Buddhism which, more than most, might appear to have distanced themselves from all soteriological or devotional preoccupations.

Indian philosophical thought is also blamed for lacking any personal impulse, any search for truth without some kind of preestablished directions. In actual fact, it is undeniable that the Indian philosopher gives the impression of being already 'born' a *vedāntin* or *sāṃkhya* and that his acceptance of one world view or another is merely the natural development of his belonging by family or culture to a certain milieu. This impression is bolstered by the almost total lack of private testimony: the Indian thinker does not confess his thoughts to his diary, does not keep any kind of notepad, and does not write letters.[11] The westerner, used to following step-by-step his philosopher's hesitancies, enthusiasms and changes of direction, is legitimately perplexed by the virtual absence of conversion in India, whether philosophical or religious, with the exception of those all-too-numerous ones described in edifying biographies. Here, indeed, we find throngs of faithful passing from one religion to another, or prominent philosophers suddenly acknowledging their blindness on impact with

[11] The exception represented by the edifying letters written to sovereigns or disciples by the Buddhist philosophers Nāgārjuna, Mātṛceta and Candragomin is only apparent, constituting a mere literary topos (cf. Dietz 1984; Hahn 1999).

the character that the 'biography' aims to extol. When we examine the facts, however, i.e. the works that the philosophers have left us and the centuries-old debates to which they have given rise, we realise that whoever is born — for example — a *naiyāyika*, dies a *naiyāyika*. The two shining exceptions that, until a short while ago, I could have cited, have been reduced by recent studies to just one, and that not without ambiguities and suspect legend-making manipulations: I refer to the case of Maṇḍana Miśra (eighth century), with his intellectual peregrinations between the Pūrvamīmāṃsā and the Vedānta. The second case could have been that of an illustrious kāśmīri author of the tenth century, Śaṅkaranandana, the 'great brahmin' of Tibetan sources, his conversion being assumed from Buddhism to Śaivism, or viceversa, comforted by the fact that his works, even those with a general Buddhist flavour, were cited not only with profound respect but at times even with approval by the illustrious *śaiva* master Abhinavagupta.[12] A case apart, unique in the Indian context, is that of the great polygraph, already mentioned, Vācaspati Miśra. Vācaspati is the author of commentaries, all of great importance, on the principal classical *darśana*s, and gives the impression, on each occasion, of accepting each one.[13] Well-deserved is the appellation by which he was known for centuries: *sarvatantrasvatantra*, 'at ease among all systems'.[14]

[12] However, if my reading of a crucial and much-debated passage of the *Īśvarapratyabhijñā-vivṛtivimarśinī* ('Considerations on the long commentary to the Verses of Recognition of the Lord') by Abhinavagupta (vol. II, p. 299) is correct, Śaṅkaranandana is not appreciated by the Śaivas as a result of his conversion from Buddhism to Śaivism, but because, although a Buddhist, specifically *śaiva* motifs emerge from his works, the subliminal heritage of being born into a family that had been *śaiva* for centuries. V. Eltschinger's current research on the Sanskrit manuscripts of Śaṅkaranandana's works that have recently come to light in China shows that he was the author of Buddhist works only (furthermore, it is anything but rare for a Buddhist author to come from a brahmin family).

[13] It is interesting to note that, in commenting on the *mīmāṃsaka Vidhiviveka* he fiercely criticizes any possibility of a special power of insight in the yogin, while in commenting on *Yogasūtra* and *Bhāṣya* he takes it for granted.

[14] One is tempted to replace this translation with the other theoretically possible: 'independent of all systems'. Also endowed with this qualification a few centuries later is another famous polygraph, the *vedāntin* philosopher Vedāntadeśika (cf. Hardy 1979: 277).

Vācaspati thus represents an isolated case of an independent philosopher, taking sides against Buddhism in an intelligent defence of the Brahmanic world. His non-acceptance of any one system in particular should not be understood in a Mozartian fashion ("*L'uno val l'altro, perché nessun val nulla*", i.e. "One is as good as the other, because none is any good"), but rather as an implicit admission of the substantial unitariness of the Brahmanic river in which the currents of the single systems run. This is therefore considered more significant than the great disparity — and often irremediable doctrinal contrast — that opposes, for example, the realism and pluralism of the Nyāya-Vaiśeṣika against the absolutism of the Vedānta, or the radical dualism and evolutionism of the Sāṃkhya against the absolute non-dualism and 'illusionism' of the Vedānta, or else the timeless gaze of the Vaiśeṣika against the incessant spatial-temporal mobility of the Sāṃkhya, and so on and so forth.

Thus, in operating within the tradition in which he is 'born', the prevailing attitude of the Indian thinker may well be represented by the famous preamble of the *Nyāyamañjarī* ('Bunch of flowers of logic'), by the kāśmīri Jayanta Bhaṭṭa (ninth century C.E.):

> This subtle fragrance is extracted from the forest of herbs of the Nyāya system; it is extracted from the investigating science (*ānvīkṣikī*) like butter from milk. How could I be capable of devising something new? At the most, it is permissible to aspire to some novelty in presentation...[15]

Contrary examples of thinkers who state their own unicity with pride, sometimes veined with feverish bitterness, do exist, but are extremely rare: one might recall the Buddhist epistemologist Dharmakīrti (seventh century C.E.),[16] the materialist Jayarāśi (seventh

---

[15] *Nyāyamañjarī*, vol. I, p. 5, vv. I.7-8. It should be said that, as it appears to our eyes (and as it appeared to the eyes of contemporaries), the *Nyāyamañjari* is anything but a work of clever cosmetic art: it is one of the most penetrating and innovative works in the whole of Indian thought.

[16] All Dharmakīrti's works betray the haughtiness of someone convinced of indubitable intellectual superiority. The two verses found at the end and beginning respectively of his *magnum opus*, the *Pramāṇavārttika* ('Gloss on the means of correct

century C.E.), the neo-logician Raghunātha Śiromaṇi (sixteenth century C.E.).[17] The discipline of logic, like any other discipline, or more generally any structured form of human activity, must be based on timeless teaching, given once for all at the outset of each cosmic age and taking the form of a text or body of texts (*śāstra*). In the *śāstra*, everything is already present (cf. Pollock 1985); what is new must already be contained in parts of it that have not (or not yet) come down to us. Innovating means widening one's awareness to

---

cognition'; recognised as being authentic in the Miyasaka edition, as well as being attributed to him by Indo-Tibetan tradition), are the most eloquent testimony to it: I.2: "Mankind is attached to what is dull and vulgar and does not care about refinement. Not only are they disinterested in profound sayings, but in addition are swollen with pride and marred by envy. Consequently neither do I care to offer my work for their benefit. If I have composed it, it is only because in it I find my satisfaction, since my love for long and deep meditation on words well-spoken has been gratified by it." IV.286: "My work will find none in this world capable of grasping its profound sayings. It will be absorbed in my person and with it will perish, just as a river vanishes into the ocean. Even those endowed with a not negligible intellectual perspicacity will be unable to plumb its depths. But not even those endowed with the most exceptional intellectual perspicacity, not even they will be able to grasp its ultimate meaning" (cf. Stcherbatsky 1930-32: vol. I, pp. 35-6).

[17] Of the proud and troubled Raghunātha the compilations of his followers narrate many anecdotes. One of the many recounts that, as a student, Raghunātha expounded in public his reservations on a theory maintained by his master Pakṣadhara, the *sāmānyalakṣaṇāpratyāsatti* — or the indirect connection of the sensory organs with the universal by means of their direct connection with the concrete and specific individualization of the universal — and that Pakṣadhara had cruelly mocked him in front of everyone. That same night Raghunātha, grasping a sword, made his way to his master's house, decided to obtain acknowledgement of his own superiority or to kill him. The master was saved only because Raghunātha, already lying in wait in the dark, heard him say to his aged wife, while together they contemplated the heavens illuminated by a splendid moon, that that day a yet more splendid moon — that of Raghunātha — had risen in the heaven of the Nyāya... His main works, such as the *Tattvacintāmaṇi-dīdhiti* ('Ray of light that illuminates [or: comes from] the Gem of the Desires of True Nature' [of the means of knowledge, the work by Gaṅgeśa; see below]) or the *Padārthatattvanirūpaṇa* ('Description of the true nature of categories'), abound in persistent claims of his own excellence and originality: "Whatever the sages of the past have agreed in deeming right or wrong", one reads in his commentary on the capital work by Gaṅgeśa mentioned above, "will all be open to question now that I am speaking" (cf. Ingalls 1988: 9-14).

include what in reality has never begun or ceased to be. This is why, says Vācaspati Miśra at the beginning of his commentary on the *Yogasūtra* ('Aphorisms on Yoga'), two treatises like the *Yogasūtra* and the *Aṣṭādhyāyī* ('Treatise in eight lessons'), so different in purpose but just as seminal in their respective dominions — Yoga and grammar —, start in the same way: *atha yogānuśāsanam* ('Here is the teaching of Yoga') and *atha śabdānuśāsanam* ('Here is the teaching of words'), both choosing, out of many possibilities, the particular term *anuśāsanam*. This term — whose current meaning is simply 'teaching' — should be interpreted, according to Vācaspati Miśra, in the pregnant sense of 'teaching' (*-śāsanam*) 'subsequent to', 'conforming to' (*anu-*), i.e. deriving from a totality of normative knowledge that precedes it and feeds it like an inexhaustible spring. According to two different orientations, which are however subtly complementary, the *śāstra* too has its own course: a virtually infinite and all-inclusive text that gradually fades away, shortened by some divine transmitter worried by the progressive decline in men's faculties, or else an originally brief and scintillating text that gradually becomes diluted, getting longer and more complex so as to offer a hold to those same declining faculties of those living in the calamitous times of the *kaliyuga* (the present age, the fourth and last of a series in progressive involution). So as to avoid becoming unseemingly mechanical, practice must be a direct or indirect emanation of the *śāstra*. If an action, a speculation, or a concept is 'right' without the *śāstra* having any part in it, this is not due to some impossible self-regulating power of the individual, but to his being imperceptibly penetrated, as it were drop by drop, by the *śāstra* with which his social life is somehow imbued. The borderline case of 'right' action truly without any root in the *śāstra* is not, owing to its exceptional nature, in any way significant: "It is like a letter of the alphabet that one may see cut into the bark of a tree", says Yaśodhara (thirteenth century C.E.) using this beautiful image in his commentary on the *Kāmasūtra* ('Aphorisms on Love'; the text providing rules for the erotic sphere!), "the unknowing fruit of the gnawing of termites" (cf. Pollock 1995). In all this, it is impossible not to perceive the complex and all-embracing strategy of social and cultural control operated by the Brahmanic class, a numerically insignificant élite mostly uninvolved directly in political or economic power, but with immense prestige, within which almost all this sapiential literature arises.

One of its effects is to obscure any diachronic perspective: in a certain sense, the new is always behind or by the side of the old, immersed in an eternal present. Of the old and the new, it is the old that is intrinsically more prestigious, and it is consequently very rare for any author or work to advocate their importance by laying claim to 'novelty'. For this to happen, with a certain frequency, we must wait until the seventeenth century (cf. Pollock 2001), when various disciplines felt the need of refounding themselves, or just believed that they had done so;[18] some centuries earlier, there was the isolated case of the new Nyāya (*navyanyāya*; see below), whereas now, more or less simultaneously, we find a new poetics and aesthetics (*navyālaṅkāraśāstra*; cf. Bronner 2002), a new Mīmāṃsā (McCrea 2002), a new Vyākaraṇa ('Grammar'), a new Dharmaśāstra.[19] Such dynamics can be clearly identified in the *vyākaraṇaśāstra*, the *śāstra* of grammar or, more widely, the sciences of language. Linguistic

[18] It is interesting to note that this 'novelty' is often no more than an invitation to return to the ancient founding texts, thanks to the rediscovery and re-meditation of which the discipline enjoys 'new' vigour; cf. for the Nyāya in the fifteenth century, Preisendanz 2005: 74; for the Mīmāṃsā, Pollock 2002: 434.

[19] This does not mean that previous authors (whom we would call 'classic', if such a concept were not so laden with ambiguity in the Indian context that it ends up being unusable) did not also use this concept, albeit in an evaluative context well exemplified in Utpaladeva's work the *Īśvarapratyabhijñā-kārikā* or °*sūtra* ('Verses on the recognition of the Lord'; first half of the tenth century C.E.). In closing this capital work of Śaiva Tantrism, Utpaladeva states, "By me a new and easy way has been elucidated in this work, just as it was expounded by my great master in the treatise called *Śivadṛṣṭi* ('Vision of Śiva') [...]". An explanation of how the epithet 'new' should be understood in qualifying a way of liberation that, as such, is assumed to be vouched for by atemporal revealed scriptures, is given by Abhinavagupta in his *Īśvarapratyabhijñā-vimarśinī* ('Considerations on the Verses on the recognition of the Lord'): "By 'new', we mean that this way, already contained in all the esoteric writings (*rahasyaśāstra*°), was not yet in the public domain by reason of its being hidden in them" (vol. II, p. 271).

investigation, albeit of remarkable penetration, has not established any temporal differentiation between the two main strata of the Sanskrit language — the Vedic and the so-called classical. Although this would have been the most obvious thing to do, even for a less perspicacious eye than that of an Indian linguist, the same effect is substantially obtained by placing them side-by-side in an eternal spatialised present, distinguishing only their fields of application (Vedic is not labelled as the language of the past, but as a specialised language for ritual purposes); cf. Deshpande 1993: 53-74. The passage of time is thus replaced by a synchronic stratification of 'presents'.[20]

[20] And it is precisely in the domain of the *vyākaraṇaśāstra* that we encounter a contradiction (merely apparent, I believe) to the above-mentioned principle: the criterion known as *uttarottaraprāmāṇya* '[gradually increasing] authoritativeness of the more recent over the more ancient', according to which, among the great triad of sages who founded the grammatical tradition — Pāṇini (fifth-fourth century B.C.E.), Kātyāyana (third century B.C.E.) and Patañjali (second century B.C.E.) — in the event of any doctrinal clash, the third must prevail over the second and first, and the second over the first. The question, linked to the possibility of recourse to current linguistic sensitivity and usage in the event of a clash of the rules of grammar, has recently been the subject of lively debate, the two protagonists being leading modern specialists of *vyākaraṇa* (Deshpande 2005, Aklujkar 2002-2003; see also Vergiani 2005), and is too complex to be dealt with here. I shall merely remark that the principle of the primacy of what is earlier seems valid only for scriptural texts or mythical or semi-mythical authors *ṛṣi* or *muni*, such as the authors of the *sūtra*s at the root of the various disciplines), whereas as a rule no difficulty is encountered in criticizing previous 'human' authors. The principle of *uttarottaraprāmāṇya* is valid solely in the case of this triad of grammarians and is not extended to any subsequent author (not even the great Bhartṛhari!). The explanation for this apparent inconsistency seems to be a double one. Firstly, medieval tradition attributes a semi-divine status to the three great grammarians responsible for the *vyākaraṇaśāstra*, which, from this point of view, places them on the same level: thus, they may be considered as successive moments of a progressive manifestation (or self-manifestation) of the primordial *śāstra*. The fact that the process of semi-deification ends with them can be related to the gradual fading of Sanskrit as a living language. Whereas up to Patañjali, grammatical rules can always be invalidated by recourse, in the last resort, to checking the spontaneous usage of the language by 'authorised' speakers, after him the criterion of correctness coincides with consistency with established grammatical rules. Grammatical tradition is henceforth divided into two sides: on the one, we find the 'divine' grammarians, defined as 'those whose eye is turned exclusively to the subject of the rules (i.e. language)' (*lakṣyaikacakṣuṣka*), while on the other, all subsequent grammarians have 'their eye turned exclusively to the rules' (*lakṣaṇaikacakṣuṣka*).

This apparent shrinking from innovation and need to place the centre of gravity as far back as possible so as to provide the whole with stability and endurance is already reflected in the form of the texts, and first and foremost philosophical texts. Starting from the example of the *darśana*s, the classical philosophical systems or world views (although the prototypes of the genre are to be sought in the science of the rite and grammar), we find at the outset a mostly self-referencing root-text, the work of an 'omniscient' sage, drafted in an extremely synthetic and often intentionally obscure form and purposely incomplete (*sūtra*). The *sūtra* attracts a remarkable number of commentaries, and commentaries on commentaries, belonging to precise genres, such as the *vṛtti,* the *vārttika*, the *bhāṣya*, the *ṭīkā*, each with its own characteristics and functions (see below pp. 173-175). This succession of commentaries, which may be dated several centuries later than the *sūtra*, provides a continual introduction of the new without ever explicitly disavowing the root-text, whose perennial validity is strongly affirmed, ignoring or pretending to ignore its progressive fading away. The Jains go still further: the *sūtra* is like the amorphous clay, destined to become a vase only after the industrious labour of the vase-maker/commentator (Dundas 1996a: 78). A different strategy prefers, rather than a sometimes over-arduous re-interpretation, a furtive recasting of the *śāstra*, as in the case described by Dagens (2002: 903-907) of the sections devoted to architecture in the śivaite Tantric scriptures. Once temple construction activities and styles change, according to the changing tastes of their royal patrons and artists, and the divergence between the prescriptive texts and the architectural reality becomes too accentuated, instead of seeking to halt the present, it is more realistically decided to modify the *śāstra* surreptitiously by no longer copying the obsolete chapter and replacing it with a new one that actually follows current reality while claiming to be its immovable foundation.

This, moreover, is the peculiar way in which India comes to terms with history, by means of its virtual negation. The fundamental role attributed to commentaries is distinctly felt by Indian civilisation as a whole. With a paradoxicality that becomes only apparent in the light of these considerations, we see the Jaina Śvetāmbaras ('Clothed in white') who, faced with a potential catastrophe that would completely destroy their scriptural canon, are more concerned with the loss of the commentaries than with that of the original scriptures (cf. Dundas 1996a: 83).

At the root of every *śāstra*, we find the *śāstra par excellence*, the Veda, a non-human revelation (it is *śruti*, 'hearing') on which all human activities are based: impersonal knowledge which, according to most 'orthodox' positions, is not even the work of a god (as claimed, for example, by the Nyāya), but is the direct manifestation of the Absolute in text form. Such conditioning of speculation by revelation has appeared fatal to western critics, traumatized by the clash of reason and faith that has accompanied so many centuries of European thought. In actual fact, in India, the relationship between philosophic speculation and revelation is much more fleeting and also strongly diversified. The most typical position is perhaps that of Kumārila (seventh century C.E.), precisely because the school to which he belongs, the Pūrvamīmāṃsā, or 'Ancient Exegesis', sets itself up as the first bastion of the Veda and the 'official' tool for its interpretation and utilisation. According to Kumārila — an upholder moreover of the absolute impersonality of the Veda, which has no author either human or divine —, the authority of revelation is absolute only in the sphere of *dharma* — meaning the religious universe. This, however, is limited to injunctions relating to the ritual sphere for which no other authoritative source is available, whose effects do not belong to the sphere of experience (*adṛṣṭārtha*). For whatever is *dṛṣṭārtha* ('with visible effect'), on the other hand, human intellect is the arbiter. The result is that, in the works of Indian philosophers, rarely does one see such an extensive and sophisticated use of rational argument as in this very champion of the Veda's authority, for which he is severely reprimanded by the most representative master of the rival-twin school, the Vedānta or Uttaramīmāṃsā ('Later Exegesis'), the almost contemporary Śaṅkara. The authority of the Veda, says

Śaṅkara, also extends to the content and processes of our knowing, for which it provides that substrate and necessity which they cannot provide by themselves. Revelation does not therefore concern only what man must 'do' — starting from the highest meaning of the term, ritual action — but also what he 'is', what is the nature of the universe, etc. Such teachings are dealt with particularly in the extreme segment of Vedic revelation, the Upaniṣads or *vedānta* ('end of the Veda'), which Kumārila on the other hand treats as mere illustrative digressions (*arthavāda*) as compared to the higher truth of the ritual injunctions (*vidhi*). For the individual, the means of valid cognition (*pramāṇa*) and, more widely speaking, his rational reasoning (*tarka*) are as it were self-referencing tools that continually risk leading into cul-de-sacs and producing, at the best of times, provisional truths destined to be undermined by a more informed subsequent use of the same tools. The great grammarian-philosopher Bhartṛhari (fifth century C.E.) formulated this principle once and for all in an oft-quoted verse from his *Vākyapadīya* ('On sentence and words'): "An object, with an effort defined according to a certain nature thanks to inferential reasoning by skilful reasoners, by others yet more skilled can be ascertained in a different way" (I. 34).

This concern that autonomous reasoning may end by triggering a delirium of omnipotence, or merely debase itself in the self-satisfaction of a technique aimed especially at wearing down opposing ideas (this is a frequent meaning of *tarka*)[21] is also common to currents foreign to Vedic revelation, such as Buddhism or Jainism. In traditional philosophical circles, the term *tarka* is frequently associated with the adjective *śuṣka* ('arid, dry, without juice'). This does not mean, however, as often repeated, a rejection of rationality *tout court*, since a kindred term — *yukti* ('congruity [of reasoning and interpretation], intelligibility, etc.') — which, like *tarka* belongs to the same broad semantic field as western 'reason', enjoys, on the other hand, almost universal appreciation. Recourse to Vedic revelation

[21] On the multiplicity of meanings of this important term in Indian philosophy, cf. Oberhammer, Prets, Prandstetter (1996, *s.v.*).

satisfies the need to provide a solid anchor for cognitive and speculative activity, a foundation outside itself. It is also in this less immediate sense that we can consider the so-called parable of the 'tenth man', recounted by Śaṅkara in the *Upadeśasāhasrī*, ('The thousand teachings'). Ten young men crossing a river on a raft are assailed by the doubt that one of them has been swallowed up by the waters, so one of them starts counting and does so several times with great care, each time reaching the number nine. From the consternation into which they all fall, they are freed by one who does not belong to the group and is crossing there by chance: from outside, it is easy for him to see that the young men effectively number ten and that the one counting, not out of lack of attention, but perhaps due to excessive involvement, had forgotten to count himself.[22] As confirmation of the complexity of the Indian cultural world and, generally speaking, its reluctance to accept overly coercive schematization, one encounters sporadic eulogies on the absence of rooting (*apratiṣṭhitatva*), seen as a stimulus to critical investigation and to a continual calling to question (Halbfass 1991: 147).

In actual fact, the nature and results of this stated dependence on Vedic revelation probably have much less impact than western critics may fear. This depends firstly on the nature of the Veda, which contains no definite and univocal doctrines, still less any definite dogmas, which makes its impact much less intrusive, even on the thought of those, like Śaṅkara, who although a decided minority in the body of Indian thinkers overall, tend to extend the prescriptive nature of the Veda to all human activities and not just to the sphere of *dharma*. The Veda is not a form of experience, but rather gives form to experience (Mohanty 1992: 282). Its plasticity gives rise to inexhaustible possibilities of re-interpretation, or of introducing new

[22] The fable is concisely recounted in the section in verse of the *Upadeśasāhasrī* (XII.3 and XVIII.172-176). The tenth man is none other than the common man, incapable by his own forces alone of perceiving his own identity with the *ātman-brahman*. The commentator Ānandagīri adds that only the teaching of revealed scriptures and of his master makes this radical act of self-recognition possible (p. 105, *śāstrācāryopadeśa*°).

matter, unlike that other great component of tradition, the *smṛtis*, 'memories', which are subordinate to the Veda and much more structured than it is, with a tendency toward rigidity. Rather than supplying content for cognitive experience, Vedic revelation provides it with a vast field of reference, which supports it without suffocating it.[23] Dependency on tradition is in any case itself subject to investigation, to problematisation by the same 'orthodox' philosophers, who as it were bring it into the open air, incessantly remodelling its range and meanings. It is also highly interesting to note that, despite the fact that whole branches of knowledge — such as grammar, with its great prestige as the model science — arise from a sacred environment and are strictly linked to the Veda, this does not in any way prevent their developing in wholly independent and 'secular' ways.

On the other hand, the western critic himself is increasingly aware that 'pure' theory, free from conditioning, which by contrast is claimed to characterise western thought, is in actual fact nourished and guided by unconscious paradigms, and inevitably conditioned by contexts and cultural models. Furthermore, as Popper has said on several occasions, human knowledge is distinguished by being always a gradual modification of previous knowledge.

Having stated these necessary premises, our presentation of the essential lines of Indian philosophy will partly follow the traditional model centred on the six classical Brahmanic systems (Nyāya, Vaiśeṣika, Sāṃkhya, Yoga, Mīmāṃsā and Vedānta) to which are added Pratyabhijñā (the school that constitutes the theoretical bases of non-dual Śaiva Tantrism), Lokāyata, Jainism, and Buddhism. The reduction of the systems to six appears already

[23] For centuries, India has debated whether or not the Veda has a 'meaning', seriously discussing the negative hypothesis formulated first by Kautsa (before the fifth century B.C.E.). It should also be borne in mind that, at the time of Yāska (fifth century B.C.E.), long lists (*nighaṇṭu*) were in circulation of words in the Veda that were already found incomprehensible by contemporaries. They form the basis of the capital work by Yāska, the *Nirukta*, deemed to be the root text of the science of etymology — or, rather, semantic analysis — '*nirukta*' in Sanskrit. On the totally different approach to revelation in the Kashmirian Śaivādvaita, see Torella forthcoming C.

well-grounded in the work of the first major doxographer, Haribhadra (eighth century C.E.) — although his list comprises Buddhism, Nyāya, Sāṃkhya, Jainism, Vaiśeṣika and Mīmāṃsā, with an appendix on Lokāyata materialism [24] — and was to become the most current, besides other works that tend to present more differentiated views, such as the *Sarvadarśanasaṃgraha*, describing as many as sixteen *darśana*s. In its doxographic presentation, each *darśana* appears as it were embalmed in a definitive form, unaccompanied by any reconstruction of its formation process. Despite the fairly considerable variety of positions, the followers of the single *darśana*s view themselves as belonging substantially to a common tradition,[25] which mostly includes in its widest sense both Jains and Buddhists, and even the universally vituperated Lokāyatas, the 'Materialists'.[26] Yet again we are surprised by Kumārila, the champion of the ultra-orthodox school specialising in the hermeneutics of the Veda, who shows an unexpected

---

[24] As a conclusion, Haribhadra proposes a set of six, which he achieves by incorporating Nyāya and Vaiśeṣika and adding the Lokāyatas ('Followers of worldly matters?') as the last. The absence of the Vedānta is worth noting, which, together with Yoga, seems to be counted among the *darśana*s relatively late on, and in any case not earlier than the thirteenth century (Gerschheimer 2007: 239). Although this is understandable for Yoga, which tends to be considered as a 'theist' version of Sāṃkhya (*seśvara-sāṃkhya*), the omission of Vedānta is less clear, since it is considered as a definite school of philosophy as early as the sixth century and was subjected to detailed critical analysis (*vedāntatattvaviniścaya*; cf. Qvarnström 1989) in what may be deemed, together with the epic Buddhist text *Manimekhalai*, one of the forerunners of the doxographic genre, the already-mentioned *Madhyamakahṛdaya* by Bhavya.

[25] The motive for the substantial concordance of the various *darśana*s spreads with particular insistence starting from the sixteenth century, when Indian philosophy had already left behind its most creative phase, in the works of Vijñānabhikṣu, Madhusūdana Sarasvatī and Appaya Dikṣita (cf. Halbfass 1991: 358).

[26] Almost all the doxographies that have come down to us give space to the three heterodox traditions. Sporadic and late exceptions include the *vedāntin*s Madhusūdana Sarasvatī (sixteenth century) and Vallabha (fifteenth-sixteenth century), Rājaśekhara II (fourteenth century), etc.; cf. also the contemptuous rejection of the Lokāyatas by the *naiyāyika* Jayanta Bhaṭṭa at the beginning of the *Nyāyamañjarī* (cf. Gerschheimer 2007: 246-247)

tolerance toward the supporters of doctrines other than those of Mīmāṃsā, so long — of course — as they do not touch the praxis, the rite.[27] With respect to this multiplicity of viewpoints and doctrines, several basic positions can be identified, ranging from total rejection to various forms of conditional acceptance. Strict adherence to a single school and rejection of any other position is relatively rare, mingled with sectarian connotations of a religious kind (see the Vaiṣṇava *ekāntavādin*s, the 'absolutists'); or else, as in the case of the Lokāyatas, is determined by their position of radical and critical isolation. Rejection of the theses of adversaries in Madhyamaka Buddhism should be seen as the programmatic rejection of any thesis as such, including — if it existed — their own. Much more widespread is a sort of limited acceptance, provided that the rival school — to which a certain validity is ascribed — is willing to take its place on a rigidly hierarchic scale, at the top of which only one's own doctrine is enthroned.[28] Such a position, in which tolerance is only a façade, is often accompanied by the concept of double truth (one's own, absolute, while that of others is relative), or adaptation by grading the truth to the qualitative differences of human beings. Lastly, we have the so-called 'perspectivism' of Bhartṛhari (Houben 1997), which accepts the multiplicity of points of view as a direct result of the nature of reality, considering each one an object worthy of attention and capable of bringing its contribution to the attempt to tackle the

[27] Quite telling are the different tones (harsh/fair) used by Kumārila to address Buddhist opponents in the ritualistic *Tantravārttika* and the theoretical *Ślokavārttika*.

[28] This theme frequently recurs in the texts of dualistic and non-dualistic Śivaism in Kashmir: the various *darśana*s are placed on an ascending ladder of principles that constitute the real, according to the Śaivas. Cf. for example, the verse quoted in the *Pratyabhijñāhṛdaya* ('Heart of Recognition', p. 18) by Kṣemarāja (eleventh century C.E.), who associates Buddhism with the 'mind' principle (*buddhi*), Jainism with the principle of 'constituent qualities' (*guṇa*), Vedānta with the principle of 'soul' (*puṃs*), the Pañcarātra of the Viṣṇuites with the 'non-manifest' principle (*avyakta*). See, more in general, the whole commentary of Kṣemarāja on *sūtra* 8 of *Pratyabhijñāhṛdaya*: "The positions of all *darśana*s are stages of Him" (*tadbhūmikāḥ sarvadarśanasthitayaḥ*).

complexity of the real.[29] This agrees well with the prevailing position of Jain philosophy, known as the 'doctrine of non-univocity, or non-absolutism' (*anekāntavāda*; see below pp. 132-133). The disparity of positions is viewed not as a mark of bewilderment and chaos, but as a source of enrichment for the intellect, which, thanks to it, perfects its ability to discriminate (*Vākyapadīya* II. 487-489).

Thus, partially following doxographic tradition, our presentation of the *darśana*s turns particularly on 'philosophic' themes, leaving religious components aside as far as possible. In fact, as we shall see, in some cases in which the soteriological dimension appears to be a wholly late, secondary addition, its omission does no significant violence to the unitary meaning of the system. The main, closely interconnected themes are: the nature of the real, causality, the means of valid knowledge, language and verbal knowledge.

[29] The reluctance (or perhaps lack of interest) of Bhartṛhari to identify with any specific ontological and metaphysical option is linked directly to the status of his discipline. This extraordinary theorist of language, echoes of whom can be found in the work of Saussure, emphasises on various occasions that the grammarian, even if a grammarian-philosopher, must not concern himself with things, but with the words that describe them. His field of research is the universe of language, seen as an indispensable diaphragm between subject and object. Indeed, it is only thanks to the linguistic filter that things can be thought: language and knowledge are merely two sides of the same coin.

Part One

BRAHMANIC PHILOSOPHY AND ENVIRONS

The Nyāya System

The Nyāya system (lit. 'method', later also 'logic') presents itself as the continuator of two distinct traditions, the *ānvīkṣikī vidyā* ('science of investigation and critical examination'), and the *vāda* ('debate'), whose methods were classified and its rules established in India from the earliest times. Indian culture has featured learned debate on the most disparate subjects throughout its history even up to the present (just take part in one of the still frequent *paṇḍitasabhā*s, 'meetings of scholars'). This has left unequivocal traces on the very form of the texts and on the ways of developing a theme, in which dialogue form decidedly prevails, whether direct or more or less disguised as a highly intricate game of presenting alternative positions, provisional solutions followed by other objections, until the established doctrine (*siddhānta*) is reached. Unsurprisingly, given the position enjoyed by grammar as *the* model for the sciences, it is in a grammatical work — the *Mahābhāṣya* ('Grand Commentary [on Pāṇini's *Aṣṭādhyāyī*]') by Patañjali (second century B.C.E.) that we find the most prestigious and immensely influential example of the articulation of scientific argument.[1] Debate, learned dispute (for which the almost synonymous terms *kathā* and *saṃbhāṣā* are used),

[1] The first critical edition of this labyrinthine work, published in 1885, we owe to the philological genius of F. Kielhorn, the fruit of enormous labour carried out side-by-side with Indian paṇḍits. It ranks as one of the monuments of modern Indology.

which have a Vedic precedent in the *brahmodya* (disputes in the form of enigmas, sometimes not dissimilar from the Zen *koan*) and in the *vākovākya* (disputes in dialogue on theological subjects), find their earliest codifications in medicine and liturgical science. Closely linked to the rules of debate are the so-called *tantrayukti*s, 'rules for the composition of a scientific treatise', whose earliest and most prestigious codifications are found in texts belonging to widely different contexts, such as politics and medicine, underlining their character as general standards that can be extended to all branches of knowledge. The following description is from a medical text, the *Suśrutasaṃhitā* ('Collection by Suśruta'; second-third century C.E.?), substantially shared by the *Arthaśāstra*, and also found, with the addition of four elements, in the other great classic of medicine, the *Carakasaṃhitā* ('Collection by Caraka'; first century C.E.): 1) subject of the discourse (*adhikaraṇa*); 2) correct combination of words (*yoga*); 3) determination of the meaning of a polysemic word according to context (*padārtha*); 7) general instruction (*upadeśa*); 8) presentation of a logical reasoning (*apadeśa*); 9) solving a present difficulty by analogy with a past one (*pradeśa*); 10) expectation of a future event on the basis of some present indication (*atideśa*); 11) exception (*apavarga*); 12) completion of the meaning of a sentence thanks to the context (*vākyaśeṣa*); 13) implication (*arthāpatti*); 14) contrary assertion (*viparyaya*); 15) reference to things repeatedly described in another section (*prasaṅga*); 16) absolute affirmation (*ekānta*); 17) admission of a different point of view (*anekānta*); 18) provisional thesis (*pūrvapakṣa*); 19) verification [by question and answer] (*nirṇaya*); 20) implicit acceptance [of an opposing position, if mentioned without any criticism] (*anumata*); 21) arrangement according to a previously established order (*vidhāna*); 22) anticipation of subjects for future development (*anāgatāvekṣaṇa*); 23) reference to previously discussed subjects (*atikrāntāvekṣaṇa*); 24) doubt (*saṃśaya*); 25) elaborate description (*vyākhyāna*); 26) technical use of a term (*svasaṃjñā*); 27) etymological explanation (*nirvacana*); 28) exemplification (*nidarśana*);

29) direction (*niyoga*); 30) putting two or three subjects together (*samuccaya*); 31) presentation of alternatives (*vikalpa*); 32) comprehension based on the context of what is not expressed (*ūhya*) (Solomon 1976: 72).

To the presentation of themes deriving from the earliest eristic, the Nyāya root-text (*Nyāyasūtra*) adds an in-depth treatment of the means of valid cognition (*pramāṇa*) — dwelling in particular on the formulation of inferential reasoning — and a comparatively summary ontological setting, with a soteriological coda at the end.

It is on this repeatedly reinterpreted text that classical Nyāya is built, later on profoundly renewed and questioned by the so-called 'New Logic' (Navyanyāya), which still today has a prominent place in circles of traditional knowledge. Starting from Udayana (tenth-eleventh century C.E.), Nyāya transformed its path into something largely parallel to Vaiśeṣika, creating a confluence and becoming a single school.

The textual corpus of Nyāya is thus based on the *Nyāyasūtra*, a heteroclite collection of brief aphorisms, which assumed its (relatively) definitive form in the fourth century C.E., starting from an original nucleus that can be dated to the second century C.E. Its author is deemed to be a sage named Akṣapāda, who is later on (from the tenth century onwards) designated as Gotama or Gautama. His historical existence is rather doubtful and everything known about him has a legendary air, starting from the meaning attributed to the name Akṣapāda ('he who has eyes in his feet'). This derives from a special gift of the gods, worried by his repeated accidents (falls, etc.) due to his continual absorption in profound and learned study (this may remind us of the analogous remark by Theophrastus about Thales). The first commentary that has come down to us is by Pakṣilasvāmin, alias Vātsyāyana (second half of the fifth century C.E.), entitled *Nyāyabhāṣya* ('Commentary on the Nyāya[*sūtra*]'). It was the object of a major sub-commentary, the *Nyāyavārttika* ('Gloss on the Nyāya') by Uddyotakara (sixth century C.E.) planned as a reaction to the reviews of Nyāya by the rising logical-epistemological school of Buddhism, led by Dignāga. The *Nyāyavārttika* was in turn extensively commented on first by a group of commentators (the so-called *ācārya*s, 'masters') whose works have not come down to us, and then by the polygraph Vācaspati Miśra (tenth century C.E.), who, as already stated above, devoted himself to the elucidation of disparate *darśana*s not belonging univocally to any school. His *Nyāyavārttikatātparyaṭīkā* ('Long commentary on the purports of the gloss on Nyāya') was in turn commented on by Udayana, in his long and difficult *Nyāyavārttikatātparyapariśuddhi* ('Accurate clarification of the purports of the glosses on Nyāya'), the whole of which has not come down to us. It should not be thought however that the commentaries on the *Nyāyasūtra* end with Udayana's prestigious work.[2] The latter was in turn commented on by Vardhamāna (*Nyāyanibandhaprakāśa*, 'Illustration of the compilation of Nyāya'), Vardhamāna by Padmanābha Miśra (*Vardhamānendu*, '[Light of the] moon on Vardhamāna'), Padmanābha by Śaṅkara Miśra (*Nyāyatātparyamaṇḍana*, 'Ornament to the purport of Nyāya'). Besides the direct commentaries on the root-*sūtra*, some independent treatises deserve special mention, starting with the *Nyāyamañjarī* ('Bunch of flowers of Nyāya') and the *Nyāyabhūṣaṇa* ('Ornament of Nyāya'), respectively by Jayanta Bhaṭṭa (second half of the ninth century C.E.) and, slightly earlier, Bhāsarvajña, both kāśmīris. The former work, composed — according to the author — while he was in prison and seeking some way to pass the time, is noteworthy for its objective presentation of opposing theses and exemplary elegance of style. The latter, discovered only recently, in the form of a commentary on another work by the same author, the *Nyāyasāra* ('Essence of Nyāya'), presents strongly personal positions, somewhat eccentric as compared to the current tradition of Nyāya, later picked up by the masters of the New Logic. Of considerable importance are also two works by Udayana, the *Ātmatattvaviveka* ('Discrimination of

[2] For an accurate examination of the tradition of the commentaries on the *Nyāyasūtra*, see Preisendanz 2005.

the nature of the ego'), devoted to confuting the negation of the self by the Buddhists, and the *Nyāyakusumāñjali* ('Handful of flowers of Nyāya'), an articulated demonstration of the existence of God with a rebuttal of the atheism of Buddhists, Materialists, Sāṃkhyas and Mīmāṃsakas.

Bhāsarvajña and Udayana may be considered as the last great exponents of classical Nyāya and, together, as the link between ancient and new logic. The establishment of the Navanyāya can be attributed to the revolutionary work by Gaṅgeśa, the *[Pramāṇa]Tattvacintāmaṇi* ('Gem of desires regarding the true essence [of the means of right knowledge]'), composed in about 1325. In those almost three centuries separating Udayana from Gaṅgeśa several interesting thinkers are found, such as Maṇikaṇṭha, Śrīvallabha and Śaśadhara, dedicated in particular to revising the teaching of Udayana. The *Tattvacintāmaṇi*, which comprises as many as 12,000 verses, is divided into four chapters, each devoted to one of the means of right knowledge accepted by Nyāya, marking a first distancing from classical doctrine with its subdivision into sixteen categories (cf. below pp. 39 ff). Many of the classic problems are dropped in order to focus exclusively on the themes of epistemology and logic. Gaṅgeśa's work gave rise, for over three centuries, to an impressive quantity of commentary literature, focused mainly on the far most important chapter of the whole work — devoted to inference — in turn divided into a 'section on pervasion' and a 'section on knowledge', respectively defining inference and the invariable concomitance on which it is based, and the subject of inference and the fallacies of inferential reasoning. Of the other chapters, the one dealing with verbal testimony also received considerable attention. Because of the peculiar conciseness of Gaṅgeśa's style, extremely brief passages of his work, or even single assertions, frequently form the subject of lengthy and elaborate commentaries. Extreme care taken in definitions is one of the identifying traits of Navanyāya which, starting from Gaṅgeśa, developed its own complex and articulated terminology that came to prevail in practically every branch of knowledge. Starting from

Gaṅgeśa's work, we also encounter a radical change of interlocutor in the critical discourse of Nyāya. Its 'natural' adversaries — the Buddhists — having vanished from India, arguments concentrate against the doctrines of Mīmāṃsā and — not by chance — in particular against one of the two main schools: that of the followers of Prabhākara who, more than most, had been influenced by the final season of Buddhist philosophy.

The last great exponent of Navyanyāya is Raghunātha Śiromaṇi (first half of the sixteenth century), whose highly unusual image for the Indian world is that of a scorner of tradition and audacious innovator, aware of the excellence of the intellectual talents that placed him above his contemporaries (cf. above p. 21). His main works are the *Anumānadīdhiti* ('Ray of light on inference'), a highly penetrating investigation of the homonymous section of the *Tattvacintāmaṇi*, and the *Padārthatattvanirūpaṇa* ('Description of the true nature of categories'), in which he profoundly alters, with additions and eliminations, the Vaiśeṣika doctrine of categories, incorporated in Nyāya. His main contributions are an analysis of concomitance in inferential reasoning and the various forms of negation. As proof of the by-now almost exclusive interest — during the last season of Navyanyāya, which still survives today in India — in formal logic, midway between linguistics and philosophy, and repeatedly commented on in following centuries, we have the *Anumānadīdhiti*, a work whose extreme conciseness and acuteness together with the inflexible rigour of its style make it one of the most arduous in the whole of Indian philosophical literature.

In what has become their canonical form, the *Nyāyasūtra* consists of five chapters (*adhyāya*, 'lesson'), each divided into two sections (*āhnika*, 'day'). According to the interpretation of the commentator Vātsyāyana, they contain an indication (*uddeśa*) of the fundamental concepts of Nyāya, their definition (*lakṣaṇa*) and critical examination (*parīkṣā*). The first chapter is devoted to stating and defining the sixteen basic categories; the second, to a critical examination of the means of achieving valid knowledge (*pramāṇa*), preceded by an examination of what is the necessary precondition, i.e. doubt. The third chapter is devoted to a critical examination of the first six of the twelve objects of knowledge; in the fourth, the first section examines the other six and refutes opposing theses, whereas the second, following a much less linear path, again deals with the validity of knowledge, followed by the theory of atoms, several themes concerning yoga, and two kinds of discussion and debate deemed incorrect; lastly, the fifth chapter is devoted to 'futile objections' (*jāti*) and 'cases of immobilization' (*nigrahasthāna*), i.e. the circumstances under which one of the two dialectic contestants must acknowledge defeat.

The textual history of the *Nyāyasūtra* has been particularly tortured, starting from an original nucleus of chapters one and five, in which the eristic theory is concentrated, with subsequent additions concerning epistemological, logical and ontological themes and lastly, a soteriological appendix, poorly integrated with the rest. It may well have been the uneven nature of the text, for centuries exposed to additions or deletions, that finally decided Vācaspati Miśra to compose, at a fairly late date (a not frequent occurrence: the text is dated 898 but unfortunately without indicating the era to which it refers; of the two possible dates, the later one, 976/7, appears more probable) a brief work known as the *Nyāyasūcinibandha* ('Compilation of the index of the *Nyāya[sūtra]*'), which is both an analytical index and definitively fixes the canon.[3]

The sixteen categories presented by Nyāya are firstly the fundamental categories of debate, thus acting as a frame for the whole system, containing within them the means of knowledge deemed valid (*pramāṇa*, mentioned first) and the objects of valid knowledge

---

[3] It should be noted however that recent studies tend to discredit the hypothesis that the *Nyāyasūcinibandha* should be attributed to the better known Vācaspati. If the assumed date is much later, it has to be explained why the above date is indicated at the end of the text. As noted by Muroya (2007: 420), we are dealing with a single manuscript, examined only by its editor, which for the time being can no longer be traced.

(*prameya*, in second place).[4] Under these two categories are discussed epistemological theory and logic, on the one hand, and ontology on the other. The latter is viewed in terms of realism and pluralism, recognizing that the object has an existence that is independent of the knower. The knower is expected to record accurately the fact with which he comes into direct or indirect contact, without projecting upon it any subjective structures. The object is viewed as a substance with inherent qualities: its component parts do not however constitute the totality of the object, since the whole is considered as a distinct entity transcending the accumulation of its parts. This original form of ingenuous realism, however, very soon had to face the subtleties of Buddhist phenomenalism, culminating in the thought of Dignāga and Dharmakīrti (cf. below pp. 159 ff). An impassioned debate ensued, culminating in the work of Udayana, in which Nyāya realism does not change radically, but lucidly accepts a conscious problematisation. The Nyāya view ends by representing a kind of formalization of common sense, widely accepted, at least at the level of practical reality, by the Brahmanic schools in general, but not only by them, if one considers that even the thought of Hindu Tantrism (cf. for example, Utpaladeva and Abhinavagupta),[5] apparently so distant, deems that Nyāya doctrines, all things considered, are the most adequate in accounting for empirical reality and for orienting oneself within it.

---

[4] According to the *Bhāṣya* to *Nyāyasūtra* I.1.1, *prameya* does not refer to just any object of knowledge, but only to those ('the self, etc.') of which proper knowledge leads to liberation. In this context, the *Nyāyabhāṣya* mentions the four *arthapada* ('significant statements?' in which the two lemmas of the compound *padārtha*, usually translated as "category', have been intentionally inverted), corresponding to "what has to be eliminated" (*heya*), 'the causes of what has to be eliminated' (*hānahetu*), 'elimination (*hāna*) and 'means of elimination' (*hānopāya*); on this quadripartition, see below p. 95. The different interpretations of this passage, not lacking in ambiguity, given by subsequent Nyāya tradition are attentively examined in Wezler (1984: 324-37).

[5] Cf. the explicit statement by Abhinavagupta in his commentary (*vimarśinī*) on the *Īśvarapratyabhijñākārikā* by Utpaladeva (vol. I, p. 25). Cf. below pp. 214-215.

The sixteen categories are set forth in the very first verse of the *Nyāyasūtra:*

> Leading to achievement of the supreme good is knowledge according to reality: 1) of the means of right knowledge (*pramāṇa*), 2) of the objects of right knowledge (*prameya*), 3) of doubt (*saṃśaya*), 4) of motivation (*prayojana*), 5) of the example (*dṛṣṭānta*), 6) of established doctrine (*siddhānta*), 7) of the members of inference (*avayava*), 8) of hypothetical reasoning (*tarka*), 9) of definitive ascertainment (*nirṇaya*), 10) of [loyal] debate (*vāda*), 11) of diatribe (*jalpa*), 12) of quibbles (*vitaṇḍa*), 13) of fallacious logical reasons (*hetvābhāsa*), 14) of deliberate distortion [of contrary theses] (*chala*), 15) of futile objection (*jāti*), 16) of the points of immobilisation (*nigrahasthāna*).

Those admitted as means of right knowledge are specified in *sūtra* I.1.3: "The means of right knowledge are perception, inference, analogy and verbal testimony". Examination of the means of right knowledge, the nature of valid knowledge, the logic of inference and its articulation in syllogism gradually constitute the central element of Nyāya, finally becoming the exclusive element in Navyanyāya. Notwithstanding the inclusion of eristic-related themes, as also, secondarily, of soteriology, Nyāya is widely identified as the system that specialises in logic and epistemology.

As in all Indian thought, the means of knowledge par excellence, accepted by all, is direct perception (Matilal 1986). *Sūtra* I.1.4 provides the following definition: "Perception [is that knowledge that] arises from contact between the senses and the object; it cannot be expressed in words; it is not deviant; it has a definite character". Each of these four requisites has been subjected to careful — and often divergent — analysis by commentators (Jayanta even deems that they could be extended to all means of knowledge). "What is born from contact between the senses and the object" is the least problematic feature, even though, as Uddyotakara is the first to propose, it needs to be divided into six types in order to account for all forms of direct perception other than that — the most usual case — of an external object. The first type is, naturally, when the senses perceive the external object as substance; the second, when a quality or universal of the substance in contact with the senses is perceived ; the third, when the universal of the said quality belonging to the object is perceived (the blueness of a blue lotus); the fourth, belonging, for example, to the sense of hearing — which is essentially ether — when it perceives the sound that is ether-based; the fifth, when a definite quality is perceived inherent in the sound that is in turn inherent in the ether; lastly, the sixth, when perception of an empty space makes us perceive the absence of a vase that was previously there.

The second requisite "it cannot be expressed in words" is the most debated among Nyāya exegetes (Jayanta gives six different interpretations of it). While its original meaning probably aimed at clearly distinguishing perception from other *pramāṇa*s, such as inference or authoritative testimony, in which verbal articulation is fundamental, Vācaspati Miśra makes it the keystone of his peculiar interpretation of the whole *sūtra*. For him, Akṣapāda-Gotama is defining two different types of perception, one that is immediate and coincides with pure sensation, and the other, already articulated in perceptual judgement in which concepts and words play a central role. Through brazen distortion of the text, making it say what would become current in Indian philosophy only after the Buddhist Dignāga (ca. 480-540), and even altering the word order, Vācaspati understands *Sūtra* I.1.4 as saying, "Perception [is that knowledge that] arises from contact between the senses and the object; it is not deviant; [it possesses two forms, of which one] cannot be expressed in words, [while the other] has a definite character". The presence of two distinct phases in perception, one with and one without conceptualisation (*sa-vikalpaka*, *nir-vikalpaka*) was to become one of the cornerstones of Nyāya epistemology. According to Jayanta, such conceptualisation essentially consists of the appearance of a verbal element, thanks to which perception becomes knowledge proper ("this is a vase"). Although all Nyāya philosophers agree in considering both moments as perception, thus in opposition to the Buddhists, their positions vary as regards the internal articulation of these two phases. The theory of Vācaspati, according to which the particular ('this') and the universal ('vase') are already known at the very moment of the sensation and are merely not related as subject and predicate, was to prevail in the subsequent history of Nyāya. It was accepted and developed by the founder of New Logic, Gaṅgeśa, who gave the doctrine its definitive form: 'this' and 'vase', albeit perceived from the very first moment, are placed in a qualificand-qualifier relationship only in the subsequent phase, and before that occurs the sensation remains substantially out of reach (*atīndriya*). Beside ordinary perception (*laukika*), according to the New Logic (anticipated however by Jayanta), extraordinary perception (*alaukika*) also exists, characterised by non-ordinary contact with the senses (*alaukikendriyasannikarṣa*) and distinguished in three forms. The first, through a universal perceived in a particular individual, perceives all individuals belonging to that class; the second allows a present object to be perceived through a past perception ("I see a piece of scented sandalwood", in which the present perception is fed by the past perception); the third arises from yoga practice and, by way of example, makes it possible to view extremely small and distant objects (cf. below pp. 96-99).

Of the last two requisites mentioned in the *sūtra* that defines perception, the first ('non-deviant'), according to most commentators, is to exclude perceptive errors, while the second ('it has a definite character'), taken in its simplest meaning, is to eliminate indistinct or doubtful perception.

The second means of right knowledge, inference (*anumāna*), is defined in the next *sūtra* (I.1.5), which if anything is even more problematic than the previous one: "Then comes inference, which is preceded by that [perception] and is of three kinds: with an antecedent [as *probans*] (*pūrvavat*), with a consequent [as *probans*] (*śeṣavat*) and as established on the basic of generic [or general] correlation (*sāmānyatodṛṣṭa*)". Of all these characteristics, the only one without any ambiguity is the first. Indeed, in the general context of Indian philosophy, inference is mostly viewed as a cognitive process that compensates the momentary lack of direct perception (although there are also objects that are intrinsically inaccessible to perception and only inferable, *nityānumeya*) and bases its validity on a similar direct experience in the past. Furthermore, a component of actual direct perception is always present in the inferential process, acting as essential support as well as trigger (cf. below pp. 178 ff).

In view of the multiplicity of interpretations to which this *sūtra* gave rise over the centuries, we shall start from the one provided in the most ancient commentary of those that have come down to us. According to the *Bhāṣya* of Vātsyāyana, for inference of the *pūrvavat* type, the effect is inferred from the cause, which is — naturally — the 'antecedent' (e.g. "When we see clouds rise, we infer that it will rain"). In inference of the *śeṣavat* type, the cause is inferred from the effect ("When we see that a river has risen, we infer that it has rained upstream"). In inference of the *sāmānyatodṛṣṭa* type, the repeated previous observation of similar cases allows us to establish something even if it escapes our direct observation ("We have seen that whenever something is found in different positions from its earlier ones, it is because a movement has occurred; therefore, even if we cannot see it directly, the sun moves").

This, however, is not the only set of interpretations presented by Vātsyāyana. *Pūrvavat*, he continues, could also be said of an inference based on previous (*pūrva*) direct perception of two things as being inseparably connected. When, later on, only one of the two is perceived, the presence of the other is also inferred. *Śeṣa* in *śeṣavat* could also be understood in the sense of 'remaining'; an inference of this kind is based on what 'remains' after any other objects have been eliminated and others have been previously established as irrelevant. For example, suppose we are wondering about the nature of sound, i.e. to which of the six categories (substance, quality, action, universal, particularity and inherence; cf. pp. 63 ff) it must belong.

Ascertainment that sound exists and is non-eternal immediately excludes the last three, while for the others, we proceed by elimination. Sound cannot be substance, because if it were, it could not have a single substance as its inherent cause; nor action, because it is the cause of a subsequent sound. Hence, it can only be considered as a quality. In *sāmānyatodṛṣṭa* inference, the relationship between *probans* and *probandum* is not perceptible, and the *probandum* is determined on the basis of the similarity of the *probans* to another entity. Of this kind is inference of the self based on desire: desire is a quality and we see that all qualities are inherent in a substrate; it follows that the substrate of qualities, such as desire itself, is the self.

As we can see, even the most ancient of the extant commentaries appears hesitant about assigning a definite meaning to this *sūtra*. Over the centuries, subsequent commentators have accumulated an incredible number of divergent interpretations, to which may be added those given by other schools, such as Vaiśeṣika, Sāṃkhya or Mīmāṃsā, in which the three terms — sometimes in slightly different versions — are also recurrent. We should at least mention here the commentator immediately after Vātsyāyana, Uddyotakara, who in his *Vārttika* proposes two other sets of interpretations, different from each other and radically different from those provided by the *Bhāṣya*. According to the former, the three terms mean respectively: a) inference based exclusively on concordance (*kevalānvayin*: "the vase may be the object of verbal designation because it is knowable"; indeed, for Nyāya, whatever is knowable is also namable); b) inference based exclusively on difference (*kevalavyatirekin*: e.g. "the element earth differs from other elements because it is endowed with smell"; it is known that none of the other four elements has smell); c) inference based on a combination of concordance-difference (*anvayivyatirekin*: "On the mountain there is fire because there is smoke"; whenever there is fire, there is smoke; whenever there is no fire, there is no smoke). In the second interpretation, however, the three terms aim at establishing the conditions on which any kind of inference is based. This means that the *probans*, in the case in question, must have been observed in the past as invariably accompanied by the *probandum* (*pūrvavat*); the *probans* must also have been observed as invariably accompanied by the *probandum* in the remaining similar cases (*śeṣavat*); the third term (*sāmānyatodṛṣṭa*), analysed with great artifice, is taken as referring to all inferences not based on causality ("in this region there must be water because herons can be seen"). Lastly, following a procedure that is typical of Indian commentators, Uddyotakara even manages to see in the laconic description of *sūtra* I.1.5 the two conditions that are normally required by inference, i.e. not to clash either with direct perception or with revealed scripture: they are implied by the last word of the *sūtra* (*ca*, 'and').

Recent studies have put forward some sound arguments for interpreting the three terms, seemingly first mentioned in the *Ṣaṣṭi-tantra*, in the light of similar classifications of inference found in ancient Buddhist texts. Lastly, we should emphasise the analogy with the description of inference by the medical schools. The *locus classicus* is the *Carakasaṃhitā* (Sūtrasthāna XI.19-20), according to which three types of inference can be distinguished, according to whether it concerns present, past or future, exemplified respectively by inferring fire from smoke, an accomplished sexual relationship from the conception of a foetus, the future production of a certain fruit from the presence of a certain seed.

The third of the four means of right knowledge — analogy (*upamāna*) — is defined in the next *sūtra* (I.I.6). "Analogy is the means that leads to the knowledge of an object by virtue of its similarity to another commonly known object". According to the classical example, even someone who does not know the features of the bovine called a *gavaya* — but is told that it is similar to a cow — is capable of identifying it. Nyāya tradition distinguishes three main types of analogy: by similitude; by difference; and by peculiarity of attributes. The first is exemplified by the case quoted above. The second obtains when the object denoted by a certain name is described on the basis of its marked dissimilarity from another class of well-known objects. The third, when, for example, a certain animal is identified —

described as a long-necked quadruped, with prominent lips, that feeds on thorns — as a camel. Considering analogy as a valid means of knowledge and, in particular, as a means of independent knowledge, not traceable to anything else, has been greatly contested, both within and without Nyāya (Bhāsarvajña even denies it totally, thus reducing the number of the means of knowledge to three). Adversaries of Nyāya point out that, in the case commonly quoted as an example, there are three distinct components: knowledge of similarity to the cow derives from authoritative testimony (a distinct *pramāṇa*, the fourth); the view of the *gavaya* is clearly an act of perception; attributing its proper name to it is a matter of inference. Some of these objections (followed by their confutation) are even voiced in the *Nyāyasūtra* itself. As mentioned above, some of the arguments used by adversaries are deemed valid by Bhāsarvajña: analogy should be eliminated from the list of the means of knowledge because it boils down to the cooperation of verbal testimony and memory. Exemplary in defining the dynamics of the *śāstra* is the way in which Bhāsarvajña manages to make such a drastic innovation on a fundamental point of Nyāya doctrine — such as the number of the means of knowledge — without questioning the authority of its mythical founder Akṣapāda.

The fourth and last means of knowledge is verbal testimony (*śabda*, lit. 'word', 'language'), thus defined by *Nyāyasūtra* I.1.7 : "Verbal testimony is an instruction coming from an authoritative source". Objections to this means are not lacking either, in part similar to those raised by analogy. As pointed out by Akṣapāda himself in the second *adhyāya* (I.45 *et seq.*), devoted to a critical examination of the *pramāṇa*s, it could be objected that verbal testimony is only a particular case of inference (this is, for example, the position of the Buddhist Dignāga), since — as with inference — something currently not accessible to perception is known by means of a sign, i.e. the word that designates it. Furthermore, the relationship between word and meaning is of the same kind as connects logical reason to the object of inference. The Nyāya response is on two levels: the two relationships are not the same, because the first derives solely from linguistic convention, whereas the second belongs to the natural order; furthermore, the true foundation of verbal testimony is not to be found in the word itself, but in the authoritativeness of the person pronouncing it. On what constitutes 'authoritativeness' or 'reliability' (*āptatva*), the philosophers of Nyāya and all the other schools, Brahmanic and otherwise, have long disputed. The question cannot however be put without considering what is added by the following *sūtra:* "This [verbal testimony] is of two kinds: its object may be perceptible or not perceptible" (I.1.8). The definition of a person worthy of trust, says Vātsyāyana in his *Bhāṣya* (*ad* I.1.7), as one who has direct knowledge of an object and is motivated by the desire to communicate the object exactly as he himself has directly perceived it, is applicable equally to a seer, a nobleman or a barbarian, while the authority about what is not accessible to the experience of the senses (in other words, it is not of this world) is reserved for seers, persons endowed with special powers of spiritual penetration, who in far distant times acted as go-betweens for the manifestation of the Veda.

The autochthonous nature of classical Indian logic has long been debated, with a nuanced range of positions, from peremptory affirmation of direct subordination to the thought of Aristotle (Vidyabhusana) to total autonomy (Matilal). A certain superficial affinity between the two traditions notwithstanding, it seems fairly clear that Indian logic is the outcome of gradual development, starting from the techniques used in learned discussion from the earliest times, with a long history of progressive adjustments and blind alleys, involving not only philosophical or religious-philosophical and liturgical contexts, but also — and to greater effect — the scientific environment, with medicine in the forefront.[6] The hypothesis

---

[6] On this line, major research is being carried out by a team of scholars under the direction of K. Preisendanz (their aims also include producing the first critical edition of one of the great classical Indian medical texts, the *Carakasaṃhitā*).

advanced with incredible nonchalance by Vidyabhusana (1920: 511-2) of works by Aristotle translated into Sanskrit in the first centuries of the Common Era meets with no confirmation of any kind.

In the Indian context, logical research essentially concerns how best to divide and formally present the inferential process. This is not required when recourse is made to inference, as it were for 'internal purposes', since this way of knowing through mediation belongs to the primary spontaneous mechanisms of human cognitive activity. Different is the case in which the result of this knowledge has to be communicated, so that all passages leading to it have to be made explicit, for the chief purposes of convincing — here once more raising the hypothesis of an eristic origin to this discipline — others who have not personally experienced the said process, or remain aloof or keep their distance, either out of intellectual torpor, or out of willful acceptance of different assumptions (e.g. the followers of some rival doctrine). From 'inference for oneself' (*svārthānumāna*) we thus pass on to 'inference for others' (*parārthānumāna*), a distinction that is emphasised particularly by the masters of Buddhist logic. Although this theme is tackled by all schools, it is deemed to be the privileged field of Nyāya (as we have seen, the term *nyāya* is also given the meaning of 'logic' *tout court*).

In the classical form of Nyāya, inference for others is presented as the concatenation of five propositions, the result of simplifying a more ancient set of ten, also within the Nyāya tradition, of which mention is made by Vātsyāyana (for the purpose of criticism) in his *Bhāṣya*; a different set of ten members is mentioned by the Jain Bhadrabāhu in the *Daśavaikālikaniryukti* (cf. p. 136). The first member of the syllogism is represented by the hypothesis (*pratijñā*, lit. 'promise') or assertion that is the object of the demonstration. The classic example is "there is fire on the mountain", which however is usually expressed in the form of a nominal phrase as a subject-predicate relationship: "the mountain is endowed-with-fire" (*parvato vahnimān*). The subject (*pakṣa*) is thus predicated by the property that is to be demonstrated (*sādhya*). The second member is the logical reason (*hetu*), meaning the affirmation of the presence of a certain sign (*liṅga*) in the subject that will also involve the necessary presence of the assumed property: "because it is endowed-with-fire". The third member is the example (*udāharaṇa*), which in actual fact consists first and foremost of the assertion of a necessary correlation (*vyāpti*) between the sign and the property to be demonstrated and, secondly, of exemplification in both positive (*sapakṣa*) and negative terms (*vipakṣa*): "Indeed, whatever is endowed-with-smoke is also endowed-with-fire, like a kitchen; and, vice-versa, whatever is not-endowed-with-smoke is also not-endowed-with-fire, like a lake". The fourth member, synthesising the second and third, is the application (*upanaya*) to the case in question of the general principle expounded in the third part: "like the kitchen, the mountain too is endowed-with-smoke", or else: "unlike the lake, the mountain is not not-endowed-with-smoke". The fifth member is the conclusion (*nigamana*), wholly similar to the first part, except for the fact that what was presented as a thesis to be demonstrated in the first part is now given as an acquired fact.

Five is thus also the number of terms playing a role in the five members of the syllogism: subject (*pakṣa*), corresponding to the minor term of the first figure in Aristotelian syllogism; the property to be demonstrated (*sādhya*), corresponding to the major term; the sign (*liṅga*), corresponding to the middle term; the positive example, or example by similarity (*sapakṣa*); the negative example, or example by difference (*vipakṣa*). In actual fact, this scheme, definite in appearance only, leaves open various points that are subjects of debate that has gone on for centuries, focusing particularly on the precise nature of the object of inference and how the necessity for correlation of property and sign can be determined. The Nyāya position on the first question is variable: according to the case, it can be the minor term as linked to the major term ("the mountain is endowed-with-fire"), the major term as linked to the minor term ('fire as being linked to the mountain'), or the middle term, taken in its individual dimension, as linked to the major term ('the smoke [whose precise location is unknown] as linked to fire'). In reality, the solutions put forward by Nyāya philosophers are fairly diversified, but it will only be possible to give an account of them after presenting the Buddhist position (starting from Dignāga, cf. pp. 159 ff), which is largely responsible for their critical examination of the whole question.

Equally important, the second point deals with the necessary characteristics of logical reason (*hetu*), the number of which classical Nyāya establishes as five. The first is its constituting a property of the minor term (*pakṣadharmatā*; 'the mountain is endowed-with-smoke'); the second is its presence in other cases similar to that of the minor term (*sapakṣasattva*; "whatever is endowed with smoke [as is the minor term] is endowed with fire, such as the kitchen"); the third is its absence in all dissimilar cases (*vipakṣasattva*; whatever is not endowed-with-smoke, unlike the minor term, is not endowed-with-fire, such as, for example, a lake); the fourth is its not concerning whatever has already been established as non-existent or false (*abādhitaviṣayatva*); the fifth is its not being such as to clash with other logical reasons leading to opposite conclusions (*asatpratipakṣitva*). If a logical reason does not satisfy these five conditions, it ceases to be such and becomes a pseudo-reason (*hetvābhāsa*). Similar fallacies may also be ascribed to the other parts of the inference, but, as Jayanta points out, since logical reason is the very core of inference, it is not worthwhile spending time on analysing possible fallacies in the other parts with the same attention. A pseudo-reason will thus suffice (*Nyāyasūtra* I.2.4-9 examines the five main types) to determine a pseudo-inference.

However, this consideration in analytical terms appears insufficient to explain the existence of inference as a cognitive fact. The five members must be made to belong to a dynamic continuum by the knower and synthesized in a complex notion, known as 'consideration of the logical sign' (*liṅgaparāmarśa*; Uddyotakara *ad Nyāyasūtra* 1.1.5). Indeed, according to Nyāya, neither knowledge of the sign in itself, nor knowledge of the universal concomitance (*vyāpti*) between the sign and the element to be inferred — as required by the followers of Mīmāṃsā or Vedānta — can alone provide the trigger producing inference. As stated later on by New Logic (Navyanyāya), the inferential process involves not one but three successive 'considerations of the logical sign' and only with the third is the inference complete. Returning to the classical example, the logical sign — smoke — is considered firstly as being invariably linked with fire, at some time previous to the inference; secondly, when it is directly perceived on the mountain; and lastly, the third time, when the smoke present here and now is associated with the prior notion of the invariable concomitance of all smoke with fire.

The concept of 'invariable concomitance' has also received considerable attention from Nyāya philosophers, reaching its acme in the work by Gaṅgeśa. If logical reason is the essential core of inference, the invariable concomitance between the major and middle terms is the source of its validity. This concept has been variously presented and formulated, both by and outside the Nyāya school, sometimes as 'non-deviance' (*avyabhicāra*; cf. Śrīdhara), sometimes as 'impossibility of reciprocal absence' (*avinābhāva*; cf. Praśastapāda, etc.), and again as 'generic relation' (*sambandhamātra*; cf. Bhāsarvajña). The most widely accepted term, even if variously qualified, is eventually 'pervasion' (*vyāpti*) which thus invests the said major and middle terms of inference with the respective roles of pervader (*vyāpaka*) and pervaded (*vyāpya*). They may be represented as two concentric circles; the term of lesser extension (here: 'being-endowed-with-smoke') is encircled by the term of greater extension ('being-endowed-with-fire'), in the sense that the former cannot exist without the latter (while, as we shall see, the contrary is untrue). The two terms do not necessarily have different extensions, as in this case; the two circles may also coincide and, according to case, alternately perform the role of pervader and pervaded. Even what is here the term of greater extension could be used as the logical sign in an inference, but only so long as certain conditions are satisfied.

Fire, in other words, may be used to establish the existence of smoke, so long as we are not dealing with a generic fire but with the product of a specific type of fuel (e.g. leaves); indeed we know that metal can be made incandescent by fire without producing smoke. On the basis of this consideration, Nyāya was induced to specify that the relationship between pervader and pervaded must contain no condition (*upādhi*) — understood as meaning a property that must necessarily be present in all possible cases in the major term and, on the other hand, only in some cases in the middle term — but must be innate or natural (*svābhāvika*), i.e. unconditionally present in all cases. The various possible implications of the concepts of *upādhi* and *vyāpti* are dwelt on considerably by Maṇikaṇṭha Miśra (thirteenth-fourteenth century C.E.). They are continued and further developed later by Gaṅgeśa, who, in his *Tattvacintāmaṇi*, discusses as many as twenty-nine different definitions of *vyāpti*, rejecting twenty-one of them one by one. Among the remaining eight deemed acceptable, he focuses finally on one (in actual fact, so intricate is Gaṅgeśa's argument that even the number of definitions studied and rejected is a matter of debate). According to the surviving definition, pervasion is "an invariable and unconditional relationship between the middle and major terms".[7]

It remains an open question, however, as to how the existence of such a relationship can be ascertained. Nyāya's considered answer has to tackle two extreme criticisms: that of the Lokāyatas (Materialists) and that of the logical-epistemological school of Buddhism. According to the former, human knowledge can in no case rise above the particular and thus any possibility of generalization is excluded. For the latter, such a relationship is possible, but its range is restricted only to relationships of causality or identity (cf. pp. 168-169). The final position of Nyāya, itself the result of the stratification of various solutions proposed over time by its exponents, may on the whole be formulated as follows. Pervasion is ascertained

[7] On the concept of 'pervasion' in Navyanyāya, see Wada 1990.

by repeated experience (*bhūyodarśana*) of both positive and negative concomitance — i.e. presence-presence and absence-absence — of the two elements under various circumstances, assisted in dubious cases by recourse to hypothetical reasoning (*tarka*). Nyāya does not however hide the difficulty of entrusting to simple perception — however extended — of particular cases the determination of a relationship of a general order, and then seeks to overcome it by assuming that perception has a specific quality, that of grasping in the object not only its individual form, but also its dimension as belonging to a class, thus legitimising the process of generalization. This theory is known as *sāmānyalakṣaṇapratyakṣa* 'perception that grasps the general character', presented by Jayanta as an example of extraordinary perception (cf. p. 43).

The advent of Navyanyāya (cf. Wada 2004) gave rise to a profound and lasting change, firstly in philosophical language, in which the highest degree of precision was required as compared to the ambiguities of ordinary language (cf. Wada 2001). This is obtained by recourse to a constellation of technical terms and by exploiting to the full the intrinsic disposition of the nominal phrase in Sanskrit to express any imaginable level of abstraction. This is possible thanks also to the facility of coining abstract expressions by adding secondary suffixes, attached not only to single lemmas (e.g. *jñeya* > *jñeyatva* 'knowable > knowability'), but also to long and complex nominal compounds. The result is a strongly distinctive language and, in appearance at least, an extremely complicated one, in which the expressive power of daily communication is wholly sacrificed to what is perhaps unattainable univocity and total adherence to the content of logical-epistemological analysis — a fatal temptation, also well known to Western philosophy. The following are some examples. A cognitive act may be presented in ordinary experience as "this is a vase", or "this vase is blue". The Navyanyāya philosopher starts by identifying two levels: the content of the cognition (*viṣaya*) and the cognitive act or knower to which this content belongs (*viṣayin*). The 'content' dimension is in turn divided into three distinct elements: a qualificand, a qualifier and the specific type of relationship that binds them. In the first example, 'this' is the qualificand, 'vase' the qualifier and the relationship one of identity. In the typical language of Navyanyāya, the common expression "this is a vase" becomes: "that knowledge that possesses a qualificand residing in 'this', defined by adjective-ness residing in a vase defined by relation-ness residing in identity". Thus, at the cost of a wearisome proliferation of words, what is aimed at is to identify precisely the roles performed by each of the elements that the nominal sentence would leave ambiguous: the vase could, for example, be — as it is in other contexts — the qualificand, and so on. A central role is played by the concept of 'delimitor' (*avacchedaka*) and 'delimited' (*avacchinna*)[8] that, in the most restricted way in which they are employed, delimit or identify relational abstracts; these — as stated above — in Sanskrit can be created with great facility. An expression such as the one occurring in the classical example of inference: "there is fire on the mountain", usually presented as "the mountain is endowed-with-fire", lends itself to the following analytical presentation: "the nature of qualificand ('qualificand-ness') residing in the mountain is a qualificand-ness limited by mountain-ness, defined by fire; and the qualifier-ness residing in the fire is a qualifier-ness delimited by fire-ness and defined by the mountain". In the previous analysis of the proposition "this is a vase", the intervention of the delimitor-delimited concept allows a further clarification: "it is that knowledge that possesses a qualificand residing in 'this', delimited by this-ness, defined by adjective-ness residing in a vase, delimited by vase-ness, defined by a relation-ness residing in identity". Indeed, the vase may be portrayed in the cognition/ proposition in one of many aspects: as a substance with inherent qualities; as a generic material object; as an object made of clay; as a tool for performing certain actions; as the mere presence of something as opposed to the absence of anything; etc. Saying "a vase delimited by vase-ness" means in this case restricting the reference to

[8] Also important is the concept of 'definer', 'describer' (*nirūpaka*); cf. Wada 1988.

the general conformation of the object and thus to its specific and overall identity.

Returning to the expression "there is fire on the mountain" / "the mountain is endowed-with-fire", Navyanyāya analysis points out at least three possible structures: in the first, there is a qualificand modified by a qualifier; in the second, there is a subject to which a predicate is attributed; in the third, there is a substrate on which an entity resides. The property (*dharma*) that identifies the mountain — 'mountain-ness' — thus acts as 'delimitor of substantive-ness', 'delimitor of subject-ness', 'delimitor of substrate-ness'; on its own side, the property of fire (or of being-endowed-with-fire) — 'igneity' — may act as a 'delimitor of adjectivity', as a 'delimitor of predicativity', as a 'delimitor of the fact of residing on a substrate'. The relationship between the substrate and what resides there may in turn be partial or total, according, that is, to whether the substrate is pervaded (or occupied) partly (*avyāpyavṛtti*) or wholly (*vyāpyavṛtti*). The same expression is also used for another type of pervasion, mentioned above, pervasion between the middle term and the major term (*hetu* and *sādhya*) in inference. In a work belonging to recent Navyanyāya literature, the proposition "the vase is blue" is analysed in as many as ninety-six constituent elements...

The Vaiśeṣika System

> While in the systems hitherto considered particularly in the Vedānta, Sāṃkhya and Yoga, there runs a strong religious and even poetical vein, we now come to two systems, Nyāya and Vaiśeṣika, which are very dry and unimaginative, and much more like what we mean by scholastic systems of philosophy, business-like expositions of what can be known, either of the world that surrounds us or of the world within, that is, of our faculties or powers of perceiving, conceiving or reasoning on one side, and the objects which they present to us, on the other.
>
> (F. Max Müller)[1]

Of the Indian philosophical systems, Vaiśeṣika most lends itself to representing a kind of philosophy of nature, prompted by the intent of constructing a reliable image of the outside world, understood first and foremost as its complete cataloguing. Although this basic attitude, as we shall see, is also found in various kinds in other schools — like Sāṃkhya, Jainism, Buddhism, Mīmāṃsā, the Materialists — in Vaiśeṣika it appears to assume its purest form, least conditioned by other factors, such as the soteriological need, which in the end influences even those disposed to deny it (like Mīmāṃsā and the Materialists). Ancient Vaiśeṣika, at least according to Frauwallner's reconstruction (1978: II, 3-180), seems to have been totally deaf to it, and to have proposed the total elimination of all mythological and scriptural stuff, entrusting itself only to the cold gaze of reason — which appeared so pedestrian and discouraging to Max Müller (at least as much as, on the other hand, it was exalted and, perhaps, mythicised in turn by Frauwallner) — to orientate itself in the existing. Another aspect that characterises Vaiśeṣika is its decided preference — and this goes still more for classical Vaiśeṣika

[1] *Cit.* in Faddegon 1918: 6.

— for a synchronic or horizontal description of the real (Halbfass 1992: 49-51), withdrawing from cosmogonic questions that are probably deemed to be intrinsically connected with myth. This, in the end, becomes a much wider attitude of marginalizing time — not to speak of history — and with all becoming, an attitude all the more unexpected in a so-called philosophy of nature. Indeed, on closer examination, the nature of Vaiśeṣika consists solely of 'things' and not of processes, at the opposite end from philosophies, such as Buddhism to a great extent, for which reification is as a rule the major enemy. This attitude may serve to explain why Vaiśeṣika never opened to science as such, remaining increasingly entangled in the snares of a kind of 'scientific scholasticism'. The Vaiśeṣika world view is based on a few axioms (Bronkhorst 1992), each responsible for major consequences — even if sometimes not immediately identifiable — in the economy of the system: a) a complete enumeration of the existing is possible; b) the whole is a different and independent entity from its component parts; c) there is direct correspondence between words and things; d) spatial (as also temporal) extension can be reduced to atomic dimensions.

The foundation of the Vaiśeṣika system is the *Vaiśeṣikasūtra*, deemed to have attained its current form between the first and second centuries C.E. Its author — and the system's mythical founder — is the sage Kaṇāda ('Eater of grains', or, according to others, 'Eater of atoms', with an allusion to his championing of the atomic theory), who is presented by tradition as a mysterious and secluded character (another of his names is Ulūka, 'Owl'). The *Vaiśeṣikasūtra* comprises about four hundred short and often enigmatic aphorisms, divided into ten *adhyāya*s ('lessons'), the first seven of which are in turn divided into two *āhnika*s ('days'). This corpus is far from possessing any univocal form and presents considerable variations from one commentary to another of those that have come down to us. The commentary literature itself does not possess that compactness that distinguishes its twin system, Nyāya, and, on the contrary, appears problematic. Up to the mid-twentieth century, the *Vaiśeṣikasūtra* was read in the light of only one commentary, the late *Vaiśeṣikasūtra-upaskāra* ('Ornament of the *Vaiśeṣikasūtra*') by Śaṅkaramiśra, composed in the fifteenth century. This was soon accompanied, published within a few years of each other, first by a *Vyākhyā* ('Explanation') by an anonymous author — but certainly more ancient than Śaṅkaramiśra by several centuries — and then by a major *Vṛtti* ('Brief Commentary'), authored by Candrānanda, and datable between the ninth and tenth centuries. Lastly, an epitome of the *Vārttika* ('Glosses') by Bhaṭṭa Vādīndra was composed around the thirteenth century. Of other older commentaries we find traces only in quotations: among these stands out the *Kaṭandī*, ascribed to Rāvaṇa. It is earlier than the fifth century (the date of the *Nayacakra*, 'Wheel of Philosophical Standpoints', by the Jain Mallavādin, which it mentions), and may coincide with the *Bhāṣya* ('Elaborate Commentary'), an illustration of the most ancient commentary of all, the *Vākya* ('Sentences'), which accompanied the *sūtra*s (it has also been suggested that the *Kaṭandī* comprised both the *Vākya* and *Bhāṣya*). The *sūtra*, the *Vākya* and the *Bhāṣya* were then in turn the subject of an analytical commentary (*ṭīkā*) by Praśastamati, which has also been lost. The appearance of a brilliant and well-constructed work, the *Padārthadharmasaṃgraha* ('Synthesis of the Properties of Categories') by Praśastapāda (fifth-sixth century) soon came to dominate the system, even pre-empting the root-*sūtra* and certainly contributing to the eclipse of the abundant existing commentaries. While making constant reference to the *Vaiśeṣikasūtra*, the *Padārtha-dharmasaṃgraha* presents itself as an independent and often decidedly innovative work. Of the same kind is the *Daśapadārthaśāstra* ('Treatise on the Ten Categories') by Candramati, dating approximately to the same period, as shown both by its Chinese translation — which alone has come down to us, the sole evidence of this probably marginal work, in any case wholly neglected in its Indian context both as quotations in other works and manuscript tradition are concerned. Confirmation of the importance of the *Padārthadharmasaṃgraha* is shown by the fact that in turn it has triggered a considerable commentary literature, in which stands out the *Vyomavatī* ('Wide-ranging [explication]'), a pun on the name of its author Vyomaśiva (early ninth century), the *Nyāyakandalī* ('*Kandalī* Tree [of scented white flowers] of the Nyāya') by Śrīdhara (tenth century) and the *Kiraṇāvalī* ('Bundle of luminous Rays') by Udayana (tenth-eleventh centuries).

The initial aphorisms of the *Vaiśeṣikasūtra* (quoted here according to Candrānanda) open immediately onto the system's central teaching but, as we shall see, the first of them also provides an opportunity for some assessment of its original nature.

> We shall now illustrate the *dharma* (*athāto dharmaṃ vyākhyāsyāmaḥ*)" (I.1.1). "That, thanks to which worldly well-being and the highest good is realised, that is *dharma*" (I.1.2). "The authoritativeness of tradition [whence the previous assertion] derives from the fact of having been enunciated by Him [the Lord]. (I.1.3)

The following *sūtra* is introduced by the commentator Candrānanda with these words: "The own form of *dharma* has thus been stated as well as its definition; we shall now go on to expound the means for its realisation, meaning substance, qualities and actions. Among these..."

> "Earth, water, fire, wind, ether, time, space and the ego: these are the substances" (I.1.4). "Shape-colour, taste, smell, touch, number, dimension, separateness, conjunction and disjunction, distance and proximity, notions, pleasure and pain, desire and aversion, effort: these are the qualities" (I.1.5). "Raising, lowering, contraction, expansion and going are the actions" (I.1.6).

It has been noted (by Frauwallner; discussed in Halbfass 1992: 69-70) that in two of the commentaries on the *Padārthadharmasaṃgraha*, the *Vyomavatī* and the *Kiraṇāvalī* mentioned above recurs the quotation of a phrase, with some variations, that closely recalls the formulation of the first *sūtra*. It differs however on a fundamental point: "everything possesses the character of being, all this will I state" (e.g. Vyomaśiva: *yad bhāvarupaṃ tat sarvam abhidhāsyāmi*). This has led to the hypothesis that any soteriological preoccupations — or 'religious' in a wider sense — must have originally been foreign to this system, born with the aim of pure scientific investigation into the nature of the physical world and only more recently given a philosophical-religious 'respray', probably in order to compete more easily with other prestigious traditions, like the Buddhist and Jaina, which right from the start had been intimately marked by such far-reaching concerns. At the same time, there has been no lack of critics of Vaiśeṣika who have pointed out this strange discrepancy between the declared intent at the beginning of the *Vaiśeṣikasūtra* and its actual content. Although there is no doubt as to the particularly troubled history of the *Vaiśeṣikasūtra* text, as mentioned above, it must be taken into account that if this system's orientations have been modified, this did not take place recently, since as early as the fifth century Bhartṛhari shows that he knows the initial *sūtra* in the form in which the — relatively late — extant commentaries have handed it down to us. The almost total lack of certain data, as well as of textual bases, makes any reconstruction of the ancient phases of Vaiśeṣika largely conjectural.

What is certain is that the system's basic attitude and interests place it on the 'minority' side of Brahmanic thought. One passage from the *Kaṭha Upaniṣad* (II.1) lends itself excellently to an attempt to trace a line of demarcation between two different modes of thought and experience: "The Self-begotten Lord made openings [the senses] facing outward: this is why man looks outward and not within himself. But a wise man, aspiring to non-death, turned his eye inward and saw the inner Self". While one trend, destined to assume a pre-eminent role in Indian philosophical tradition, is thus oriented toward introspection and the search for an absolute unitary principle before which the manifest world inevitably pales, claims of an exactly contrary nature are not lacking, featuring the investigation of the outside world, the intent of focusing on its every specificity: concrete facts rather than the recondite spiritual principle underlying them. One of the explanations of the term Vaiśeṣika given by commentators makes reference to this very orientation toward differentiation and the particular (*viśeṣa*).

To the 'naturalistic' side belongs, for example, the famous dialogue between Bharadvāja and Bhṛgu in the *Mahābhārata* (XII.183-187), to which Frauwallner (1973: 98-106) calls attention. To Bharadvāja's questions about the origin and nature of the universe, Bhṛgu replies by outlining an analytical scenario starting from a primordial situation in which only ether exists, from which are born water, air, fire and, lastly, earth. These five elements constitute everything; to each of them belong two sets of specific qualities, i.e. providing space, movement, heat, fluidity and solidity, on the one hand, sound, tangibility, visibility, taste and smell, on the other. Each of these qualities then possesses various modalities, the subject of long lists. From appropriate combinations of these primary elements (*bhūta*) are also formed living beings, both animal and vegetal. Even vital principles and sensory faculties are merely combinations of elements, particularly of fire and air.

From these and other similar speculations Vaiśeṣika philosophy developed. It seems however to differ owing to its disinterest — to become increasingly marked, up to the system's classical formulation — in the evolutionary form that as a rule characterises this kind of concept and in the long run maintains communication with the religious sphere and mythical cosmogonies already outlined in the Veda. In a manner not dissimilar, for example, from the Buddhist Abhidharma schools and the Sarvāstivādin, and from Jainism — albeit apparently without their motivations which, in any final analysis, are of a soteriological order — Vaiśeṣika has systematically devoted itself to a kind of cataloguing of whatever relates to or is part of 'being' or 'reality' (*bhāva*, *sattā*) — complex terms and concepts and, as we shall see, inevitably ambiguous — paying little heed to creationist or theological questions. As a result, it is regarded by Brahmanical 'orthodoxy' — at least in its Vedāntic component

— with a certain suspicion: though never being explicitly disavowed, it is usually relegated to unflattering positions in doxographic classifications.

The Vaiśeṣika classificatory effort does not stop with numbering single entities, culminating in the identification of a limited number of general principles or rubrics, known as *padārtha*, commonly translated as 'categories' (lit. 'word meaning'). The literal meaning of the term should not lead one to think of any standpoint on nominalism, which would moreover be rather incongruous with the marked Vaiśeṣika realistic option, of which one of the tacit axioms is trust in the capacity of knowledge and language to mirror and express things for what they are. Most probably, the term should be understood according to its less pregnant meaning, widespread in common use, of 'entity' or 'thing', designated in the most generic and abstract terms, around which 'discourse' is possible. In the classical form of Vaiśeṣika — corresponding to the settlement achieved by the *Padārthadharmasaṃgraha* — the number of categories is established as six: 1) substance; 2) quality; 3) motion; 4) universal; 5) particularity; 6) inherence. They are listed in a verse included in the *Vaiśeṣikasūtra*, which however appears most likely to have been a later addition, seeing that neither the text commented on by Candrānanda, nor the one commented on by Vādīndra mentions it (it is found only in the text commented on by Śaṅkaramiśra in the fifteenth century). Furthermore, the initial *sūtra*s of the *Vaiśeṣikasūtra*, quoted above, mention and describe the first three only. This consideration, together with the fact that the two triads appear to be as highly heterogeneous as they are homogeneous internally, leads to the conclusion that categories 4) universal, 5) particularity, 6) inherence belong to some later stage of the system. While it is true, as stated in the *Padārthadharmasaṃgraha*, that all six categories possess 'reality' (*astitva*), 'knowability' (*jñeyatva*) and 'linguistic denotability' (*abhidheyatva*), only the first three, on the other hand, have any 'relation to [factual] existence' (*sattāsambandha*). The opposition of *sattāsambandha* and *astitva* — this latter term being mentioned by Praśastapāda on a single occasion and without any explanation, which subsequent commentators and authors have sought to do in the most disparate ways (Halbfass 1992: 154-158) — appears similar to that of concreteness and abstraction of being, the former belonging to the world of objects, while the latter is of much wider application, including the sphere of cognition and the linguistic universe. As an example, only *astitva* pertains to the effect prior to its effective production, configured precisely as the attainment of *sattāsambandha*.

If, with Frauwallner, one admits that the original number of categories was restricted to three, in the classical arrangement given to Vaiśeṣika by the *Padārthadharmasaṃgraha*, they are firmly established as six, later becoming seven with the addition of *abhāva* ('non-being, absence') in the work of Udayana, the first to present Vaiśeṣika explicitly in union with Nyāya. The number of categories remains open to criticism, however, both inside and outside Nyāya-Vaiśeṣika, and there is no lack of those who underline the intrinsic arbitrariness of any enumeration of the basic components of reality that claims to be exhaustive. It should not be forgotten that another Vaiśeṣika work, more or less contemporary with the *Padārtha-dharmasaṃgraha*, establishes the number as ten, as shown by its very title *Daśapadārthaśāstra* ('Treatise on the Ten Categories'), adding 'causal efficiency' (*śakti*), 'lack of causal efficiency' (*aśakti*), 'specific universal' (*sāmānyaviśeṣa*) and 'absence' (*abhāva*). Lastly, in the *Padārthatattvanirūpaṇa*, Raghunātha Śiromaṇi subjects the entire system of categories to radical criticism, eliminating, for example, space, time and 'existence' itself (*sattā*), and adding others, such as causality and number.

According to the *Padārthadharmasaṃgraha* (pp. 43-44), the first three categories have in common, beside their relation to existence (*sattāsambandha*), other characteristics as well: they may have both universals and particularities; from the specific Vaiśeṣika point of view, they may be called 'things' (*artha*); and they are capable of producing merit and demerit. The other three categories (*ibid*. p. 49)

— universal, ultimate particularity and inherence — on the other hand have intrinsic existence, i.e. not dependent on relation (included with *sattā*), are revealed solely by the intellectual faculty, can be neither causes nor effects, have neither universals nor peculiarities, are eternal and cannot be indicated by the word 'thing'.

According to the *Vaiśeṣikasūtra* (I.1.4), the nine substances — earth, water, fire, wind, ether, time, space, inner sense, soul — have three common characteristics: they may be endowed with motion and with the quality of being 'inherent causes' (indeed, Vaiśeṣika distinguishes inherent or 'material' causes, non-inherent causes and efficient causes. In the case of the product 'pot', these are represented respectively by the clay and its component earth atoms, the qualities peculiar to the inherent cause, determining analogous qualities in the effect, and by the potter's wheel and hands). This last feature is reformulated in *sūtra* I.1.8: "Substances create other substances". The substance produced is an assembly of parts (*avayavin*), a whole, deemed entirely different from the parts or factors that produced it, a doctrine drawing an interminable series of criticisms onto Nyāya-Vaiśeṣika, *in primis* from the Buddhists, who on the contrary maintain the wholly fictitious nature of any 'compound'. All substances, except for those made of parts, also possess the characteristic of not being dependent and of being eternal.

The Vaiśeṣika concept of substance is not univocal, and has at least three different meanings. In the first, 'substance' is the equivalent of the seat of qualities and motion, and is what *sūtra* I.1.7 refers to; the second is the substrate that continues to exist through any accidental change; the third is that of the entity's ability to exist independently. To the question as to whether such an entity, divested of all qualities or any other attribute, could continue to have any 'concrete' reality and, as such, be an independent object of perception, Vaiśeṣika thinkers replied in positive terms, albeit with various nuances and not without some hesitation, which also derived from the unclear distinction between the ontological level of 'substrate' (*āśraya*), of qualities, etc. and the logical/ linguistic level of the subject to which predicates refer (Halbfass 1992: 98).

According to the section of the *Padārthadharmasaṃgraha* devoted to analogies and differences among the categories, to which we have several times referred, the substances 'space' and 'time' have in common the fact of possessing the same five qualities — number, dimension, separateness, conjunction and disjunction (cf. pp. 69-71) — and of being the instrumental causes of whatever has an origin. They are not understood as dynamic elements, but as the static and reified coordinates of the universe. Space and time also share with ether omni-pervasiveness, infinite dimension and the fact of constituting the common receptacle of all material things endowed with parts.

Every element (*bhūta*) possesses a permanent aspect in the form of atoms and an impermanent one in the form of aggregate. Beside the seven qualities that are common to all the elements (number, size, separateness, conjunction and disjunction, distance and proximity), they also possess others, in progressively decreasing number, belonging to a set of four (taste, smell, shape and tangibility; earth possesses all four, while air has only the last). As an aggregate, the 'earth' element is part of the bodies of creatures, of the sensory organs and objects. While the bodies of a few privileged creatures (e.g. the gods, or seers) are born directly from earth atoms, as a rule other bodies are born in the maternal womb or from an egg, as a result of the mixture of male sperm and female menstrual blood. The organ formed by it is that of touch. With regard to objects, both mineral and vegetal are constituted by the 'earth' element. The 'water' element, as an aggregate, is the essential component of a special class of bodies living in the world of Varuṇa, and forms the organ of taste; as far as objects are concerned, it forms seas, rivers and lakes. As an aggregate, 'fire' (*tejas*) forms, mixed with earth, the bodies found in the world of the Sun; it forms the organ of sight. In the world of objects, its presence is quadruple: it is the ordinary terrestrial fire, feeding on common fuels; the celestial fire, whose fuel is water, which forms the sun and stars; as the abdominal fire, it is responsible for digestion and for transforming food into vital fluid; as underground fire, it takes the form of gold and other metals. As stated above, 'air' (*vāyu*) forms the bodies that live in the world of Wind; it forms the organ of touch. As an object, it is not directly perceptible, but can be inferred from the effects it causes, like the motion of clouds, rustling, sounds, etc. In the body, it is present as breath, distinguished in many kinds, and performs important functions, such as the circulation of essential fluids (*dhātu*).

In actual fact, 'ether' (*ākāśa*) has little in common with the four material elements with which it is associated. Its existence is inferred from that of sound, which would otherwise be a quality lacking a substrate. Ether is reached by exclusion, after progressively examining and discarding all other substances. Even sound, on its own side, presents marked peculiarities as compared to the other qualities, which are also objects of perception. Ether is conceived of as infinitely great, since sound can be perceived everywhere. It does not possess a plurality of forms of manifestation, being infinite, unitary and not made up of atoms. Its function as a sound-perceiving organ is thus fairly problematic: in this connection, Vaiśeṣika has constructed a somewhat abstruse theory, stating that the organ of perception is ether, or at least that portion of ether circumscribed by the auditory canal, which owes the development of this otherwise inexplicable perceptive faculty to — yet again — the intervention of the 'invisible' (*adṛṣṭa*): invisible power, generated by ethically positive or negative actions, whose range of action goes well beyond the dimension of the individual subject and incarnates a mysterious force that governs the natural events of the entire universe.[2] Consequently, deafness cannot be attributed to a defect of ether — by definition infinite and unalterable — but to a deficiency of *adṛṣṭa* (Frauwallner 1973: 148-149).

---

[2] Frauwallner defined *adṛṣṭa* as "an idea that had already made its appearance during the ancient period of Vaiśeṣika, where it acted as a foreign body, disturbing the compact edifice of the ancient Nature philosophy" (Frauwallner 1973: 60-61). On *adṛṣṭa*, cf. Frauwallner 1973: 62-64; Houben 1994: 738-740.

The four elements are in turn constituted by atoms (*paramāṇu*: 'extremely small'), which cannot be divided further and are capable of combining together in increasingly more numerous aggregates — bi-atomic (*dvyaṇuka*), tri-atomic (*tryaṇuka*) and so on — thus becoming accessible to perception as molecules, etc. Indeed, the quality technically called 'smallness' (*aṇutva*) is peculiar only to atoms, taken alone or as a couple, with the difference that 'smallness' is permanent in the former and impermanent in the latter. 'Largeness' (*mahattva*), or macroscopicity, starts only from ternary aggregates. Atoms are eternal and unalterable, identical in shape (*parimaṇḍala*, 'rotund'), and are distinguished by the qualities specific to each element. Qualities are also deemed to be permanent.

There is consequently no real and actual birth or destruction of the universe in the composite picture outlined by the *Padārtha-dharmasaṃgraha* (cf. Frauwallner 1973: 146-147). When the stasis phase that follows the periodic dissolution of atom aggregates forming the material world reaches the end of the one hundred 'years of Brahmā', the 'invisible power' (*adṛṣṭa*) adhering to souls starts functioning again, causing first of all motion in the air atoms, which aggregate in a great mass of wind. Thundering, it invades and fills space. In the same way, from the water atoms is formed an immense ocean, in which the earth collects little by little. From the ocean there develops a great mass of heat: fire. Fire and earth are the elements from which the Supreme Lord forms the universe, the so-called 'egg of Brahmā' (*brahmāṇḍa*), which progressively fills with creatures. At the end of a further one hundred 'years of Brahmā', the Supreme Lord, having reached the close of his mandate, resolves to destroy the universe and, to this end, suspends the power of the *adṛṣṭa*, which was the ultimate source of the dynamism of the created. As a result, motion rises in the atoms, leading to the progressive disaggregation (*vibhāga*) in bodies of their component elements, until the elements themselves disintegrate and the entire world ends up as isolated atoms.

Eighth in the numbering of substances comes the soul, or 'self' (*ātman*). Their number is infinite; they are inaccessible to perception, owing to their subtle and all-pervasive nature; the soul is the object of inference only, starting, for example, from the impossibility of conceiving any other possible substrate for quality, such as knowledge (*buddhi*), firstly, and then for pleasure, pain, attachment, aversion and effort. Lastly comes the 'inner sense' (*manas*), which coordinates the activities of the various senses and is the only one capable of perceiving qualities such as pleasure or pain. Of atomic dimensions, it possesses unlimited speed, but cannot unite with other atoms.

The 'quality' category (*guṇa*) comprises, according to the *Vaiśeṣikasūtra* (I.1.5, mentioned above), seventeen elements: shape, taste, smell, touch, number, size, separateness, conjunction, disjunction, distance, proximity, notion, pleasure, pain, desire, aversion and effort. To these, the *Padārthadharmasaṃgraha* adds a further seven: weight, fluidity, humidity, disposition (*saṃskāra*, differentiated in turn as speed, elasticity and as the mark left by previous experience and cognition), merit, demerit and sound. Qualities always depend on a substrate in which they inhere (substances), while they cannot inhere in other qualities (thus, strictly speaking, we should not even speak of 'number' relating to qualities, since number itself is a quality) or to motions. They can inhere in a single substrate, either occupying it partially (as in the case of sound and the qualities of the soul), or in several substrates (in the case of conjunction and disjunction) which are consequently, thanks to them, united or separate.

Vaiśeṣika authors dwell at length — as we cannot — on the nature of the qualities and their various subdivisions, as well as their role — whose formulation is rather complicated and debatable — in relation to causality. Noteworthy, for example, is the concept of *apekṣābuddhi* ('dependent notion'), on which depend qualities that intrinsically assume an observer as point of reference, such as distance and proximity, number and separateness. Such qualities — together with extension, conjunction and separation — belong to the so-called 'common' qualities (*sāmānya*), in opposition to the others, known as 'specific' (*vaiśeṣika*), since they are reserved, as we have seen, only for certain substances. Among the 'common' qualities, we should clarify the clear distinction of meaning between 'separateness' (*pṛthaktva*) and 'disjunction' (*vibhāga*): whereas the former quality guarantees a thing's identity and individuality, so that it can be distinguished from all others, the latter is the condition, destined to last just an instant, that immediately follows the cessation of a previous conjunction. Although in common usage, the two Sanskrit terms *guṇa* and *dharma* are substantially synonymous, the *guṇa* of the Vaiśeṣikas has a much more restricted meaning, reserved to a small set of 'objective' qualities, whereas *dharma* embraces every possible attribute with which a subject can be predicated, without any need for some kind of reference to reality.

Particularly interesting is what Vaiśeṣika, and especially the *Padārthadharmasaṃgraha* and its commentaries, has to say about the 'sound' quality. Every sound, including that of human language itself, has only three possible origins: it can be produced by a conjunction, by a disjunction, or by another sound. In the case of language, we have a flow of breath that rises from our lungs and, in the oral cavity, comes into contact with the places and organs of articulation, in turn conjoined with or disjoined from each other, and connected with the ether. The quality 'sound' that arises from ether lasts only an instant and takes place at a greater or shorter distance from the perceiver's ear. Since, according to Vaiśeṣika, for perception to occur, there must be contact between the organ and its object, we can only surmise that sound reaches the ear physically by means of a chain. Each sound, in itself instantaneous, must therefore have the power of generating an identical sound, which immediately destroys the previous sound, and so on, until it reaches the ear. To take into account the fact that sooner or later every sound ends, we must add that the penultimate sound has the property not only of destroying its cause, but also its effect.

Like quality, every motion must be related to a certain substrate (substance) and can therefore not be a substrate for other motions or qualities. This and other analogies led Bhāsarvajña to consider it not as a separate category, but as a subspecies of quality. Motion can be produced by weight, fluidity, effort or conjunction, and can in turn produce conjunction and disjunction. Motion with an unidentifiable definite cause is ascribed to 'invisible power' (*adṛṣṭa*). Motion generally recognised as having an instantaneous duration is classified as five kinds: raising, lowering, contraction, distension, to which is added 'going' (*gamana*) for cases in which no precise spatial direction is foreseen (such as, for example, the motion of the atoms). The inevitability of any spatial direction excludes from motion all substances deemed omni-pervasive, such as ether, the soul, time and, naturally, space itself.

Although the term *sāmānya* recurs several times in the *Vaiśeṣika-sūtra*, no definition of it is given. Yet again it will be useful to turn to the *Padārthadharmasaṃgraha* (pp. 741-743), which assigns the following characteristics to the universal: it is present in a multiplicity of individuals, maintaining its own intrinsic unity; it determines the notion of the continuity of its presence in an indefinitely large number of individuals; it can be absolute or relative (i.e. it can embrace a content of greater or lesser extension). According to another definition, accepted by most followers of Nyāya-Vaiśeṣika, it is a unitary and eternal entity, present in many individuals by means of a special kind of relationship with them, called 'inherence' (*samavāya*, cf. pp. 74-75).

The problem of the universals, which traverses the whole of Indian thought — neither more nor less than it does through all Western philosophy, from Plato onward — requires a preliminary clarification of terminology. Indeed, to complicate an already fairly complex scenario of positions and debates among the various schools, we find an overlapping of three terms with ambiguous outlines, often greatly diversified from one school to the other: *sāmānya* (lit. 'commonness, generality'), *jāti* (lit. 'birth, kind') and *ākṛti* (lit. 'conformation, configuration'). In the Nyāya-Vaiśeṣika context, *sāmānya* and *jāti* cover substantially the same semantic area, with the difference that specifically Nyāya texts show a preference for the former and specifically Vaiśeṣika ones the latter. Pakṣilasvāmin, in his commentary on the *Nyāyasūtra* (pp. 111-112) understands *jāti* as a form of *sāmānya*, but with a more restricted extension (the term, as we have seen, having the basic, more concrete, meaning of 'birth'), meaning the 'specific universal' of Vaiśeṣika; *sāmānya* is defined as 'what causes the continuity/ continuation of a notion'. The term *ākṛti* on the other hand seems to refer as a rule to a decidedly more concrete level than *sāmānya* and *jāti*, that is, to the way in which common elements making it possible to define two or more objects as similar or belonging to the same class also appear even externally as possessing an analogy of structure or conformation. Such a differentiation in the meanings of the said three terms is valid only for some schools, like Nyāya or the Grammarians, whereas in others, such as Mīmāṃsā, they tend to be confused (Halbfass 1992: 120-121). Vaiśeṣika was the first to introduce a hierarchy among the universals: the universal 'cow', which links many individuals, none identical to the other, is subordinate — i.e. of lesser extension — than the universal 'quadruped', which in turn is less extensive than 'animal', and so on, until we reach the universal that cannot be included by any other: *sattā*, 'the fact of existing, existence', an abstract formation (*-tā*) from *sat*, 'existing'. This is the absolute universal (*para sāmānya*) spoken of in the *Padārthadharmasaṃgraha* (pp. 29, 741).

The Vaiśeṣika conception of the universal presents a few inevitable paradoxes: the universal is eternal and undivided, and is therefore contained integrally in every particular individual; in fact, its sole *locus* is particular individuals. This however does not mean that if all particular individuals perish the related universal perishes too, since it is by definition eternal. It will continue to have some sort of indefinable, latent existence. Although the *Vaiśeṣikasūtra* I.2.3

considers it, together with the 'particularity' category as *buddhyapekṣa* ('dependent on the intellectual faculty') and the *Padārthadharmasaṃgraha* attributes to it the quality of *buddhilakṣaṇa* [3] ('having as a means of characterization/ definition the intellectual faculty'), subsequent texts — and, albeit not without ambiguity, the *Padārthadharmasaṃgraha* itself (cf. Halbfass 1992: 99-102) — concur in considering it as the object of direct perception, thereby implicitly stating that the universal is not a phantasm of the intellect, the fruit of its autonomous and unconnected power of abstraction, but that on the contrary any abstract concept of similarity, etc. finds therein its *ubi consistam*, an objective basis that will also be the ultimate guarantee of the validity of the object-knowledge-language equation, the axiom on which the whole Vaiśeṣika edifice tacitly rests. These features of the universal according to Vaiśeṣika refer, especially by way of contrast, to those of the Platonic universal. For Platonism too, universals — 'ideas' — have their own real existence, independent of particular objects; they do not reside in the said particular objects, but in a space beyond the heavens; objects are merely an imperfect copy of them. If, notwithstanding their imperfection, men manage to have some notion of ideas/ universals, this is only because their souls, prior to being involved in their earthly adventure, have been able to contemplate the 'originals'.

The fifth category (*antyaviśeṣa*, 'ultimate particularity') is the one that has most given rise to diverse interpretations, first of all owing to the widespread ambiguity of the texts themselves. The *Vaiśeṣikasūtra*, while mentioning it, provides no definition. After distinguishing (I.2.3) the universal (*sāmānya*) from the particularity (*viśeṣa*), considering them both, however, as we have seen, as the function of a certain attitude of knowing (*buddyapekṣa*) — which the commentator Candrānanda (in the same terms as Praśastapāda) later defined respectively as 'inclusive' (*anuvṛttibuddhi*) and

[3] A quality that shares in the 'peculiarity' and 'inherence' categories.

'exclusive' (*vyāvṛttibuddhi*) (p. 8) —, and having said that universals such as those of substance, quality and motion (but not 'existence') may also be viewed as particularities, he states (I.2.6) that in no way can the character of universal be attributed to 'ultimate particularities' (*antya-viśeṣa*). *Viśeṣa*, explains Candrānanda (p. 8), owes its name to the function of 'diversifying' (*viśeṣakatva*). Being present by means of a relationship of inherence in permanent substances — such as atoms, ether, etc. —, it determines the notion in terms of exclusion for objects with similar conformations and qualities: this is one thing; that is another. The ultimate particularity, as further clarified by the *Padārthadharmasaṃgraha* (pp. 765-770), is the extreme factor of identification, present only in the atoms of the four elements, in ether, time, space, the soul, and the inner sense, and perceptible by the yogins. Indeed, they alone can discern the differences between elementary and virtually identical entities, such as the single atoms of the various elements or liberated souls, and are even capable of recognizing a certain atom seen in another time and space. Atoms, all having the same nature, cannot themselves be responsible for such distinct cognition. They become so thanks to their association with the ultimate peculiarities, just as, adds the *Padārthadharmasaṃgraha* (p. 771), impure substances, such as cow- or horse-meat, make other substances impure, which would not otherwise be so, by virtue of their sole contact with them. The *Daśapadārthaśāstra*, on the other hand, appears to reserve this factor of identification, among the permanent substances, only to those that are also unitary, like ether, space and time. The concept of ultimate particularity is sometimes confused with 'separateness' (*pṛthaktva*), which has a much wider application; ultimate particularity too, for example, is qualified by 'separateness'.

Inherence ends the list of categories according to classical Vaiśeṣika, and the *Padārthadharmasaṃgraha* too closes with the investigation of inherence. Inherence is a special type of connection between two elements, an eternal and necessary connection, unlike that occasional and provisional connection known as *saṃyoga* ('conjunction'). An example of *saṃyoga* is the connection between a jug and milk, whereas the connection of the universal with particularities or of the part with the whole belongs to inherence. According to the formulation of the *Padārthadharmasaṃgraha* (pp. 773-774), inherence differs from conjunction for four reasons: 1) because in the relationship the two members are inseparably connected; 2) because it is not caused by the action of its members; 3) because it does not cease with the separation of its members; 4) because the relationship in which its members are placed can only be that of container-contained (*ādhārya-ādhāra*). Inherence cannot be the object of perception (except by yogins: cf. p. 98), and is unique, differing in this from conjunction. Thanks to inherence, the universal 'substance' resides in the various substances, the universal 'quality' in the various qualities, the universal 'motion' in the various movements. Yet again, inherence binds ultimate particularity to permanent substances. Despite this apparent character of extreme abstraction, inherence proceeds from the very idea of 'here'. As noted by Halbfass (1992: 75), it serves to account for the mixing of the different and ontologically heterogeneous components in the concreteness of the empirical world. While analysis in terms of categories dissolves the unity of the thing, inherence establishes the *ratio* for its reconstitution. Conversely, since no category is isolated, it is only starting from the notion of inherence that we can analyse the various components, which in experience appear inextricably connected (Bronkhorst 1992: 97).

The Sāṃkhya System

To a young American student who had just informed him that he had come to Banaras to study one of the Indian philosophies, Sāṃkhya, one of the great sages of traditional India of the last century, Gopinath Kaviraj, replied with a certain impatience that Sāṃkhya is not *one* of the Indian philosophies, but *the* Indian philosophy (Larson 1987: XI). It should be stated that the young student was Gerald Larson, who went on to become one of the best known scholars of this *darśana*. Gopinath Kaviraj's affirmation, which might seem overly decisive and over-simplifying, is anything but lacking in justification. Not only is Sāṃkhya the most ancient of the *darśana*s, it also constitutes the first attempt to give some coherence to the speculations expressed, first and foremost, in the Upaniṣads and hand them down, grafting them into the very weft of Indian civilisation.[1] In the end, India adopted, in an almost subliminal manner, the most characteristic of Sāṃkhya ideas and — what appears even more significant — did so seemingly unaware of their original provenance (macroscopic, for example, is the case of Tantrism; see Torella 1999a).

The entire Sāṃkhya structure rests on a few extremely 'strong' motifs, characterised by decidedly archaic traits. The universe can be reduced to tension between two antithetic principles: on the one side, unitary matter (*prakṛti*) without beginning, dynamic (and 'female'), which evolves incessantly in an infinity of forms by virtue of the imbalance of its three basic components, or 'qualities' (*guṇa*): *sattva* ('light, distension'), *rajas* ('dynamism, passion') and *tamas* ('obscurity, heaviness') (cf. p. 83); on the other, we find a spiritual principle (*puruṣa*), static ('male'), fragmented into a plurality of

---

[1] For an updating on the most recent status of studies on Sāṃkhya, reference to the volume edited by J. Bronkhorst is obligatory, as a collection of the contributions at the meeting organised by him at Lausanne in November 1998, published the following year in *Asiatische Studien / Études Asiatiques*, 53, 3.

souls, consisting solely of the light of consciousness and without action. The world's drama and pain arise substantially from a misunderstanding: the soul appears to be snared in the painful play of psyche and body, only to discover, once liberation is attained by means of an 'isolating vision' (*viveka*) that separates it definitively from matter, that there has never been any real involvement and that the soul had never ceased to be free and out of reach. The Sāṃkhya philosopher reaches this conception of the world, not on the basis of any revelation, but following independent reflection through which he enucleates and 'counts' the ultimate principles of the real (25, in the classical version of the system). 'Number, enumeration' is the current meaning of the word *saṃkhyā*, of which Sāṃkhya is a derivative: 'connected with, based on, enumeration', although any examination of the ancient occurrences of this root makes the meaning 'intellectual, ratiocinative investigation' seem decidedly more probable. In actual fact, however, the two meanings do not exclude each other, since enumeration is a primary means of giving a *ratio* to the confused multiplicity of the real. It is well known moreover that *ratio* itself, used regularly by Cicero to translate the Greek *lógos*, contains in what was its original nucleus the idea of 'computation' (Houben 1999: 495). It was probably this aspect, together with the exclusion — at least by most of its schools — of the figure of a divine creator and its often highly critical attitude toward the Veda, that made Sāṃkhya seem the very incarnation of Indian rationalism (which is the subtitle of the pioneering treatise devoted by R. Garbe in 1918 to this system),[2] disregarding the powerful soteriological impulse from which Sāṃkhya rises and its undisguised sapiential roots. If this label has to be given to anyone, Vaiśeṣika rather than Sāṃkhya would be the ideal candidate.

Right from its first mentions in the *Mahābhārata* (evidence of Sāṃkhya terminology is however already found in the *Kaṭha Upaniṣad* II.11 *et seq.* and it is also mentioned in the *Arthaśāstra*, p. 13),

[2] *Die Sāṃkhya-Philosophie: Eine Darstellung des Indischen Rationalismus nach den Quellen.*

concentrated particularly in the Mokṣaparvan ('Section on Liberation'; (Brockington 1999, Bakker-Bisschop 1999), Sāṃkhya is associated with Yoga or, to be more precise, the association is of *sāṃkhya* and *yoga* terms, the contours of which are not easy to identify with any precision. Rather than two distinct systems, they appear to be two different spiritual methodologies, one based on the saving power of pure knowledge, the other on that of a special kind of 'action'. This initial schematic opposition is bolstered by a series of other — not always coherent — connotations, such as the contrast between intellectual — even bookish — knowledge, reasoning, emphasis on intellectual faculties, on the one side, and direct experience, ecstasy, spiritual realisation, power, exploitation of bodily and psychic resources, on the other. Although *sāṃkhya* and *yoga* are often seen as being in conflict or even considered as alternatives, solemn affirmations as to their fundamental unity are not lacking, such as the famous passage which, for its exemplariness, is worth quoting in full:

> *Sāṃkhya* knowledge has been expounded by me. Now bring your mind to bear on *yoga* knowledge as I have seen and heard it, O best of kings, according to truth. There is no knowledge to equal *sāṃkhya*, there is no power to equal *yoga*. Both form a single path, both are said to be limitless. While men of scanty intellect see them as two separate things, O King, we for certain see them as one thing only. The same thing that the followers of *yoga* see, that do the followers of *sāṃkhya* also. He who sees *sāṃkhya* and *yoga* as a unity is he who knows according to truth.
>
> (*Mahābhārata* XII.304.1-4)

Proliferation of different schools and doctrines has accompanied Sāṃkhya throughout its long history. As late as the seventh century C.E., the Buddhist pilgrim Kuei-chi records the existence of as many as eighteen Sāṃkhya schools; Sāṃkhya, it should be remembered, was one of the subjects studied at the Buddhist university of Nālandā. According to the great Buddhist poet Aśvaghoṣa (second century C.E.), who gives a detailed description of it in his *Buddhacarita*

('Deeds of the Buddha'), the Buddha himself made a prolonged study of Sāṃkhya.

An attempt at reconstructing the prehistory of Sāṃkhya, i.e. of Sāṃkhya prior to its relatively late arrangement as a definitive *darśana*, was made by E. Frauwallner (1973: I, 217-392), with results as brilliant as they are intrinsically hypothetical. According to Frauwallner, the first stage is represented by the Adhyātmakathana ('Spiritual Tale'), included in the Mokṣadharma, in which no evolutionary theory yet appears, and the point of departure is seen as the five major elements which, created by the individual ego (*bhūtātman*), in turn produce the sensorial faculties, their objects and organs of action. To these five elements are added three other principles: *manas* ('internal sense'), *buddhi* ('intellect'; but with features leading one to think rather of *prakṛti*), and, lastly, *kṣetrajña* (lit. 'knower of the field'), i.e. the conscious and spiritual principle, also called *sākṣin* ('witness').

The second phase, connected with the teaching of Pañcaśikha — along with Kapila and Āsuri, one of the mythical founding fathers of Sāṃkhya —, as indicated yet again in the various chapters of the Mokṣadharma, sees the emergence of the concept — also found in the classic form of the system — of a unitary *prakṛti*, formed by the equilibrium of three components or qualities (*guṇa*s), and of 24 principles which (bar the spiritual principle) all evolve from it. The teachings that the *Mahābhārata* attributes to Pañcaśikha, characterised by recurrent emphasis on 'disgust' for the world (*nirveda*) considered as the point of departure for philosophic research, albeit highly diversified and even contradictory (Motegi 1999), seem however recalcitrant to this kind of structuring.

The third phase appears to be characterised by the so-called 'sixty doctrinal themes' (*ṣaṣṭitantra*), which also seems to be the title of a specific work attributed to Vārṣagaṇya that has not come down to us, but of which various quotations are extant in the works of rival schools, testifying to what must have been its importance and representativeness. The 'sixty doctrinal themes' comprise the ten basic subjects (*mūlika*) of Sāṃkhya doctrine: existence, unity, finality, serving another's ends, alterity, inactivity, conjunction, disjunction, the plurality of souls and the continuance of the body's existence (after liberation). To these are added the fifty 'ideas, notions' (*pratyaya*), i.e. the basic components of the individual's intellectual and psychic life. The *Ṣaṣṭitantra*, composed most probably at the outset of the fourth century and then provided by Vindhyavāsin with a major commentary, must have enjoyed great prestige, since it managed for several centuries not to be overshadowed by the appearance of what was to become the system's standard work, the *Sāṃkhyakārikā*. This may also have been due to the fact that the themes of epistemology and logic, given only a fleeting mention in the concise stanzas of the *Sāṃkhyakārikā*, are dealt with extensively in the *Ṣaṣṭitantra* and were long considered an integral part of the system's doctrine.

Taken as the reference text for the Sāṃkhya *darśana*, the *Sāṃkhyakārikā* is distinguished from the root-texts of the other *darśana*s from various points of view, the first being that it is not a self-referencing text, since its last verse acknowledges its dependence on the *Ṣaṣṭitantra*, the contents of which it enucleates, leaving aside its narrative digressions and disputes with rival doctrines. The *Sāṃkhyakārikā* is a tract of about seventy verses (not *śloka*s, much more widely used for this kind of work, but the more refined and elegant *āryā* verses), authored by a certain Īśvarakṛṣṇa, of whom almost nothing is known. The number of verses — given as seventy by the *Sāṃkhyakārikā* itself (although it is anything but infrequent in Indian texts for the number of verses to be rounded off) — is in actual fact seventy-two or seventy-three in its commentaries. With regard to its date, we have a *terminus ante quem* of 557-569, being the period of the literary activity of Paramārtha, who translated it into Chinese; the trend is to place the *Sāṃkhyakārikā* between the fourth and fifth centuries C.E. The clear and concise *Bhāṣya* by Gauḍapāda (eighth-ninth century?) has been considered its standard commentary and even now accompanies editions of the text of the *kārikās*. Very probably more ancient is the *Māṭharavṛtti* ('Brief commentary by Maṭhara'), which has several points in common with the commentary translated by Paramārtha into Chinese, together with the *kārikās*. The great polygraph Vācaspati Miśra (tenth century) also devoted a commentary to the *Sāṃkhyakārikā*, the *Sāṃkhyatattvakaumudī* ('Moonlight [that illuminates] the true essence of Sāṃkhya'), a text much read and in turn repeatedly commented on over the centuries, even though its capacity for in-depth examination and mastery of Sāṃkhya scholasticism appears on the whole rather modest. Vācaspati gives the impression that, rather than illustrating the specific doctrines, he is more concerned with piloting the whole of this ancient and prestigious system toward a harmonisation-integration with Vedānta. Of quite different calibre and of fundamental importance for an understanding of the *Sāṃkhyakārikā*, and more generally also for knowledge of ancient Sāṃkhya history — but, in spite of its merits, much less fortunate than Vācaspati's *Kaumudī* — is the *Yuktidīpikā* ('Illustration of Reasoning'), divided into eleven *āhnikas* ('days'), composed by an unknown author in about 680-720 C.E., a critical edition of which appeared just a few years ago (Motegi-Wezler 1998).

An interesting phenomenon of the revival of a doctrine that appeared to have entered on a progressive decline, and confirming the lasting presence of Sāṃkhya philosophemes, is the appearance at a late period of two works that can be assigned to the *sūtra* genre, the *Tattvasamāsa* (about fifteenth century?), which is brief and obscure, and the much more extensive *Sāṃkhyasūtra* (about fourteenth century?), both recent compilations although certainly incorporating ancient material. It is interesting to note that it is not on the *Sāṃkhyakārikā*, but on the *Sāṃkhyasūtra* that Vijñānabhikṣu (sixteenth century) leans in his attempt to draw the Sāṃkhya definitively into the Vedāntic orbit, exploiting its more cosmology-oriented formulation and integrating it in a view compatible with theistic Vedānta. His commentary performs this operation also by the expedient of multiplying quotations taken from epic and puranic texts, thus creating an 'orthodox' stream in which to dilute much of the hardness and intractability of the original Sāṃkhya.[43] At the same time, the appearance of a creator god — which this text does not, however, seem to authorise — is not a novelty in the long history of Sāṃkhya, being evident for example in some of its more ancient versions. The equation, which becomes current starting from the *Sarvadarśanasaṃgraha*, of *nirīśvara-sāṃkhya* ('atheistic Sāṃkhya') = Sāṃkhya, and *seśvara-sāṃkhya* ('theistic Sāṃkhya') = Yoga does apply to the classical and pre-classical period, in which actual Sāṃkhya schools of both trends are attested (Hattori 1999).

The *Sāṃkhyakārikā* opens by proclaiming the uselessness, for making pain cease, both of the various kinds of worldly knowledge and practices and of those enjoined by Vedic revelation, and claiming the sole effectiveness of discriminative knowledge "of the manifest, of the non-manifest and of the knower" (*kār*. 2), terms that refer respectively to principles ranging from the intellect to the earth, to primordial 'nature' (*prakṛti*) and to the soul. Uncreated and non-manifest root-nature (*mūlaprakṛti*) constitutes the ultimate matrix not only of the whole material world, but also of the psychic and intellectual dimension of the individual. Although not falling under the senses, its existence is established through its effects, i.e. the intellect, etc. (*kār*. 8). The principle of causality invoked at this point is based on five criteria: what does not exist cannot be produced; an adequate material cause is necessary to produce the effect; it is not possible for all to be produced by all; a thing can be produced only by someone/ something capable; and, lastly, the effect must be co-

[3] That Vijñānabhikṣu does nothing to hide his piloted 'revitalisation' of what was by then an almost defunct *śāstra*, but rather vaunts it, can be seen in the introductory verses to his *Sāṃkhyapravacanabhāṣya* ('Elaborate Commentary explaining Sāṃkhya doctrine'): "Only a small part [a digit] remains [of the Moon] of Sāṃkhya tradition, which contains the ambrosia of knowledge; the rest has been devoured by the Sun of Time. Through the ambrosia of my words, I shall bring it yet again to its fullness" (p. 1).

essential with the cause (*kār*. 9). Paradoxically, what starts up the entire evolutionary process is actually the presence of the soul, which albeit inactive and intrinsically alien to any real involvement with becoming, nevertheless acts as its indispensable catalyst. Using a motif the essence of which will later be used by the Tantric school of the Śaivasiddhānta, the universe comes into being, in the final analysis merely so that the soul may recognise its extraneousness from it and isolate itself in its self-identity. Even this recognition is made possible by the action of *prakṛti* itself, which thus finds in its own negation its ultimate reason for existence. Īśvarakṛṣṇa gives an account of it, using an elegant and well-constructed simile:

> Like a dancer who withdraws from the scene once the play has been performed before the audience, so *prakṛti* withdraws after manifesting itself to the soul. Lavish with help of various kinds and endowed with qualities (*guṇa-vat*), it operates without minding its own interest in the interest of the soul, which for its own part is lacking in qualities (*a-guṇa*) and is concerned with nothing and no one. There is nothing more delicate than *prakṛti*, I deem, who, knowing that it has been seen, no longer shows itself to the eye of the soul. (*kār*. 59-61)

The text plays on the double meaning of *guṇa*: 'qualities, artistic talents' in referring to the dancer, and on the three 'components' or qualities — *sattva*, *rajas* and *tamas* — in referring to *prakṛti*. These latter are simultaneously states of mind and cosmic forces (ambiguities unsolved in classical Sāṃkhya, which is heir to highly differentiated ancient doctrines), present in various concentrations in all aspects of the manifest world. *Sattva* is characterised by joy and light, and is gentle and enlightening; *rajas* is characterised by absence of joy and by dynamism: it is unstable and stimulating; *tamas* is characterised by inertia and restriction: it is heavy and obstructive.

Fluctuating similarly between the microcosmic level (in many ways, indeed, the creation of the universe seems that of human individuality) and the macrocosmic is the following evolutionary process, summarised in a single verse: "From *prakṛti* arises the Great (*mahat*), from this the Sense of the Ego, from this the group of sixteen. Moreover, from five of the sixteen arise the five major elements" (*kār*. 22). The first principle, the 'Great', i.e. the intellect (*buddhi*), is particularly important since it acts as the interface between the sentient soul and the ensemble of the insentient world. Indeed, it is within the *buddhi* that the presuppositions for a meeting and coalescence are created, however ultimately unreal, between spirit and matter, which would otherwise remain wholly incommunicable, thus disrupting the development of the universe itself. In the intellect, the cognition process reaches its acme with 'decision' (*adhyavasāya*; "this is a vase") which, in order to realise itself fully lacks only the light of awareness that belongs to the soul. The intellect is also the seat of the eight 'dispositions' (*bhāva*). The second principle is sense of ego, i.e. referring psychic and cognitive events to a personal individuality (*ahaṃkāra*, which, rather than 'fictitious or empirical ego', as it is often translated, means first and foremost 'to say: I'). From the sense of ego there develop in turn two distinct sets of principles: the first comprises eleven elements (inner sense, the five senses of knowledge and the five senses of action); the second comprises the five 'subtle elements', from which the five major elements finally develop. The sattvic nature of the first set and the tamasic nature of the second rest on a common energetic foundation represented by *rajas*, which characterises the sense of ego as a whole. The inner sense (*manas*) acts as coordinator (*saṃkalpaka*) of the senses of knowledge (eye, ear, nose, tongue and skin, not to be understood as organs but as sensory faculties) and of action (speech, hand, foot, excretory organs and sexual organs), and of the data transmitted by them which, thus coordinated and managed, it transmits in turn to the two upper faculties, the sense of the ego and the intellect. The subtle elements (*tanmātra*), arising from the sense of ego impregnated by the *tamas* component, are entities with somewhat fleeting identification: they are listed as sound, tactility, shape/colour, taste and smell. From each of these then evolves the corresponding gross element (ether, air, fire, water and earth), whose principal (and distinguishing) quality is that of the *tanmātra* that generated it. The confusion often made between *tanmātra*s and qualities is thus not without justification. The *Sāṃkhyakārikā* however is quite clear in contrasting the generality of the *tanmātra*s with the specificity of the gross elements (*kār*. 38). The taste *tanmātra*, for example, consists of a kind of quintessential and undifferentiated quality (the literal meaning of *tanmātra* is, in fact, 'only that' or else 'that one in its mere generality'), matrix of the earth element, whose concrete form is first qualified by taste, but this time in all its various possible modulations. According to the classical theory of the 'accumulation of qualities', the gross elements possess the single qualities in increasing number, starting from ether, which has only sound, to earth which has all five. The thirteen principles from intellect to the senses of action, supported by the five *tanmātra*s, form the *liṅga-śarīra*, a kind of subtle body that summarises the person's psychic and cognitive architecture, which is the entity destined to transmigrate from body to body.

In accounting for the cognitive process, Sāṃkhya cannot avoid problematic situations, due to the radical disparity of the protagonists of this process — outer senses, inner sense, sense of ego and intellect, on the one side, and soul on the other — each of which lacks an essential feature that only the other has and which cannot be borrowed owing to the ontological abyss that divides them. Without the light of awareness, the mechanical mirroring of the object on the outer senses (*ālocanamātra*), albeit progressively refined and dynamised by the inner sense, by the sense of the ego and the intellect, can never become 'knowledge', while the translucid immobility of the soul can never procure the data on which its cognitive function can be exercised. Once more, in an attempt to explain the inexplicable, the *Sāṃkhyakārikā* has recourse to an illustration (*kār*. 21): it is the collaboration of a blind man (the principles belonging to *prakṛti*) with a lame man (the soul). A blind man and a lame man, Gauḍapāda explains in his commentary, find themselves alone in the forest, after rigands have attacked their caravan and put to flight all their other ravel companions. The lame man jumps on the back of the blind nan and points out the path they have to take. Finally, having emerged rom the forest (the *saṃsāra*), the two go their separate ways. Although this parable is introduced to clarify generally the terms of the ink between *prakṛti* and the soul that causes creation, it can also be xtended to the particular case of cognitive phenomena. In the latter, ays the *Sāṃkhyakārikā*, the organs of knowledge become 'as it were' entient by virtue of their union with the soul, and the soul, on its wn side, albeit inactive by nature, becomes 'as it were' active, owing o contagion from the three components of *prakṛti* with which it has ome in contact (*kār.* 20). This can be seen in common experience, auḍapāda further explains, when a vase becomes hot or cold through ontact with fire or ice, or when someone who is not a thief is taken or one if accompanied by thieves. Not all exponents or adversaries f Sāṃkhya found this metaphorical answer satisfactory, and many ther solutions were put forward to solve such a crucial problem. āċaspati Miśra, for example, in his commentary on the *Yogasūtra* nd the *Bhāṣya* by Vyāsa (*ad* IV.23), speaks of the intellect as a twoided mirror: one side reflects the object, while the other reflects the oul. The soul can thus make the cognitive act occur without causing ny suffering to its immaculate isolation, just as the moon can continue o shine in the heights of the night sky while reflecting in a pond.

One of the peculiarities of Sāṃkhya is the discrepancy between he importance and expansion that its doctrines must have had in the ield of epistemology and logic — in view of the evidence of its own dversaries — and, on the other hand, how little it appears in the vorks that have come down to us. The *Sāṃkhyakārikā* devotes only hree verses (4-6) to listing and defining the means of knowledge, vhich it establishes as three: perception, inference and reliable estimony. Perception (*kār.* 5a) consists of determining (*adhyavasāya*) he respective objects of the senses. Inference, which is of three kinds, nvolves a distinguishing sign and an entity distinguished by it (5bc).

Reliable testimony is a verbal communication by someone worthy of trust (5d). As far as respective limits and functions are concerned, the *Sāṃkhyakārikā* is equally laconic. Whatever exceeds the senses' range of action may be known through inference based on general observation (*sāmānyatodṛṣṭa*); whatever is super-sensitive and escapes even inference may be established thanks to revelation worthy of trust (*kār.* 6). That being so, recourse to integrations provided by commentaries is necessary, except that one realises immediately that the commentators themselves seem to have no unitary doctrine to make reference to, but only considerably differing positions: not greatly surprising, bearing in mind the already-mentioned characteristic multiformity of this system. On the nature of the first means of knowledge — perception — we have a more specific definition, handed down by the many quotations both of followers (for example the *Yuktidīpikā*, p. 5) and opponents (for example, Jinendrabuddhi in the *Pramāṇasamuccaya-ṭīkā*, p. 136): perception consists of the functioning of the ear, etc. (*śrotrādivṛttiś ca pratyakṣam*). The sources agree in assigning this definition to Vārṣagaṇya, deemed to be the author of the *Ṣaṣṭitantra*. It is a matter of the functioning, adds Jinendrabuddhi (cf. Steinkellner 1999: 669-670), of the ear, skin, eye, tongue and nose, aimed at capturing sound, tactile feeling, shape/colour, taste and smell respectively. This function is presided over by the inner sense, which performs a 'subsequent determination' (*anuvyavasāya*) on the original determination (*vyavasāya*) made by the single sense, in itself mechanical and destined to become 'knowledge' only after being subjected to progressive refinement, culminating — as shown for example by the *Sāṃkhyakārikā* — in the determinative activity of the *buddhi*, illuminated by the sentience of the soul.

Much more intricate is the situation concerning inference. On the fact that the other two types (besides *sāmānyatodṛṣṭa*), which the *Sāṃkhyakārikā* does not mention, are *pūrvavat* and *śeṣavat*, all commentators seem to agree, but provide widely different interpretations of the three terms (cf. also pp. 43-45). According to Gauḍapāda, *pūrvavat* stands for inference based on previous perception (inferring that it is going to rain after seeing clouds); *śeṣavat* stands for inference based on the final result (if this part of the seawater is salty, it means that all the sea is salty); *sāmānyato-dṛṣṭa* for inference based on an observation of a general kind (if we find the moon and stars now in one part of the sky and now in another, it means that they are endowed with motion). According to the *Yuktidīpikā* (p. 83), on the other hand, the first type refers to effect-from-cause inference, the second, to cause from effect; the third is based on observation of the invariable concomitance of the two objects, which subsequently allows the existence of one of the two to be established when the other is present. This last modality, however, as the *Yuktidīpikā* appropriately notes, should be valid for any inference. If it is mentioned as a separate kind, it is only because it is considered as the only kind of inference applicable to whatever is intrinsically inaccessible to direct perception.[4] Sāṃkhya tradition also contemplates the classification of two possible types of inference: *vīta* and *āvīta* (a classification that is certainly ancient and current in other schools, although commonly associated with Sāṃkhya), variously translated as 'direct inference' and 'inference by exclusion', or 'positive' and 'negative'. The meaning of these terms remains uncertain, as also the very form of the latter, varying in the texts from *āvīta* to *avīta* (Franco 1999).

Although the *Sāṃkhyakārikā* is very succinct in defining inference and its types, it is absolutely silent on its modes of formalization. The *Yuktidīpikā* (p. 89) advocates the ten-member form, the same mentioned and criticised by Pakṣilasvāmin in the *Nyāyabhāṣya* (pp. 29-30),[5] who retorts to those who claim that the first five should be

4 It cannot be applied indiscriminately, however (as the *Yuktidīpikā* makes a hypothetical adversary comment; p. 86). It is not valid for ascertaining the existence of consciousness, since awareness is unique and, as such, cannot be mentally associated with anything.

5 The five additional members that precede the classic set of five (cf. pp. 50-51) are: the desire to know; doubt; motivation; the capacity to obtain what is desired; the elimination of doubt. A different set of ten parts is found in the *Daśavaikālika-niryukti* by the Jaina Bhadrabāhu (cf. p. 136).

taken for granted that nothing hinders their use if they can help clarify the mechanism of inference even to those less accustomed to this kind of reasoning (*Yuktidīpikā* p. 83).

One of the pillars of the entire system is a concept of causality known as *satkāryavāda* ('doctrine of the [pre-] existence of effect'; cf. Frauwallner 1978: 303-308), closely linked to another, equally central doctrine, the *pariṇāmavāda*. According to the latter, development of the various principles from primordial *prakṛti* should be seen in terms not of the creation of what was not previously there, but of change, the real transformation of something that does not, however, cease to exist in its substantial identity, even within different structures. Effect must in some way already exist in the cause because, if it were totally non-existent, it would even lack those distinctive features correlating it to a particular cause, and thus everything could be born from anything. At the same time, the change should be understood as a mere assumption of different qualities by a substance that, as such (i.e. as the related quality centre) continues to exist. Those who, like the Nyāya-Vaiśeṣika philosophers, wish at all costs to replace this concept by that of 'creation' or 'production', continues the *Yuktidīpikā* (p. 122), do so because they take too seriously something that is none other than linguistic usage, i.e. using such words to call that which, to a keener vision, would be merely a coming to manifestation of what was already potentially present, or even what is nothing but a new arrangement of pre-existent parts. But, parry the adversaries of Sāṃkhya, it is always a matter of producing something that was not there before, both in the case of coming to manifestation of what was potential, and in the case of assuming 'new' qualities. Only one Sāṃkhya author, Mādhava (ca. fifth century), shows any sign of yielding to this position, as testified by Bhāsarvajña (Halbfass 1992: 187). This was not the only one of his incautious retreats when faced by the threat of criticism: according to Jinendrabuddhi in his commentary on Dignāga's *Pramāṇasamuccaya* (p. 145), Mādhava, to react against the Buddhists who objected that a qualification of *prakṛti* by only the three *guṇa*s cannot explain the multiplicity of sensorial cognitions, ends up by admitting that five qualifications are present in it (sound, touch, smell, etc.). As a result, Mādhava, despite his good intentions, earned himself the not very flattering appellative of 'destroyer of Sāṃkhya' and, all told, rightly so. The simple and powerful edifice of Sāṃkhya does not lend itself to restoration: the replacement of even one of its archaic stones might signify the destruction of all.

The Yoga System

I have been strongly tempted to omit any treatment of Yoga in a work such as this, devoted essentially to the 'philosophy' of India. I should also have been in good company, considering that Indian tradition itself tends to treat Yoga mainly as a practice grafted onto conceptual assumptions provided by Sāṃkhya. Sāṃkhya and Yoga are thus two sides of the same coin.[1] In actual fact, the inseparable commentary that from the very beginning has accompanied the Yoga root-*sūtra*, the *Bhāṣya* ascribed to a mysterious Vyāsa (lit. 'Compiler'), calls itself the *Sāṃkhyapravacana* ('exposition of Sāṃkhya'). Furthermore, to take one of many possible examples, the Nyāya philosopher Bhāsarvajña, in quoting a series of aphorisms from the *Yogasūtra* in his *Nyāyabhūṣaṇa* (p. 442), on the theme of quadripartition (on which more below), presents them directly as *sāṃkhyānāṃ matam* ('doctrine of the followers of Sāṃkhya'). In actual fact, data concerning the very existence of Yoga philosophy (or of a Yoga system) is contradictory. Yoga is absent from the first doxography known to us, the *Ṣaḍdarśanasamuccaya* by Haribhadra (eighth century C.E.), and equally absent from the *Madhyamaka-hṛdaya* by Bhavya (sixth century), whereas both texts give ample space to Sāṃkhya. On the other hand, an ancient text such as the *Arthaśāstra*, in defining the systems in which 'investigative science' is found (*ānvīkṣikī*; cf. p. 16) mentions only three: Sāṃkhya, Yoga and Lokāyata ('Materialists'; pp. 121 ff). The Yoga-darśana is found in the *Sarvadarśanasaṃgraha* by the Vedāntin Mādhava, who ranks it highly in the system hierarchy, and is also present in later doxographies.

As a psycho-physical discipline forming part of a spiritual emancipation process, Yoga has been present in India since the remotest

[1] Cf. the passage from the *Mahābhārata* quoted above; see also *Bhagavadgītā* II.4.

times (some even claim to detect it in the Indus civilisation). It appears repeatedly in the Upaniṣads (particularly in the *Śvetāśvatara*) and in the *Mahābhārata*, and soon becomes, under various forms, an element common to all philosophical-religious experience in India, from Nyāya to Vedānta, including theistic and devotional streams, and Jainism; it is neglected only by the Pūrvamīmāṃsā. It also plays a central role in Tantrism, although the more sophisticated and extreme schools, such as the non-dualist Śivaite schools of Kashmir, look down their noses at it, as an inferior and exclusively propedeutic means (not altogether dissimilar is the attitude of Śaṅkara), reserved for followers of limited capacity and aspiration. However, although Yoga appears originally to have had the substantial aim of immobilizing the continual fluctuation of the individual body-emotions-mind complex, during its long evolution it has opened gradually to wider prospects and ambitions, including a sophisticated meditative and visualizing practice, with considerable ethical and noetic content, accompanied by the cultivation of supernatural powers.

The first text to emerge, in an already long tradition, is Patañjali's *Yogasūtra*, closely linked to its first commentary, the *Bhāṣya* by Vyāsa: together they were destined to constitute the unquestionable root of the Yoga-darśana for centuries to come. However, the questions raised by this orginal nucleus are many. Although Indian tradition does not question the fact that the Patañjali of the *Yogasūtra* is the same as the grammarian Patañjali, who in the second century B.C.E. composed the Great Commentary on Pāṇini, everything leads us to believe that the *Yogasūtra* should be dated several centuries later. While the *Bhāṣya* is nominally attributed to a distinct figure, the *sūtra-bhāṣya* complex is always deemed to be an essentially unitary entity, by a single author, Patañjali (furthermore, as stated above, the name Vyāsa, which is also the name of the mythical author of the *Mahābhārata*, merely means 'Compiler'). Later commentators — or at least the most significant of them (cf. p. 93) — never comment on the *sūtra*s alone, but always on the *sūtra-bhāṣya* complex. Yet, even on a superficial examination, between the *bhāṣya* and the *sūtra* a hiatus can be detected, occasionally emphasised by the sub-commentators themselves. For this set of uncertainties, J. Bronkhorst (1985) proposes the most radical response: the Patañjali of the *Yogasūtra* is not the author of the *Mahābhāṣya* but a homonymous Sāṃkhya master quoted by the *Yuktidīpikā* (commentary on the *Sāṃkhyakārikā*; cf. p. 81), to whom we owe not only the commentary on the root-text, but the root-text itself. This implies that he composed, starting from an indefinite number of isolated aphorisms already existing and current in Sāṃkhya circles, a passably unitary text (which he then commented on, clearly in the light of Sāṃkhya philosophy, of which he was an authoritative exponent).[2]

In the rich exegetic history of the *Yogasūtra*, four commentaries stand out: the *Tattvavaiśāradī* ('[the commentary] that enucleates clearly the essence [of the *Yogasūtra*]') of Vācaspati Miśra (tenth century), the *Rājamārtāṇḍa* ('Sun among kings') by King Bhoja of Malawa (eleventh century), the *Yogavārttika* ('Glosses on Yoga') by Vijñānabhikṣu (sixteenth century) and the *Yogasūtrabhāṣyavivaraṇa* ('Explication of the Commentary on the *Yogasūtra*') by Śaṅkara. The edition of this last work in 1952, based on the only extant manuscript, has raised a lively dispute between those that deem the author to be the great Śaṅkara (Hacker, Nakamura) and those who, on the other hand, propend toward a much later homonymic (Wezler, Halbfass, and especially Rukmani 2001). The second hypothesis appears much more plausible and does not oblige us to imagine the master of the *kevalādvaita* — who in the *Brahmasūtrabhāṣya* does not hide his lack of consideration for Yoga as a means of liberation, due to its belonging, in any final analysis, to the 'action' (*karma*) side — as a former Yoga follower, later converted to the way of sole knowledge (*jñāna*). Despite Śaṅkara, the cooptation of Yoga by Vedānta, which started as early as Vācaspati Miśra, was later completed with the work of Vijñānabhikṣu (cf. pp. 115-116).

---

[2] According to an alternative theory, the author of the *Bhāṣya* could be another major Sāṃkhya author, Vindhyavāsin (Bronkhorst 1985: 206-209).

The Yoga of the *Yogasūtra* is a complex mixture of ideas and practices of diverse provenance, which are often uneasy bedfellows. On the one hand, as we have seen, this technique aims solely at suppressing the instability of body and mind, and sometimes seems to aim at suppressing the mind itself (as was to occur in the medieval schools of *amanaska-yoga*, 'mindless Yoga'). On the other, great emphasis is given to the progressive modification of the states of consciousness and to supernormal powers. The theoretical framework surrounding the liberation process is equally ambiguous: its bearing structure is decidedly Sāṃkhya (but with an unexpected space reserved for worshipping a personal god), on which however strong Buddhist tones have been grafted.[3] To these two components we owe respectively the centrality of knowledge and of the spiritual principle last seen as consciousness without activity, on the one hand, and the identification of practices (also with a strong ethical content) aimed at the progressive wearing down of the factors responsible for the constrained condition of the individual, on the other. Indeed, one of Yoga's innovations as compared to Sāṃkhya is the attention it pays to these factors of 'affliction' or 'staining' (*kleśa*), certainly borrowed from Buddhist sources: *avidyā* ('nescience'), *asmitā* ('egotism'), *rāga* ('desire, passion'), *dveṣa* ('aversion'), *abhiniveśa* ('convulsive attachment'). Of all these, it is nescience that constitutes the nourishing terrain: "Nescience is the field of other stains, whether they are quiescent, attenuated, interrupted or in full activity. Nescience is seeing eternity, purity, felicity and the self in what is ephemeral, impure, painful and has no self" (II.4-5). Their attenuation through Yoga practice, followed by the uprooting of their subliminal impregnations (*vāsanā*, *saṃskāra*)[4]

[3] Still fundamental in this connection is the article by L. de La Vallée Poussin (1937).

[4] This theme can also be traced to Buddhist influence (cf. Frauwallner 1973: 324-329). Similarly of Buddhist origin is the requirement (I.33) of practising the four virtues (*maitrī*, 'loving-kindness'; *karuṇā*, 'compassion'; *muditā*, 'joy'; and *upekṣā*, 'equanimity'), as well as the articulation of the highest of Yoga members, *samādhi* 'absorption', either 'accompanied by' or 'exempt from' the activities of consciousness, and within the former the distinction of the four moments of 'reasoning', 'reflection', 'beatitude' and 'pure awareness of the self' (I.17-18).

through intellectual meditation (*prasaṃkhyāna*), leads to the extinction of *karma*. The mind (*citta*)[5] may thus achieve its highest state, i.e. awareness of the discrimination between soul and psyche, or in other words, liberation.

Yoga doctrine is presented as one of the most prestigious exemplifications of the so-called 'therapeutic paradigm' (cf. Wezler 1984; Halbfass 1992: 243-257), which in India unites such different traditions as Buddhism, Āyurveda and Nyāya. The liberation process is none other than a process of 'healing' from the sickness of phenomenal existence, articulated in four stages: 1) awareness of the sickness; 2) of the causes of the sickness; 3) of the status of health; 4) of the means of achieving it, i.e. what must be eliminated (*heya*); what are the causes of that which has to be eliminated (*heyahetu*); what such elimination consists of and what it results in (*hāna*); what is the means to it (*hānopāya*). According to the *Yogasūtra*, therefore, 1) "What has to be eliminated is future pain" (II. 16); 2) "The cause of what has to be eliminated is the union of seer and the visible" (II. 17); 3) "The cause of this is nescience. When the latter ceases, the union vanishes: this is elimination, meaning the isolation of the seer" (II. 24-25); 4) "The means of elimination is stable discriminating consciousness" (II. 26).[6] The same division into four stages (*caturvyūha*) appears in medical texts (*Carakasaṃhitā*, Sūtrasthāna, IX.19; cf. Wezler 1984: 309), in the Nyāya tradition (*Nyāyābhāṣya*, p. 3, *Nyāyabhūṣaṇa* p. 436), and, of course, in the formulation of the so-called 'Four Sacred Truths' of the Buddha (cf. p. 138). According to Wezler, these latter must have been the basic model for all the other quadripartitions (Wezler 1984: 322).

Without providing any detailed description of Yoga practices — the most characteristic and original part of this system — as not

[5] The abandoning of the doctrine dividing the mental organ into three parts — intellect, sense of the ego, and mind — is another major innovation of Vyāsa's as compared to classical Sāṃkhya.

[6] The *sūtra*s quoted should be read in the context of Sāṃkhya philosophy. 'Seer' stands for the power of vision, i.e. the spiritual principle, which is pure consciousness without an object.

being entirely suited to the scope of this volume, I wish however to dwell on a theme that has so far received comparatively little attention, despite its undoubted impact on the philosophic and religious thought of India: the so-called 'perception of the yogin' (*yogipratyakṣa*).[7] As we have seen, among the means of right knowledge, direct perception enjoys undoubted primacy in all schools of philosophy. Buddhist tradition, starting from Dignāga, distinguishes four varieties of direct perception: sensorial perception; mental perception; the self-perception that every cognitive or emotional event has of itself; and, lastly, the perception peculiar to the yogin. This last is defined by Dharmakīrti (*Nyāyabindu*, 'Drops of logic' I.11) as that "which arises at the end of progressive intensification of meditation on a real object".[8] In his *Pramāṇasamuccaya* (I.6cd), Dignāga defined it as the "pure and simple vision of the object (*arthamātra*°) unmixed with the teaching of any master", in which 'pure and simple' (°*mātra*°) is, according to Jinendrabuddhi (*Viśālāmalavatī*, pp. 56-57), to be understood as free from any erroneous superimposition.[9] What makes this cognitive experience unique is its paradoxical nature of 'meditation, visualisation', i.e. of something intrinsically conceptual and projective, which however becomes so vivid and clear that it is indistinguishable from sensorial perception itself.[10] This highly special form of

---

[7] See the very recent collection of essays on this and related subjects in Franco, E. (ed.) 2009 (with many bibliographic references); cf. also Torella forthcoming a, b.

[8] In his commentary on the *Nyāyabindu* (pp. 68-69), Dharmottara distinguishes three stages in this process. During the first (intense meditation), the yogin's vision starts to become clearer; in the second (the culminating moment of the previous stage), the object is as it were veiled by a subtle mist; in the third (the yogin's perception truly so-called), the object appears with the same clarity as a grain would appear on the palm of the hand.

[9] For references to the yogin's knowledge in other works by Dignāga, see the *Yogāvatāra* verses 1-6ab (quoted in van Bijlert 1989: 86-87).

[10] The opposition between direct perception and conceptual knowledge is defined (not only for the Buddhists but also for Indian epistemology in general) precisely in terms of the 'vividness' of the former (*viśada*, *spaṣṭa*, *sphuṭa* are the terms used by Dharmakīrti and followers; but see also, e.g., Utpaladeva and Abhinavagupta) and dimness (*asphuṭa*, etc.), the main responsible being the linguistic veil with which conceptual knowledge wraps the object.

consciousness possesses two other essential characteristics: the possibility of accessing spheres beyond the reach of the ordinary consciousness and the intrinsic guarantee of its authenticity. In the Buddhist context, admittance of the 'cognition of the yogin' is also closely tied to the concept of omniscience, peculiar to the Buddha and guaranteeing the truth of his teaching, which cannot (nor does it wish to) lay any claim to extra-human guarantees. It would however be a mistake to believe that such a conception arose in a circumscribed dimension and with well-defined aims, such as those now outlined. On the contrary, almost all traditions of Indian thought calmly accept that a higher form of consciousness exists and is peculiar to the yogin and to him alone, including those most intransigent about conceptual rigour and logical formalism. The sole exception is Mīmāṃsā which, on the other hand, has good reasons for keeping under rigid control any human claim, however vague, to venture into the sphere of *dharma*, apart from the sole authority of the Veda.[11] Even a school that most certainly cannot be suspected of giving way to the mystical and irrational, such as Vaiśeṣika, makes room for yogin consciousness in its root-*sūtra* (IX.13-17, according to Candrānanda). These *sūtra*s are referred to explicitly in a passage by Praśastapāda (cf. Isaacson 1993: 146-147) that adds some interesting facts to the overall scenario:

> But in the yogins — beings that are different from [superior to] us — as 'joined' [read: 'in the state of perfect absorption (*samādhi*)], by virtue of the fact that their mind is assisted by the *dharma* that arises from Yoga, there develops an infallible capacity of perception of the own nature of their

[11] Mīmāṃsaka texts abound in severe confutations of the possibility of any human 'omniscience', attacking in particular Buddhists and Jains. We should not, however, too hastily conclude that Buddhism may have ever promoted the personal confrontation of gifted individuals with ultimate truth. On the soteriological path, the *bhāvanā* ('contemplation, inner cultivation') of the Buddhist yogin has in fact rather been given an 'assimilative' function (of the truths of Buddhism; and also a 'purgative' one in that it destroys *kleśa*s), than a 'cognitive' function; cf. Torella [forthcoming a].

> own self (*ātman*), the self of others, ether, space, time, the atoms and mind, and also the qualities, actions, universals and ultimate particularities inherent in such substances, and lastly the inherence itself. In 'disjoined' yogin ['emerged from *samādhi*'], on the other hand, direct perception develops concerning subtle objects, those hidden, those remote [in space and time] ...
>
> (*Padārthadharmasaṃgraha* pp. 464-465) [12]

India, however, is also familiar with other types of 'seers', first ıd foremost the Vedic *ṛṣis*, those who 'saw' the hymns. To one *ṛṣi* r another is also attributed the composition of the root-*sūtra* of the arious branches of knowledge, and it is they who are the ultimate :positories of authority in matters of language. These semi-divine eings belong to an irretrievable past and the ontological distance :parating them from us is unbridgeable, even more than the one that :parates common man from another 'different' man, the yogin, albeit 'ith some chinks... Let us return to Praśastapāda:

> In *ṛṣis*, the founders of tradition [Śrīdhara gloss: 'the authors of the Veda'], owing to a conjunction between mind and self and to a special merit, an intuitive (*prātibha*) knowledge arises that provides them with infallible vision of objects transcending the sensory faculties, belonging both to the past and future and to the present — such as, e.g. *dharma* —, which may figure or not in the revealed texts. This is the knowledge known as *ārṣa* ('peculiar to seers'). This form of knowledge is found mainly among divine seers, but sometimes even arises in common men, as when a girl says, "Tomorrow my brother will come; it is my heart that tells me so".[13] Then there is the consciousness of the 'perfect ones', which however is not substantially different from this.[14]
>
> (*Padārthadharmasaṃgraha*, pp. 627-629)

Cf. also *Nyāyabhāṣya ad Nyāyasūtra* I.1.3 (p. 9).

This subject is also dealt with later on by Jayanta in treating the perception of yogins and *ṛṣis* in the *Nyāyamañjarī*.

The main difference, continues Praśastapāda, lies in the fact that whereas the former is spontaneous, the latter depends on a special effort, being the result of a

If we study the diffusion of the theme of intuitive knowledge (*pratibhā*, *prātibhaṃ jñānam*), we soon find ourselves in another domain, that of poetic and aesthetic speculation. *Pratibhā* is the gift that the goddess Sarasvatī grants her 'sons', the poets (*kavi*) (see Granoff 1995). In this case, *pratibhā* (Gonda 1963: 334) ceases to be just a special kind of vision (*dṛṣṭi*) and becomes simultaneously a form of creation (*sṛṣṭi*). The universe being made of 'name' and 'form', the creator of the former dimension is the poet; the creator of the latter the god Prajāpati. This statement is by Nīlakaṇṭhadīkṣita (quoted in Gonda 1963: 335). The same motif is several times expressed by the great Abhinavagupta in the *Abhinavabhāratī*, "Like the creator Prajāpati, so too the poet is able to create a world according to his desire [...]" (ibid. p. 343). Tantric thought, however, advances beyond literary creation. Utpaladeva, the philosopher of absolute non-dualism, with the intent of giving an account of the creation of the physical universe by the supreme Śiva — none other than Supreme Consciousness — employs an example, i.e. something close to everyone's experience: "Truly, the Conscious Being, the Lord, just like the yogin, by his own will and without depending on material causes, manifests externally the multitude of things that dwell within Him" (*Īśvarapratyabhijñā-kārikā* I.5.7; Torella 2002: 116).

By way of conclusion, returning to the point of departure of this brief *excursus*, the perception of the yogin can reach paradoxical heights and see differences in objects that are identical by definition, such as (in the Vaiśeṣika conception) atoms; or else individual souls that have completed the path of liberation (Isaacson 1993: 153-154). This theme is discussed for the first time in the *Yogabhāṣya* (*ad Yogasūtra* III.53). It is the same Section III of the *Yogasūtra* devoted to supernormal powers (*vibhūti*) that provides the most ancient and fundamental treatment of the powers peculiar to the yogin. One of the powers that the *Yogasūtra* (III.19) recognises in the yogin — the ability to know the mind of others and its content (*paracittajñāna*)

'perfection' process employing ointments and other magical substances. On the knowledge of the perfect ones, see also *Yogasūtra* III.32.

— causes a certain embarrassment to the philosophers of non-dual Śivaism. This theme is included by Utpaladeva in a highly intricate context, which I shall not reconstruct here, come down to us in a fragment of his *Īśvarapratyabhijñā-vivṛti* (cf. Torella 2007c, 2007d, forthcoming b). According to his hypothetical objector, this fact, accepted by all, shows that it is not true that consciousness cannot be objectified (one of the axioms of Śivaite thought on the other hand is that any cognitive act exclusively illuminates itself, *svaprakāśa*, and can never become the object of another cognitive act). Utpaladeva's answer is that in the yogin the process of identification with Śiva — the supreme and only I — is so far advanced that it brings about the progressive fading of the notion of multiplicity and diversity among various individual subjects. For such a yogin, knowing the thoughts of 'others' substantially means knowing his own thoughts, something that occurs as a rule without objectivation, but from within, by introspection.

The basis for defining the relationship between Sāṃkhya and Yoga is the same stated above based on the passage from the *Mahābhārata*, quoted in full: on the one side difference, on the other complementarity (many other passages of the epic could be added; see, too, the centrality of Sāṃkhya and Yoga in the *Bhagavadgītā*). The main points of the theoretical framework of Yoga coincide with those of Sāṃkhya. Even the final point of arrival is the same: achieving a vision that discriminates spirit and mind (or nature). To reach this final point of arrival, however, Yoga develops a process of spiritual and psychophysical discipline (lacking in Sāṃkhya), in which the Buddhist tradition has a significant part, centered on two keywords: *abhyāsa* ('repeated practice') and *vairāgya* ('detachment').[15] From a strictly doctrinal point of view, Yoga differs from Sāṃkhya mainly

[15] Cf. also *Bhagavadgītā* VI.35cd. It is precisely against the centrality of repeated practice and detachment that śivaite Tantrism mobilizes itself, countering them with instantaneousness and passion respectively (Torella 2000: 402, fn. 38; 2007f: 30-32).

on three points. 1. Yoga conceives of the mind as a unitary entity (*citta* or *manas*), omnipervasive (*vibhu*) and not distinguished in three dimensions (*buddhi*, 'intellect'; *ahamkāra*, 'egoity'; *manas*, '[mind understood as] inner sense'); the Sāṃkhya concept of a 'subtle body' (*liṅgaśarīra*) is absent. 2. Yoga attaches central importance, in the constitution of individuality immersed in the flow of *saṃsāra*, to the role of *karma* in the form of latent impregnations (*vāsanā*) and conditioning impulses (*saṃskāra*) and to that of 'afflictions' (*kleśa*). 3. The idea of a personal god (*īśvara*) is introduced, to whom however no active role is attributed in the creation of the world, or even in the direct salvation of the individual. It is merely a single soul, always free, which, at each (autonomous) regeneration of the world, once more proclaims the doctrine of Yoga and acts as a support for meditation, thus assisting the yogin in his process of liberation.

THE MĪMĀṂSĀ SYSTEM

Mīmāṃsā, too, already had a long history behind it before constituting an independent *darśana*. The term *mīmāṃsā* (lit. 'intense application to reflection') frequently occurs in the ancient lists of traditional knowledge. Its subject is Veda exegesis, particularly the ritual prescriptions found in the Vedic literature in the widest sense of the word, not so much to extract their hidden meanings as to determine the principles leading to their proper execution. In actual fact, interpretation of their symbolic and noetic content also belongs to the Mīmāṃsā field of action, but quite early on tended to become the specialisation of a distinct school-discipline, which in turn gave rise to the *darśana* called Vedānta, otherwise known as Uttara-Mīmāṃsā ('further, recent, Mīmāṃsā'),[1] contrasted, often severely, with properly so-called Mīmāṃsā, denominated Pūrva-Mīmāṃsā ('previous, ancient, Mīmāṃsā'). Strange though it may seem, its domain of application has never given it the status of *vedāṅga* ('ancillary science of the Veda'), probably because it was felt that it would not be proper to give it the rank of an 'ancillary' or 'subordinate' discipline (which is implicit in the overall meaning of *aṅga*). On the contrary, this science has been considered so close to the Veda as to be deemed more of an appendix than a subsidiary tool (this, for example, is the position clearly expressed by Jayanta in the *Nyāyamañjarī*, vol. I, p. 8). The area of sacrificial science is indeed represented amongst the *vedāṅga*s by the Kalpa, with which Mīmāṃsā is in close contact but without ever converging.

Anyone expecting from such premises a sapiential and 'mystical' discipline would be profoundly surprised, if not disappointed. What we are dealing with is a realism in some ways even more pronounced

---

[1] On possible motivations of such a denomination, which however came into use rather late on (apparently not earlier than the eleventh century), see Bronkhorst 2002/2003.

than Nyāya, bringing it very close to the Vaiśeṣika environmen Mīmāṃsā lacks the peculiar Vaiśeṣika classificatory obsessior which in the end mixes concrete data and intellectual projection together under the single and ambiguous rubric of the 'real'. Whil thinkers of classical Mīmāṃsā do adopt, with some modification: the Vaiśeṣika doctrine of categories (cf. Harikai 1997) — agai confirming the basic affinity of the two systems — Mīmāṃsā neve gives up its preference for the concrete, the individual, safeguarde by a strong dose of elementary common sense. This moreover neve fails to amaze once seen applied, not to some everyday banality, bu as a rule to the most abstruse and complex liturgical lucubrations.

Mīmāṃsā is constructed with adamant consequentiality on a fe\ principles, of which it also seeks to provide some demonstration, bu all having the air of axioms that can in no wise be relinquished withou causing Mīmāṃsā's *raison d'être* to vanish at the same time. Fir: and foremost, Mīmāṃsā deals with the theory and practice of sacrific which generates and supports the universal *dharma* and ensures t the patron of the sacrifice happiness in the next world and tot liberation from the cycle of rebirth.[2] To make this scenario 'work everything must be absolutely clear and firm, so as to expel the mai enemy: doubt. Paradoxically, just one element remains hazy: the go or gods to whom the sacrifice is offered. In the end, they are no mor than an expedient or convention, a mere name in the dative th completes the package of the liturgical act, which itself contains i own power and dispenses it only if it is properly carried out. Th sole source for knowledge of *dharma* is Vedic revelation. To affir its validity and safeguard it from any possible doubt, Mīmāṃsā doe not follow the path adopted by Nyāya (the Veda is authoritative becaus it is promulgated by the Lord himself), still less the one adopted b

[2] Rebirth and liberation, however, appear to have become part of Mīmāṃsā at relatively late date and are wholly absent in Śabara (fifth-sixth century), the mo: ancient author of commentaries on the *Mīmāṃsāsūtra* that have come down to u: They start to be found only in the work of Kumārila (*Ślokavārttika*, sambandhā kṣepaparihāra, 106-110; cf. Bronkhorst 2002/2003: 113).

Buddhists and Jains for their respective scriptures (the Buddhist or Jain canons are authoritative because their *human* authors — the Buddha and Mahāvīra — are omniscient).[3] For the latter, Mīmāṃsāka thinkers, first of all Kumārila (*Ślokavārttika*, codanāsūtra, 111-144), reserve harsh words, aimed at cutting down to size any human claim to omniscience, recalling mankind to a realistic and bitter awareness of its limitations. With regard to the Lord, Creator of all and also of the Veda, Mīmāṃsa is not willing to admit his existence. If one wishes to maintain that a god created the universe, as Kumārila argues in the *Ślokavārttika* (saṃbandhākṣepaparihāra, 47-59), one has to admit that by so doing he intends to realise some purpose, and consequently that beforehand it was intrinsically imperfect — even if such a purpose had been for his own amusement. If he did so merely because such was his nature (*svabhāva*), one must conceive of a context of total autonomy, which does not fit very well with the parallel hypothesis that *karma* (of whom?) should be fulfilled. If he created the world to allow its creatures to emancipate themselves in the end from the pain of *saṃsāra*, could he not rather have created them happy? And so on. Mīmāṃsā, moreover, knows fully well the snares that beset any demonstration of the absolute reliability of an individual from whom verbal knowledge can be derived, even when the individual concerned is divine. The Mīmāṃsā position is thus as follows: the Veda is authoritative because it has no human author (*apauruṣeya*; *Ślokavārttika*, codanāsūtra, 97ab) — or even better, because they have no author at all (cf. *Ślokavārttika*, codanāsūtra, 68), being without beginning and without end (they are *nitya*, 'eternal'; cf. saṃbandhākṣepaparihāra, 114-116). This first axiom obliges Mīmāṃsa to produce a second: any knowledge therefore, including that of the Veda, is to be deemed valid in itself (codanāsūtra, 52-53), at least until its erroneousness can be demonstrated, owing either to intrinsic defects in its formation, or to its incongruity with other

[3] Of course, Buddhists also provide a rational proof of the main tenets of Buddhism, like the Four Sacred Truths, which however allows the suspicion of being just a 'secondary' proof (cf. Torella forthcoming).

knowledge considered valid (as far as *dharma* is concerned, however, no other source of knowledge is admitted). Only the Veda, therefore, or rather, Vedic injunctions and prohibitions (the crucial term in Mīmāṃsā, *codanā*, embraces both), can provide knowledge of *dharma* (*Ślokavārttika*, codanāsūtra, 242cd-243ab). To determine what is religiously 'right' or 'wrong', there is no other means of knowledge, neither perception nor inference, still less common sense. Kumārila adds, with his peculiar sense of irony, that not even giving pleasure and happiness to others can be invoked as a criterion for identifying *dharma*, and vice-versa. Having sexual relations with one's master's wife is a very grave sin from the point of view of *dharma*, however much pleasure the faithless wife takes in the attentions of the adharmic disciple (244cd-245ab); the same can be said of drinking wine, etc.

However, if the Veda, which is a text, is to be deemed source of knowledge, this means, more generally, assuming that language has the power of conveying truth, that is to say — in order to remove any suspicion that its nature might be open to any arbitrary human or divine convention — that the relationship between word and meaning is eternal and unchangeable (Saṃbandhākṣepaparihāra, 136-137). Lastly, for every rite to lead unfailingly to its result, the world must, generally speaking, be kept within precise parameters that guarantee its proper and predictable functioning. Yet again, for the soul to benefit from the results of the rite, which ripen even long after its performance, it must be immortal. Up to this point, nothing appears to justify dealing with Mīmāṃsa in a context like that of the present work, and it would seem more congruous to include it in an exclusively historical-religious framework. In actual fact, whatever the motives that determined the assumption of the said axioms, philosophical interest in Mīmāṃsa lies in the way in which it has worked them out and justified them rationally, confronting itself in debates over the centuries with all the most prestigious philosophical currents in India (cf. Halbfass 1986-1992; Bronkhorst 1997). Even the pre-systemic phase of Mīmāṃsā — when it was still a school specialising in the exegesis of Vedic liturgies — is anything but lacking in philosophical-cultural or even philosophical-scientific relevance. The working out of a corpus of metarules to be applied so as to understand the sacrificial rules properly is homologous to the working out of meta-rules for the field of grammar, its value as a paradigm for every branch of knowledge being well known. Furthermore, it seems not improbable that the procedures of analysis and formalization used in the sciences of language received their original matrix precisely from the sacrificial sciences (Renou 1941-42).

The Mīmāṃsā root-text, the *Mīmāṃsāsūtra*, attributed to the mythical sage Jaimini, in all probability dates back to the second century B.C.E. This compilation comprises composite material, with frequent references to earlier authors, whose positions are indicated and sometimes argued with. It is of considerable size, especially as compared to the root-*sūtra*s of other systems, numbering some 2700 *sūtra*s — if a supplementary section is taken into account, the Saṃkarṣaṇakāṇḍa ('Section of Saṃkarṣaṇa'), which is apparently more recent. The work is divided into twelve 'lessons' (*adhyāya*), in turn largely subdivided into four sections or 'feet' (*pāda*), dealing with single subjects of discussion (*adhikaraṇa*), which in the end amount to about one thousand. Among the themes dealt with by the *Mīmāṃsāsūtra* are: the relationship between word and meaning; the relationship between the normative parts (*vidhi* 'injunctions') and the digressive parts (*arthavāda*, 'illustrative discourses') of the Veda; the clash between revelation (*śruti*) and tradition (*smṛti*); the analysis of the essence of verbal action particularly as concerns injunctions; the distinction between main and complementary elements in sacrifice; the order in which the various parts of the liturgies must be performed; how to apply the sacrificial model deemed exemplary to its derivative forms; how to transfer an ingredient in a particular sacrifice to the context of another; etc. As might be expected, the *Mīmāṃsāsūtra* was repeatedly commented on. The most ancient commentary of those that have come down to us is the *Bhāṣya* by Śabara (ca. fifth-sixth century C.E.), although we know of the existence of earlier commentaries, of which that of Upavarṣa is held in especial esteem; Upavarṣa might be the *vṛttikāra* ('author of the brief commentary'), repeatedly quoted also by Śabara himself. Śabara's *Bhāṣya* lays the foundations for the future development of the Mīmāṃsā system (and to him we probably owe the final editing of the *sūtra*s with their division into *adhikaraṇa*s), although it was his commentators Prabhākara and Kumārila (both active during the seventh century) who brought Mīmāṃsā to a high level of philosophical elaboration.[4] The first is known with the epithet of *guru*, in which, besides the obvious reference to his intellectual mastery, an allusion has also been seen to the excessive complexity of his theories (indeed, *guru* means not only 'master', but also 'heavy', 'verbose'). Prabhākara's main work is his long and complex commentary *Bṛhatī* ('Great [Explication]'), in which Buddhist influence is evident. Kumārila moves along lines that often diverge from his disciple — according to some traditions — Prabhākara, not only because, unlike the latter, he does not shirk from criticising Śabara whenever he deems it necessary, but also for his implacable criticism of Buddhism. Kumārila Bhaṭṭa (often simply called Bhaṭṭa), who should doubtless be numbered among the major thinkers of India, determinedly takes it upon himself to defend Vedic tradition and the superiority of the Brahmanic caste as the centre of gravity of the entire Indian civilisation.[5] His most important philosophical work is the *[Mīmāṃsā] Ślokavārttika* ('Gloss in verse [on the Mīmāṃsā]'), devoted to the first *pāda* of the first *adhyāya* of the *Mīmāṃsāsūtra*; it is followed by the *Tantravārttika* ('Gloss on the Treatise'), commenting at length on the other three *pāda*s of the first *adhyāya*, as well as the second and third *adhyāya*s, and the *Ṭupṭīkā*, a short commentary on the remaining nine *adhyāya*s. The *Bṛhatī* by Prabhākara was in turn commented on by the *Ṛjuvimalā* ('Straight

[4] A review of the three masters' positions on the most crucial Mīmāṃsā themes is found in Jha 1964.

[5] For an overall view of Kumārila's thought, see Taber 1997.

and Pure [explanation]') by Śālikanātha (mid-eighth century), who is also the actual author of a compendium of doctrines of the Prābhākara school (*Prakaraṇapañcikā*, 'Analytical Commentary on the Treatise'). The *Ślokavārttika* was the subject of the lucid commentary *Nyāyaratnākara* ('Mine of the Gems of Reason') by Pārthasārathi Miśra (tenth century?), who is also the author of an independent commentary on the *Mīmāṃsāsūtra*. The third great Mīmāṃsaka author is Maṇḍana Miśra, who, prior to his assumed conversion to Vedānta, wrote the *Bhāvanāviveka* ('Discrimination of Causal Force') and the *Vidhiviveka* ('Discrimination of the Injunction'), this latter being the subject of a lengthy commentary by Vācaspati Miśra. A third Mīmāṃsā school is linked to the name of Murāri Miśra (eleventh-twelfth century). Yielding to the by now prevailing theism, some Mīmāṃsaka thinkers were led to make room for a personal god who, although not managing to be considered the author of the Veda is however the one who 'remembers' it, and who thus — seeing that for the first time the other great dogma of the Brahmanic religions is accepted: periodic cosmic dissolution — ensures the continuity of the presence of the Veda in the universe.

For a general presentation of Mīmāṃsā doctrines with regard to epistemology and linguistic thought, cf. Excursus III 'Knowledge and truth', IV 'Linguistic speculation'.

The Vedānta System

The other denomination by which Vedānta is known — Uttara-Mīmāṃsā ('Further or Later Exegesis') — should not be understood in a strictly chronological sense. Indeed, it seems possible that originally the *Mīmāṃsāsūtra* and the Vedānta root-*sūtra* (*Vedānta-sūtra* or *Brahmasūtra*) constituted a single text.[1] Mostly the same are the ancient authors they quote (Kārśajini, Ātreya, etc.) and, among the ancient commentaries that have not come down to us, the one by Upavarṣa stands out, as referring seemingly to both texts (at least according to Śaṅkara). The same motivation that underlies the setting-up of a school to analyse the ritual part of Vedic revelation is also valid for the spiritual and speculative part, characterised by similar incoherence, obscurity, and — not seldom — outright contradiction. Despite their common course and the fact that both represent a sort of orthodoxy in the Brahmanic world — within the limits to which such a notion can be applied to the Indian context — conflicts between the two schools were nevertheless acute, as they were also within the various streams of Vedānta itself, during its long history down to our own times. The root-*sūtra*, also known as the *Śārīrakamīmāṃsā* ('Exegesis of the Incarnate Soul'), attributed to the sage Bādarāyaṇa, does not appear to be datable earlier than the first centuries of the Common Era. It comprises 555 aphorisms, divided into four *adhyāya*s ('lessons'), divided in turn into four *pāda*s which, in what are often rather obscure and allusive terms, polemicise with the principal contemporary philosophies (in particular Sāṃkhya, Buddhism, Nyāya), but without ever naming them. The main themes are the nature of the universal spiritual principle (*brahman*), the individual spiritual principle (*ātman*) and the status of the phenomenal world, invoking the authority of the Upaniṣads — especially

[1] Cf. however the reasoned objections of Bronkhorst 2002-2003.

the ancient ones, *Chandogya* and *Bṛhadāraṇyaka* in the forefront (just as their Mīmāṃsaka 'cousins' referred back to the Brāhmaṇas) — and claiming the correctness of their own exegesis of them in the face of other schools, such as Sāṃkhya, which also draw from them. To the existence of one or more Vedantic schools even prior to the first work that has come down to us in its entirety, the *Māṇḍukya-kārikā* by Gauḍapāda, there are various witnesses, including the particularly significant evidence of the *Madhyamakahṛdaya* by Bhavya, a Buddhist work abounding in doxographic material composed toward the mid-sixth century C.E. Bhavya regards Vedānta with a highly critical eye, but first and foremost with suspicion. The accusation of 'crypto-Buddhism' with which ten centuries later Vijñānabhikṣu apostrophised Śaṅkara is already encountered in the first description of Vedānta doctrines that has come down to us. Bhavya's basic criticism of Vedānta concerns, as might well be expected, its doctrine of the *ātman* or *puruṣa*, viewed as an nth declension of the concept of 'own nature' (*svabhāva*),[2] the pet aversion of every Mādhyamika Buddhist like Bhavya. The concept of a supreme self (*paramātman*), in which the *ātman* loses any connotation of individuality to rise to an absolute and ineffable dimension seems, in Bhavya's view, to be copied from the absolute according to the Buddhists: "Whatever is said rightly in Vedānta has already been said by the Buddha" (*Madhyamakahṛdaya* IV.56ab; quoted in Qvarnström 1989: 103). The *Māṇḍukyakārikā* or *Āgamaśāstra* ('Treatise on Sacred Tradition'; cf. Bouy 2000) comprises four chapters, mixing prose (twelve passages, concentrated in the first chapter) and verse (215 *śloka*s). The first three chapters contain direct quotations or paraphrases integrated by glosses, taken mainly from Upaniṣadic texts, whereas the fourth chapter has a strong Buddhist tone. The doctrine it teaches deals with the substantial unreality of the phenomenal world, like that of dreams, as against the absolute reality of *brahman*.

---

[2] On the concept of *svabhāva* in the Mādhyamika school, cf. pp. 150-151.

The history of Vedānta thought largely follows the path traced by the stream of commentaries on the *Brahmasūtra*, each polarizing one of the possible angles for reading this monument of ambiguity, which lays the foundation for doctrines and world views, each with strong peculiarities and all mutually antagonistic, ranging from extreme non-dualism to extreme dualism. One of the first major commentaries is the one by Bhartṛprapañca (fifth-sixth century C.E.), followed in order by those of Maṇḍana Miśra, Śaṅkara, Bhāskara, Rāmānuja, Madhva, Nimbarka, and Vallabha. Of the many works ascribed to Śaṅkara (first half of the eighth century C.E.), the most outstanding author in the history of Vedānta thought, only a few enjoy (almost) total consensus as being autographic, besides the above-mentioned *Brahmasūtrabhāṣya*, to which an influential commentary is devoted by the great polygraph Vācaspati Miśra: the major commentaries on the *Bṛhadāraṇyaka*, *Chandogya* and *Taittirīya* Upaniṣads and the independent treatise *Upadeśasāhasrī*. To Śaṅkara's chief disciples, Padmapāda and Sureśvara we owe respectively the *Pañcapādikā*, a commentary on the *Brahmasūtra-bhāṣya* which cuts off suddenly after the fourth *sūtra*, and a copious set of works of which the most outstanding are the *Naiṣkarmya-siddhi* ('Demonstration of the Absence of Karma'), and some imposing sub-commentaries on exegetic works by his master (lengthy and intellectually committed is his *vārttika* on the *Bṛhadāraṇyakabhāṣya*). Presenting himself as a disciple of Sureśvara is Sarvajñātmamuni, the author of the *Saṃkṣepaśārīraka* ('*Brahmasūtra* in synthesis'). A new era was opened in Vedānta history by the vigorous dialectics of Śrīharṣa (second half of the twelfth century), who devotes his extremely difficult philosophical masterpiece, the *Khaṇḍanakhaṇḍakhādya* ('Choice Delicacies of Confutation'), to the criticisms of Nyāya realism. The creative season of non-dualistic Vedānta closes with the *Advaitasiddhi* ('Demonstration of Non-Duality') by Madhusūdana Sarasvatī (sixteenth century).

With regard to the status of the manifested world, the *Āgama-śāstra* provides the most extreme solution, under the sign of absolute monism. The only wholly real entity is the Self, achieved by demonstrating the unreality of the differentiated world, based both on the authority of revealed texts (first and foremost the Upaniṣads) and on reason. The world, which presents itself as a flow of objects that rise and vanish, is totally unreal, because what is real has neither a coming-into-being nor a disappearing. The analysis of the relationship of causality leads to the conclusion that both cause and effect are unreal. The universe is thus simply not-born (*ajāta*; whence the designation of *ajātivāda* ('doctrine of non-birth'). The tension between the One and multiplicity that characterises most of the reflections on the nature of reality thus loses one of its terms: it is no longer necessary to explain how multiplicity can proceed from the One, because multiplicity simply does not exist. The multiplicity that appears in daily experience has the same degree of reality as dreams: it is the result of a mental construct based on radical nescience.

Śaṅkara's position is less extreme than Gauḍapāda's. The world of duality is not pure nothingness, but the fruit of erroneous conceptual superimposition (*adhyāsa*), which attributes to the sole absolute reality — the *brahman* — features that are not proper to it. Applying this view to the example of the rope that is mistaken for a snake, the rope is *brahman* and the snake the world of multiplicity in which our ordinary experience occurs. The reasons why individuals have made this mistake ever since — escape from which being only possible thanks to redeeming knowledge (*jñāna*) of the *ātman/brahman* identity — are ultimately inexplicable (*anirvacanīya*). *Brahman* may in turn be viewed in a perspective of knowledge (*vidyā*) or of nescience (*avidyā*). The first is the absolute *brahman*, definable not only in purely negative terms but also as 'being' (*sat*), 'consciousness' (*cit*) and 'bliss' (*ānanda*). The second is the *brahman* as a specific divine entity, the efficient and material cause of the world. *Māyā* ('wondrous power') and nescience thus assume a trans-individual and cosmogonic dimension, even though Vedānta authors are very cautious about placing them in direct contact with the lower *brahman*, who nevertheless puts the creation of the world in motion only through their effect. The solution proposed by Sureśvara, by way of example, is that nescience is proper to *brahman*, but that being ultimately unreal does not stain it. The relationship between the One and multiplicity, the ultimately real and the provisionally real (or totally illusory) becomes the crux of Vedānta thought. The intrinsic difficulty of a solution that appears truly acceptable is reflected in the continual recourse to simile and metaphor: the rope and the snake, fire and sparks, the sun and its reflection in water, the ocean and its waves, water and foam. All this however helps outline the problem rather than solving it. From such assumptions, the relationship of causality derives a peculiar formulation. While the effect must be considered pre-existent in the cause, it lacks that reality that Sāṃkhya on the other hand did not hesitate to grant it. Thus Vedānta speaks of *satkāraṇa* ('real [persistent] existence of the cause') rather than of *satkārya* ('real existence of the effect'), and of illusory modification (*vivarta*) rather than of real transformation (*pariṇāma*), it being understood that from an absolute point of view both cause and effect remain essentially unreal.

The attempt to define the status of the world that appears to ordinary experience ends up absorbing most of the speculative effort of Vedānta thinkers. A general acceptation of two levels of reality and truth — absolute (*pāramārthika*) and relative (*vyāvahārika*) (as in the case of Śaṅkara) or even of three with Gauḍapāda (*parikalpita*, 'mentally constructed'; *paratantra*, 'dependent'; and *parinispanna*, 'accomplished') — involves a differentiation of methods and objectives. Rational argument is deemed incapable of leading to the absolute *brahman*, access to which is given only by intimate experience wholly lacking any discursive representation. It must be guided and triggered by revelation, with the consequence that the affirmative parts of Vedānta doctrine provide almost exclusive exegesis of scriptural passages, while the use of reason is reserved for polemics with other schools. Thus, since the dispute is kept within the level of empirical reality, classical Vedānta ends up — for example — defending the substantiality of objective reality against Yogācāra Buddhists, who preach the sole reality of consciousness, or defending continuity and substance against the — again Buddhist — supporters of instantaneity and impermanence. The traditional debates about the number and nature of the means of knowledge, although not central, are however present, albeit marked from the start by the awareness of their being exercised on objects that are not ultimately real. Consequently, as a rule, the *pramāṇa*s admitted by Mīmāṃsā are accepted without too much discussion: perception, inference, comparison, implication, negation and verbal testimony. Even this last, albeit the only one to find space in the context of *brahman*, if only for instrumental reasons or to be able to pursue didactic aims, cannot but have a certain dose of unreality. Its function, however, as noted by Maṇḍana Miśra, remains essentially of a negative order, i.e. that of overcoming error rather than affirming the truth. In any case, no other means of knowledge can undermine scriptural authority, not even perception, which assumes duality — apart from that special case of direct introspective intuition (*anubhava*) which, on the contrary, does not depend on the intermediation of organs or tools.

A highly original contribution to Vedānta philosophy comes from the complex figure of Śrīharṣa, the refined author of the poem *Naiṣadhacarita* ('Deeds of Nala'). According to tradition, Śrīharṣa's father, Śrīhīra, after being defeated in a public debate by the great Nyāya philosopher Udayana, asked the goddess Durgā for a son who would avenge him. The whole of Śrīharṣa's *Khaṇḍanakhaṇḍakhādya* aims at demolishing the fundamental principles of Nyāya, by using extremely sophisticated negative dialectics that immediately reveals its derivation from Madhyamaka Buddhism. All notions on which the objective world rests, as presented by the Nyāya system, are subjected to radical criticism highlighting their intrinsic contradictions. With nothing left standing — belief in an external object, the principle of correspondence between knowledge and object, the reality of the universals and, lastly, the very concept of difference (*bheda*) — all that remains, by elimination as it were, is to accept the perspective of the absolute non-dual reality (*abheda*) of *brahman*.

The scholastics of Vedānta is immense and a work such as the present one cannot provide an exhaustive picture of it but merely indicate some of its guidelines. In closing, however, I should like to add a few notes about an author, whose work — although it may not have made any outstanding contribution to Vedānta speculation in the strictest sense — appears to be of considerable 'cultural' importance. We have already encountered the Vedāntin Vijñānabhikṣu [3] as commentator on the seminal works of Sāṃkhya (the *Sāṃkhyasūtra*) and of Yoga (the *Yogasūtra*). The question that springs to mind is for what reason a Vedāntin should decide to employ his philosophic energies on these two vast commentaries to texts belonging to traditions that were not his own, rather than, by way of example, joining the crowded ranks of commentators of the great Śaṅkara. Considering in particular the by then declining fortunes of Sāṃkhya in the sixteenth century, we might take literally what Vijñānabhikṣu says in the initial verses — already quoted (p. 82) — of his *Sāṃkhyapravacanabhāṣya*, and assume some pure and simple 'restorative' and antiquarian intent, were it not in conflict with what has so far been stated about the eminently 'practical' nature of Indian thought, which comments only on what is still topical and only if the commentary answers some precise requirement. In the traditional Indian context, a commentary is frequently produced on a work for two converging reasons: because the work is objectively important and because one does not agree with it. Commenting on a work thus becomes a way of remodelling it and, once remodelled, making it one's own. Not even this, however, is the case of Vijñānabhikṣu's commentaries. Reading between the lines, what really prompts him is his intention of bringing other components into the Vedantic universe

[3] On his work, see Dasgupta 1975: III, 445-495.

to act as an antidote to the prevailing teaching of Śaṅkara. Too abstract and pitilessly intellectual, Śaṅkara's teaching does not provide an appropriate framework for the new Vedānta season, signed by the growing importance of *bhakti*, or impassioned devotion to a personal god, which presupposes a greater share of reality in the individual ego and the phenomenal world in which it moves (only thus can *bhakti* find its living space). By amalgamating with Vedantic tradition the ancient traditions of Sāṃkhya and Yoga (and a similar operation is performed by Vijñānabhikṣu in connection with Nyāya-Vaiśeṣika), he automatically reduces the central role of Śaṅkara. To ensure that this is effective, Vijñānabhikṣu prefers to avoid their more challenging and extreme forms (e.g. the widespread atheistic tone of Sāṃkhya); at the same time he continually highlights the thousands of roots that link these two *darśana*s to the Upaniṣads and — more particularly — to the medieval Purāṇas, that form the connective tissue of what we now know as 'Hinduism'. Henceforth, the somewhat unpalatable champion of inflexible *kevalādvaita* ('exclusive non-dualism') ends up being pitilessly dismissed as a *pracchannabauddha*, 'a Buddhist in disguise'.

The Pratyabhijñā System

It may be surprising to find, after dealing with six major Brahmanic systems of hallowed antiquity and authority, a little known school, the Pratyabhijñā ('Recognition [of the Lord]'). A presentation of Pratyabhijñā doctrines involves, first and foremost, giving voice to one of the most original and peculiar components of India's philosophical and religious scenario from medieval times down to our own: what is known as 'Tantrism'. It will be necessary to stretch a discreet veil over the incautious remarks of a well-known scholar like George Feuerstein:[1]

> Tantrism's contribution to philosophy is negligible. Its unicity lies wholly within the practical sphere, the *sādhana*. From a philosophical point of view, there is no hiatus between Tantrism and previous traditions. Buddhist Tantrism rests substantially on the foundations of the Mādhyamika school of Mahāyāna, and its Hindu counterpart on those of the cognate Advaita-Vedānta.

In actual fact, Pratyabhijñā, which provides the theoretical bases for all Hindu Tantrism, constitutes one of the highest and most original moments of all Indian thought (it has, moreover, very little to do with Vedānta). Pratyabhijñā was born in Kashmir, the privileged land of Indian culture, in about the ninth-tenth century, when Tantric Śivaite sects, supporters of absolute non-dualism, decided to abandon their condition as more-or-less secret movements, feared for their transgressive practices, and confront the religious-philosophical culture of the time on an equal footing, aspiring to become the dominant ideology in a far wider social circle than as conventicles of ascetic nocturnal devotees of the cremation grounds. The initial nucleus

[1] Feuerstein 1974: 176-177. A very similar position is also maintained by Mircea Eliade. For a detailed presentation of Pratyabhijñā philosophy, cf. Torella (1992, 2002: IX-XLV, 2009).

comprises non-dualistic Śivaite scriptures, the Bhairavatantras, Bhairava being the terrible form of the god Śiva, in whom cruelty and violence are metaphors for rampant energy, far distant from the unmoving and bloodless deities of Vedānta. Bhairava coincides with the 'I' of every creature. In first addressing the notion of the 'I', so disliked by Brahmanic thought, non-dualist Śivaism implicitly states the centrality of free movement as against the always lurking reification of the notion of *ātman*, the self as substance. As compared to the 'I' — the Supreme Consciousness — the flow of the phenomenal world is not a (bad) dream from which one must awaken as soon as possible, but the spontaneous manifestation of the Absolute itself. The concept of *māyā*, central to Vedānta, is not eliminated: *māyā* is taken to be the power of the Lord, even his highest power, otherwise known as *svātantryaśakti* ('power of freedom'); thus *svātantryavāda* ('doctrine of freedom') becomes one of the favourite names for this school.

Although the *Śivadṛṣṭi* ('Vision of Śiva') by Somānanda (ninth-tenth century) is traditionally considered as the Pratyabhijñā point of departure, it is in the work of Utpaladeva (*Īśvarapratyabhijñā-kārikā*, 'Stanzas of the Recognition of the Lord', and commentaries) that Pratyabhijñā reaches its fullest devising, later further refined and amplified, but without modifying its essential core, by the great Abhinavagupta. Utpaladeva set up a highly sophisticated and harmonious system — a mixture of metaphysics, spiritual practice, epistemology, logic, linguistic and aesthetic speculation — with great care first selecting both allies and adversaries. The latter are first and foremost the intellectual leaders of the time, i.e. the masters of the great logical-epistemological season of Buddhism. The *Īśvarapratyabhijñā-kārikā* is largely a penetrating dialogue with Dharmakīrti and his followers, equally opposed and admired to the extent of leaving an indelible mark on Pratyabhijñā philosophy. Utpaladeva starts by provisionally endorsing the Buddhist view of an impersonal and fragmented universe, made of isolated and discontinuous instants. By using their arguments, he pursues the criticism of the realism of Nyāya — claiming the reality of the external objects and the actual existence of concepts such as relation, and so forth. After letting the Buddhist logicians demolish the Nyāya categories, he shows how the Buddhist alternative is in fact equally inadequate. It does overcome Nyāya, but remains as though suspended in mid air, since it is proved — in its fragmented and isolated universe — to be incapable of accounting for the network and circularity of human experience. The only way to save the Buddhist view from its theoretical failure is to include it in a different field of reference, represented by the omni-pervasive dynamism of a free and 'personal' consciousness that coincides with the Supreme Lord, Śiva. In this way, Utpaladeva achieves the result of both showing the superiority of the Pratyabhijñā to Buddhism and warning the Naiyāyikas (among whom the Śaiva faith was most prevalent) not to count too much on their forces alone, detached from those of the new Śaiva philosophers.

Another protagonist is the grammarian-philosopher Bhartṛhari,[2] with his doctrine of the omni-pervasiveness of language right to the very heart of consciousness, with which it substantially coincides. In order to undermine the discontinuous universe of the Buddhists, Utpaladeva decides to avail himself precisely of the latter doctrine, the language-imbued nature of knowledge, which is meant to demolish its main foundation stone, the unsurpassable gulf between the moment of sensation and that of conceptual elaboration, representing, as it were, the very archetype of Buddhist segmented reality. Thus, some of the most famous, and crucial, verses of the *Īśvarapratyabhijñākārikā* originate.

> "The essential nature of light is reflective awareness; otherwise light, though 'coloured' by objects, would be similar to an insentient reality, such as the crystal and so on." (I.V.11; cf. Torella 2002: 118). "Consciousness has as its essential nature reflective awareness; it is the supreme Word that

---

[2] For an interpretation of Utpaladeva's radical change of attitude toward Bhartṛhari, who had been fiercely attacked by his master Somānanda, see Torella 2009.

arises freely. It is freedom in the absolute sense, the sovereignty of the supreme Self" (I.V.13; cf. Torella 2002: 120). "Even at the moment of direct perception there is a reflective awareness. How otherwise could one account for such actions as running and so on, if they were thought of as being devoid of determinate awareness?" (I.V.19; cf. Torella 2002: 125).

As far as the metaphysical background is concerned, there is nothing essentially new in this doctrine, the scriptural *sarvaśakti-vilolatā* ('effervescence of all powers [in any reality]') referred to by the *Śivadṛṣṭi* (I.11b) implicitly already containing it. What Utpaladeva needed was a shared, if controversial, strong 'philosophical' argument. The omnipervasiveness of language is the epistemological version of the omnipervasiveness of Śiva, and at the same time calls for integration into the spiritually dynamic Śaiva universe.[3]

For a presentation of the complex doctrines of Pratyabhijñā, I shall give the floor to the most famous of Indian doxographers, the many-times-mentioned Mādhava, who devotes an entire chapter of his *Sarvadarśanasaṃgraha* to Pratyabhijñā (cf. in the Appendices, *From the Sarvadarśanasaṃgraha: the Pratyabhijñā-darśana*), assigning it a relatively high rank in his hierarchy of systems, close to the 'classical' Brahmanic *darśanas*.[4] Examined closely, Mādhava's chapter is none other than a skilful collage of passages, almost solely drawn from Abhinavagupta's *Īśvarapratyabhijñā-vimarśinī*. It is an interesting chance for the reader to see how an Indian doxography works and also to tackle one of the great Indian philosophical texts directly — in all its difficulty and complexity — after so much talk about them.

[3] About the Pratyabhijñā's universalistic approach to revelation, see Torella forthcoming c.

[4] Much higher, for example, than non-Śaṅkarian Vedāntins, such as Rāmānuja or Pūrṇaprajña — which come immediately after the 'negators' (*nāstika*) — but below the 'alchemists' (*raseśvaras*)!

Part Two

OPPONENTS OF BRAHMANIC CULTURE:

THE MATERIALISM OF THE LOKĀYATAS, JAINISM AND BUDDHISM

The Lokāyatas

The generic (western) designation of 'Materialists' groups together the supporters of the most radically critical positions against Brahmanic thought and, more generally speaking, against Brahmanic social and religious order, without sparing anyone, not even Buddhists and Jains, with whom however they shared the epithet of *nāstika*s ('those who say: it [god, etc.] is not') in the eyes of Brahman orthodoxy. The formulations and trends that have followed each other over the centuries, starting from the era of the Buddha and Mahāvīra — probably without ever giving rise to schools as such — present a varying mixture of hedonism, scepticism and common sense, which have received their peculiar characterization from their caustic and aggressive intolerance of the Brahmanic elite and, more generally, of any bowing to tradition.

The Materialists (Tucci 1971, Chattopadhyaya 1990) are known by three main appellatives: Lokāyatas (or also Lokāyatikas), probably 'followers of worldliness' (Lokāyata is also used to refer to the system), Cārvākas ('Of caressing speech') and Bārhaspatyas ('Followers of Bṛhaspati'). To Bṛhaspati is attributed the root-text of these schools, the *Bṛhaspatisūtra*, of which only a few fragments are extant. This divine character is also associated with the seminal text of the Indian *ars politica*, the *Arthaśāstra* ('Treatise on the Useful'), thus emphasising the link that in the perspective of classical India unites these two spheres, characterised by the same disenchanted pragmatism. Furthermore, the *Arthaśāstra*, in listing the schools that practice *ānvīkṣikī* ('investigative science'), places Lokāyata side by side with Sāṃkhya and Yoga.

The unanimous censure that the Lokāyatas have met with from all Indian philosophical systems is reflected in the loss of all their works, with the sole exception of the *Tattvopaplavasiṃha* ('Lion who upsets Principles'). It has thus been the fate of materialist doctrines to be handed down by the summary and almost always malevolent accounts of opponent schools, which marginalized them as *pūrvapakṣa*s ('opposing theses to be confuted'), not unlike what happened in the West with the Gnostics, regularly ill-treated by the Church Fathers. Their lack of fortune among the dominant philosophical schools makes the enduring presence of Lokāyata in the main axis of Indian philosophy difficult to explain, to the extent of raising the suspicion that their continually proposed liquidation belongs to some ritual plot rather than being the testimony of any genuine conflict. Another possible interpretation, on the other hand, refers to the basically unilateral nature of Indian philosophical tradition, its works coming almost entirely from an extremely restricted social circle: in such a case, the materialist schools would be just the emerging point of a much wider and more vital trend that found little acceptance in philosophical circles, but whose impact they must have felt. Confirmation of this may be found in the fact that the Jain Haribhadra, having included in his well-known doxographic work *Ṣaḍdarśanasamuccaya* only six systems (Buddhism, Nyāya, Sāṃkhya, Jainism, Vaiśeṣika and Mīmāṃsā), before concluding also gives a brief 'off-screen' account of Lokāyata doctrines.[1]

[1] As we have seen above, the Lokāyatas, albeit bitterly criticised, end up as being included in most doxographies. Exceptionally contemptuous is the tone with which they are liquidated by Jayanta, usually so moderate with adversaries: "As regards the wretched Materialists, their miserable philosophy is not even worthy to be considered" (*Nyāyamañjarī*, vol. I, p. 9, quoted in Gerschheimer 2007: 247).

The four stanzas of the *Ṣaḍdarśanasamuccaya* provide a highly colourful and significant picture:

> The Lokāyatas say that neither god nor liberation exists, that there is no action either in keeping with or contrary to the Dharma and therefore no consequence in terms of merits or demerits. The world does not go beyond the range of the senses. What all these great sages are telling us is similar, O Good Lady, to the fable that says, "Careful, here are the traces of a wolf". Eat and drink, Most Gracious One: what is past [or else 'beyond'], O Lady of the beautiful Limbs, does not belong to you; what has gone, O Timid One, returns no more. This body is but an aggregate. Furthermore: the four elements Earth Water Fire and Air are the basis of consciousness. The only means of knowledge is what is born of the senses. By virtue of the combination of earth, etc., the various entities arise, such as the body. Just as inebriating force is released from the fermenting ingredients of alcoholic beverages, so it is for the conscious principle of subjectivity [which develops from the four elements]. This is why the Cārvākas teach that it is foolish to follow the invisible abandoning the visible. For them, the joy that rises in man from accomplishing recommended actions and in fleeing from those vituperated is futile; it is no different from ether. Indeed, right conduct (*dharma*) should not be placed before satisfying desire (*kāma*).

This rejection of all transcendence and also of all ethical constriction is accompanied by a drastic reduction in man's cognitive ambitions. If the sole source of knowledge is direct perception, all human designs are vain, together with any claim to control whatever exceeds the mere present. It admits, for example, of no relationship of causality and any action based on the predictability of effects is excluded. Even if two events appear to occur with a regular sequence, the absolute necessity of their connection cannot be determined to make it extensible to past and future, both being outside the range of perception. This does not mean that the world is ruled by chance, but only that no order can be reconstructed by the limited possibilities of human knowledge. Effects are produced, various entities are born and disappear in accordance with a dynamism peculiar to their intrinsic nature (*svabhāva* — whence the name *svabhāvavādin*, 'supporters of intrinsic nature', attributed to some Materialist currents). This same kind of consideration leads to a consequence of a much wider order: no type of inference can be allowed, since to be sure of the unvarying concomitance (*vyāpti*) of *probans* and *probandum* it would be necessary to take into account an infinite number of cases. Furthermore, even admitting the possibility of inference on principle, in the specific case of, by way of example, inferring fire from seeing smoke, it cannot certainly be the universal 'fire' that is inferred, because it is already known, still less would it be possible to infer a particular fire by means of its concomitance with the universal 'smoke'.

Only direct perception therefore is deemed to be a valid means of knowledge. Such a statement makes it easy for all their adversaries (whether Brahmanic or not) to retort that without the use of reason such a conclusion could not be reached: by itself, perception is insufficient to ensure its own unique validity. The already-mentioned Jayarāśi takes up the challenge and accepts the extreme consequences: so, not even perception can be said to be a valid means of knowledge, and all ontological and ethical positions also lack any foundation, including the very ones ascribed to Lokāyata. In actual fact, as we read at the start of Jayarāśi's masterpiece, the Lokāyata root-*sūtra* did not present ideas assumed as its own, but only provisional ideas with the final aim of demonstrating their intrinsic incongruity. This task, already attempted by the author of the *Bṛhaspatisūtra*, was finally achieved several centuries later by the *Tattvopaplavasiṃha* (Franco 1994). Beneath its axe-like dialectics, all the philosophic conceptions of the time collapsed: every possible interpretation is examined and then dropped. The final outcome is quite different from that pursued by other illustrious examples of critical radicalism, first of all the *Madhyamakakārikā* by the Buddhist Nāgārjuna and the *Khaṇḍanakhaṇḍakhādya* by the Vedāntin Śrīharṣa: here is no jump into the ineffable absolute, but total scepticism. It is interesting to note that just a single manuscript of this text, albeit well-known and repeatedly quoted in its own time, has come down to us, and to save it from the oblivion to which it was most probably destined — together with all the other texts of these schools — was the famous Jaina library of Patan. While rejecting its final content, the Jaina logicians must have appreciated its dialectic effectiveness and used it to whet their already keen critical tools, with which they built up the philosophy of Non-Absolutism (*anekāntavāda*) and the multiplicity of points of view (*nayavāda*) (cf. pp. 132-135).

Jainism

The two great challenges to Brahmanic hegemony, which championed a socio-religious system dominated by Vedic sacrifice — deemed to be responsible for the very balance of the universe, and consequently raising the sacerdotal caste above all others —, both arise in the north-east of India, at approximately the same period (sixth-fifth century B.C.E), during a time of radical social and economic change that led to the ascent of the military caste (*kṣatriya*). Most probably triggered by this moment of crisis was the spread of a phenomenon that saw the abandoning of social life and the forming of hordes of 'renouncers', ascetics seeking ways other than those rigidly established by the professionals of the sacrifice. An itinerant ascetic and *kṣatriya* by birth is the historical founder of Jainism, Mahāvīra or the Jina, the last of a chain of twenty-four 'crossing-makers' (*tīrthaṅkara*), omniscient but human beings (complete enlightenment is precluded to the gods), who succeed each other through the various eras in order to proclaim the Three Jewels of eternal Jaina doctrine: right faith, right knowledge, and right action. The temporal scenario is portrayed as a twelve-spoked wheel that turns on itself, alternating a descendant and an ascendant motion, each with six distinct stages. The fifth in the descendant direction, which is where we are currently (corresponding to the Kali Yuga), will be followed, in the sixth, by the total extinction of doctrine, followed in turn by progressive rebirth. The fact that the founders of Jainism (and Buddhism) belonged to the warrior caste (*kṣatriya*)[1] is also betrayed by a certain 'military' terminology both in their social organisation and in the presentation of their teaching (Dundas 1992: 18). Paradoxically, the teaching makes non-violence (*ahiṃsā*) one of its cardinal points. Jains and Buddhists share, contrary to their

[1] Jaina tradition, however, is unanimous in saying that all Mahāvīra's direct disciples were brahmins!

Brahmanic opponents, the belief that their respective founders were human in everything and reached enlightenment counting only on their individual powers, i.e. without any divine intervention, and that their followers can do likewise. To this end, the Jina and the Buddha teach a method that leads them along the path of progressive purification, consisting of spiritual exercises, such as meditation, ethical observances and austere conduct. The latter, which in Jainism can lead to levels of almost inhuman asceticism, are however gauged differently according to whether the disciple is a monk or a layman. On other fundamental aspects of their respective doctrines, Jains and Buddhists are, on the other hand, perfectly in line with the Brahmanic universe, which they question, but from which they both, in any final analysis, derive. All share a belief in *karma*, in the cycle of rebirth (*saṃsāra*), and in the possibility of escaping from it and achieving definitive liberation (*mokṣa*). Where Jainism and Buddhism diverge is on the reality of the individual soul and the value of asceticism. For the Jains, there exists an eternal, individual principle, animating all creation, including vegetables, whereas for Buddhists any permanent individuality, every 'ego', is reduced to a continually changing combination of momentary and fluctuating mental states. The extreme asceticism championed by Jainism, for the Buddhists leads only to a self-destructive dead-end. The Buddha himself, after experiencing its substantial uselessness for the purpose of self-transformation, abandoned it in favour of a more flexible and less arid 'middle way'.

If we wish to formulate a kind of elementary Jaina catechism, we cannot leave out four elements, some of which have already made their appearance above: non-violence, the centrality of the *karma* (in the most archaic and 'primitive' form that India has ever conceived), austere conduct aimed at eradicating all emotional and passional elements, in which we are struck by what a famous scholar of Jainism, himself a Jaina, has called 'fear of food' (Jaini 1993). The fourth element concerns the mental and speculative attitude: the conviction that, in view of the enormous complexity of the real, every specific philosophical or religious position must be deemed, if not 'false', at least partial and provisional. Although apparently heterogeneous, on closer examination these four elements show that they are closely connected one with the other.

A markedly 'archaic' character, associated with a sometimes disconcerting propensity for extremism in its ethical-religious manifestations, has always distinguished Jainism. Although fated by its own elitist ethic not to take root among the masses, Jainism has managed to maintain its identity and prestige down to our own times. Albeit never playing any central role in the history of the subcontinent, it has retained its importance and, in particular, has not undergone any eclipse, leaving its highly personal mark on every aspect of culture, from philosophy to science (especially mathematics and astronomy), the figurative arts, architecture, and narrative. While their Buddhist 'cousins' progressively disappeared from India — for many reasons, of which the Muslim invasion is usually counted as one of the most decisive — the Jaina presence remained indestructible, Muslim dominion notwithstanding, established particularly in Gujarat, Rajasthan and Karnataka, and with a significant spread throughout India.

Relations between Jainism and Hinduism are complex. Too indigestible a mouthful even for the incredible assimilating capacity of Hinduism, Jainism always remains 'different' (memorable are the clashes, even sometimes bloody, with Śaivism, lasting several centuries), but at the same time its special place is recognised in the social and religious order of India, a recognition facilitated by the fact that, on its own side, Jainism, with great realism, accepted the Hindu caste system quite early on, despite a considerable conflict with its own original principles.[2]

Its corpus of scripture is distinguished according to the division of Jainism into two communities, the Digambaras ('Clothed with

---

[2] This substantial integration now finds its official recognition in Art. 25 of the Indian Constitution, which includes the Jains under the denomination 'Hindu' (together with Sikhs and Buddhists).

Space') and the Śvetāmbaras ('Clothed in White'). The former exact total nudity (but not for nuns), accept alms only on the palm of the hand (instead of in a bowl), do not contemplate liberation for women and deny that the liberated have need of food. Beside these fundamental differences, there are many others, concerning however mostly the religious sphere, for which reason they need not be examined here. It should be noted, incidentally, that the Digambara Jains are responsible for most contributions of a theoretical and logical-epistemological order. The scriptural canon accepted by the Śvetāmbaras comprises 45 texts, containing the teaching of the Tīrthaṅkaras, divided into 12 'members' (*aṅga*), 12 'sub-members' (*upāṅga*), 7 'disciplinary texts' (*chedasūtra*), 4 'root-texts' (*mūla-sūtra*), 10 'miscellanea' (*prakīrṇaka*), 2 texts of scriptural exegesis. The language is a kind of Prakrit known as *ardhamāgadhī* ('semi-*māgadhī*'), a tongue similar to the one used in Maghada (region of north-east India), where Mahāvīra lived and operated. Rather than the mark of a 'popular' origin for the Jaina creed, the use of *ardhamāgadhī* should be seen as the outcome of a deliberate distancing from Sanskrit, the language of the brahmins.[3] This canon is countered by the Digambaras with the radical affirmation that the

[3] According to tradition (cf. Dundas 1992: 60-61), Mahāvīra preached in *ardhamāgadhī*, which however reached the ears of the faithful 'translated' into the mother-tongue of each one of them. As expected, *ardhamāgadhī* was also the language spoken by the gods. Defence of *ardhamāgadhī*, as the Jains' identifying language, lasted relentlessly for many centuries (it is said that the proposal to translate the Jaina scriptures into the language of the Indian cosmopolis — Sanskrit — cost the great logician Siddhasena Divākara twelve years of exile). However, in the end Jainism — like Buddhism — had to yield to the allurement of the enormous cultural prestige of Sanskrit and accept it as the language of scholarly debate, although, even as late as the tenth century, Prabhācandra (the author of the *Nyāyakumudacandra*, 'Moon [that opens the] lotus-flower of logic') still lucidly lays claim to equality between Sanskrit and Prakrit, or even the primacy of the latter (Dundas 1996b: 144). The first major fracture in the exclusive use of the Prakrit took place as early as Umāsvāti (fourth-fifth century C.E.), and became irremediable starting from the work of Haribhadra (eighth century), which relegated the *ardhamāgadhī* increasingly to restricted circles of specialists, all belonging to the monastic community. It should however be remembered that Jainism continued to utilise various types of Prakrit (including *apabhraṃśa*) in its extraordinarily rich narrative.

original texts are to be deemed definitively lost: of them survives a pale memory in just two works, the *Ṣaṭkāṇḍa* ('[Treatise] in six parts') and the *Kaṣāya* ('[Treatise of the] Passions'). On the disappearance of this set of ancient texts (*pūrva*), attributed to Mahāvīra in person, the Śvetāmbaras also agree, maintaining however that they constitute only the third section of the twelfth 'member' of their canon, the *Dṛṣṭivāda* ('Discussion of Philosophical Systems'), which has now also been totally lost.

Jaina scriptures cover the most disparate subjects — from metaphysics to psychology and natural sciences — and draw their authority directly from the omniscience of their authors, the Tīrthaṅkaras, and in particular Mahāvīra, without fear of being proven wrong, since the last enlightened one — and therefore omniscient — was Jambū, the disciple of Mahāvīra, and in the near future, in view of the progressive decay of doctrine as a condition of the current era, the prospect of any other perfect enlightenment is precluded. The prestige of one work has greatly contributed to ensure the substantial unitary nature and absence of traumatic changes in doctrine; although not part of the scriptures, it has come to represent an authoritative synthesis of them, the more necessary owing to the vastness and dilution of the teachings they contain: the *Tattvārthādhigamasūtra* ('Treatise on Attaining the Meaning of True Reality') by Umāsvāti (fourth-fifth century C.E.); the fact of the author's being a Śvetāmbara, whereas all the principal commentaries — oustanding among which the one by Akalaṅka (eighth century) — are by Digambaras, testifies to its nature as a work *super partes*.

The worldview proposed by the Jaina philosopher is marked by a decided realism and takes a position midway between the Brahmanic schools, which variously tend to emphasise the permanence of substance, and Buddhism, dominated by a view of continual change. With its characteristic tendency toward mediation and rejection of unilateral stands, Jainism maintains the co-presence in the real of a constant element (*dravya*) and of variable modes of presentation (*paryāya*) and qualities (*guṇa*; Dixit 1971). In the universe, two fundamental categories can be distinguished: the 'living' or 'soul' (*jīva*) and the 'non-living' (*ajīva*), both subsumed under the wider denomination of 'masses of being' (*astikāya*). Particularly in the more ancient texts, the *jīva* category is poised between the spiritual and the biological.

The number of *jīva*s is infinite: they consist of pure consciousness and are endowed with omniscience, energy and bliss; they have no extension of their own, but at the same time are all-pervasive, and assume the dimension of the body to which they are connected. Once connected to a body, they can either be mobile (gods, animals, mankind) or immobile (vegetals). *Jīva*s are then classified according to the organs they possess: 'with one sense' (touch: elementary beings connected with each of the five elements); 'with two senses' (touch and taste: worms, shell-fish); 'with three senses' (touch, taste and smell: ants, gnats); 'with four senses' (touch, taste, smell and sight: butterflies, flies, scorpions); lastly, 'with five senses' are infernal beings, animals, mankind and demi-gods. The *ajīva* category includes motion (*dharma*), stasis (*adharma*) — or rather what determines motion or stasis —, matter (*pudgala*) and space (*ākāśa*); matter is presented at different levels of aggregation, starting from atoms (*paramāṇu*) which, unlike Vaiśeṣika atoms, are identical to each other.

Among the *ajīva*s, the Digambaras include time which, lacking spatial extension, is the only one to be *an-astikāya* ('lacking mass of being'). Mixing together in an absolutely inextricable manner motifs of a naturalistic, metaphysical and ethical order, the *jīva*s, the set of four *ajīva*s, together with the flow of *karma* (*āśrava*), merit and demerit (*pāpa* and *puṇya*), the blockage of *karma* (*bandha*), the impediment of new *karma* (*saṃvara*), the destruction of blocked *karma* (*nirjarā*) and liberation (*mokṣa*), form the nine basic principles of Jainism. *Karma*, which concerns as many as six of the nine principles, is conceived of as a kind of material substance generated by actions, which obstructs the powers of the soul and determine its peregrination from body to body, until final liberation. Owing to its spiritual nature, the soul would be out of the reach of *karma* — which is material — were it not for the presence of the passions that act as a kind of glue. In their most quintessential form, the passions can be reduced to four basic instincts: 1) the desire for food, which leads living beings to compete to obtain it, triggering 2) the instinct of fear. The abundant consumption of food then sets in motion 3) sexual desire, the satisfying of which again generates the desire for food. To ensure a ready availability of food, living beings develop 4) the instinct of accumulation, which leads to a hostile attitude toward other living beings with whom they are competing, a hostility that manifests itself in violent actions, at the basis of which are found the senses of attachment and aversion. Desire for food thus constitutes the basis of the condition of limitation and enslavement, facilitating *karma*'s suffocating hold on the potentially free and infinite soul. Abstaining from violence, connected in turn deep-down to the desire for accumulation, is thus first and foremost a practice of self-defence of the living being, and only secondarily responds to a gesture of active solidarity toward one's 'neighbour'. As the Jaina Amṛtacandra states without any risk of misinterpretation, "Non-violence means in actual fact only this: that attachment and the other passions do not manifest themselves; violence is likewise their manifestation. In a nutshell this is the doctrine of the Jina" (Jaini 2000: 4).

Speculations about the nature of *karma* and its infinite classifications largely keep Jaina authors busy and are one of the features of this great tradition. Of a totally different order — logical-epistemological — but equally characteristic of Jainism is another doctrine on which it is worth pondering: the doctrine of non-absolutism (*anekāntavāda*) and the other, strictly connected one, of partial points of view (*naya*; Matilal 1981, Shah 2000). Jainism starts by stating that every object possesses infinite aspects, ascribable to two radically different orders (according to the formulation of Akalaṅka, "The object is made of substance and of modes of manifestation"). A synthetic, complete knowledge would require of the subject intellectual power that is commensurate with the infinity of the related object, a power that now no longer exists. The consequences that Jainism draws from such a premise lead, not to scepticism, but to a serene and realistic acceptance of human limitations and to a systematic refusal of all absolutism — whether cognitive or ethical —, which does not spare even Jaina positions. This option is perfectly in line with the principle of radical non-violence (*ahiṃsā*) that characterises Jaina ethics and is in fact its translation in terms of epistemology. No assertion can claim to constitute the truth, and at the utmost can only be a partial aspect of it. As well as 'non-absolutism', this doctrine is also known as *syādvāda* [*syāt-vāda*] (lit. 'doctrine of 'may-be''); indeed, *syāt* — which is the optative form of *as-* ('to be') — can also express, within a wide-ranging semantic field, various nuances of possibility down to total unreality. Each assertion is broken down into seven possible alternatives, neither true nor false taken in isolation, but capable of providing an all-round knowledge of the object once brought together. Each alternative is introduced by 'perhaps' or 'maybe' — as stated, one of the possible senses of *syāt* — to which however the Jains, worried about possible sceptical values, much prefer that of 'in a certain way'. This 'seven-mode system' (*saptabhaṅgī*; cf. for example *Pramāṇanayatattvālokālaṅkāra* IV.14-21) consists of the following series: 1) [a thing, or a property, in a certain way] is; 2) is not; 3) is and is not; 4) is inexpressible; 5) is and is inexpressible; 6) is not and is inexpressible; 7) is, is not and is inexpressible. This doctrine, contained in a nutshell in one of the most ancient Jaina scriptures — the *Vyākhyāprajñapti* ('Delucidation of Explanations') —, is raised to high levels of sophistication by the philosophers of the great Jaina logical-epistemological tradition, starting from Mallavādin and Siddhasena Divākara (fifth century C.E.), continuing with Samantabhadra (sixth-seventh century), Akalaṅka and Haribhadra (eighth century), up to Yaśovijaya (seventeenth century).

A famous verse of the *Nyāyāvatāra* ('Introduction to Logic') by Siddhasena Divākara[4] is the best introduction to the complementary

---

[4] Both author and date of the *Nyāyāvatāra* have recently been questioned (Balcerowicz 2001).

doctrine of the *naya*s: "The real entity, consisting of a multiplicity of aspects, is the field of action of all cognition; the object characterised by only one of these aspects is the field of action of the *naya*s". The Sanskrit term *naya* 'conduct, principle, method, doctrine' is here taken in its technical meaning of 'partial, one-dimensional doctrine [or judgement]'. According to an image that frequently recurs in the texts, the relation between the normal knowing subject and any of its related objects is the same as that between an elephant and blind men surrounding it out of curiosity: each believes he has formed an accurate idea of what stands before him: one identifies it by the trunk, one by the tusk, one by an ear. Each *naya* retains its validity as long as its partiality is admitted and the need to bring it alongside an infinite number of others so as to reach an all-inclusive synthesis. The doctrine of the *naya*s finds its ideal accomplishment as a criterion for assessing various philosophical-religious views. The principle of non-violence, followed by Jainism also in the intellectual sphere (exemplary is the shrewd and neutral eye with which the Jaina philosopher scrutinises his adversaries' doctrines, representing them properly, without ever indulging in facile distortions), means that, for example, Sāṃkhya is partially accepted, as is Buddhism, so long as the preliminary orientation of the former on substance and of the latter on becoming is exposed. This is quite different from the ecumenism, which is only superficially similar, of the Vedānta which, in exchange for granting the rival systems a side place in the great theatre of philosophic systems, requires of them acceptance of an extremely inflexible hierarchy, of which it places itself beyond dispute at the top. The *naya*s too are classified as seven main types, in turn divided into two groups, the one concerning the 'substance' aspect (*dravya-naya*) and the other the 'modes of manifestation' aspect (*paryāya-naya*): *naigama* (viewing things as they appear at first glance, now in their general aspect and then in the specific, as does Nyāya-Vaiśeṣika), *saṃgraha* (viewing their common substrate, as does Vedānta), *vyavahāra* (viewing their individuality), *ṛjusūtra* (viewing only their present), *śabda* (making reference to various words as synonyms), *samabhirūḍha* (distinguishing a specific meaning for each word), *evaṃbhūta* (applying a given word only when the object, at that moment, effectively performs the activity it expresses).

Awareness of the limited and provisional nature of human knowledge however always lies behind the reflections of Jaina philosophers on the number and nature of the means of valid cognition (*pramāṇa*). The division between direct knowledge (*pratyakṣa*) and indirect (*parokṣa*), already present in the scriptures and developed by the most ancient authors, first of all Umāsvāti, does not correspond with what is generally understood by Indian thought in that it starts rather from the assumption that authentic knowing occurs only when the soul confronts the object directly, i.e. without the mediation of the senses or intellect. This banishes all ordinary experience, including perception, into the grey area of the indirect, setting aside direct knowledge only for the liberated. Beside the latter, called *kevala* ('isolated'), the 'direct knowledge' category also includes a further two forms, also accessible to intermediate levels of spiritual elevation: knowledge of minds, or rather, of the modifications of the minds of others (*manaḥparyāya*); and the direct intuition of entities normally inaccessible to perception (*avadhi*). Indirect knowledge, on the other hand, includes *mati* ('intellectual knowledge') and *śruta* ('auditory knowledge'). The former thus comprises sensorial perception itself, as well as inference, analogy, memory, etc.; the latter coincides with verbal knowledge, including the scriptures, always preceded by *mati*-type knowledge (e.g. auditory perception) to which is added understanding of the meaning, so that some conceive of the latter as a particular case of the former. Sensorial perception is split into four successive stages: data acquisition by the senses (*avagraha*), its determination (*īhā*), ascertainment of its specific characteristics (*avaya*) and, lastly, its definitive storing in the memory (*dhāraṇā*).

In its later development, however, Jaina philosophy ends up by accepting direct/indirect opposition in its most commonly understood sense. The same also occurs with its conception of inference, with the adoption of the division of inference into inference for oneself / inference for others (cf p. 49), as well as its articulation into five members. It replaces the former division into ten members, proposed by Bhadrabāhu in his *Daśavaikālikaniryukti* and applied in this case to proving the excellence of the virtue of non-violence (Vidyabhushana 1920: 166-167): 1) *pratijñā*, 'promise, theory to be demonstrated': "non-violence is the highest virtue"; 2) *pratijñā-vibhakti*, 'specification of theory': "it is the highest virtue according to the Jaina scriptures"; 3) *hetu*, 'logical reason': "because its practitioners are loved by the gods and are a source of merit for those who honour them"; 4) *hetuvibhakti*, 'specification of logical reason': "because its practitioners are the only ones able to live in the highest spheres of virtue"; 5) *vipakṣa*, 'contrary example': "but even those who commit violence can live well and even those who despise the Jaina scriptures can accumulate merits, as in the case, for example, of the brahmins"; 6) *vipakṣapratiṣedha*, 'confutation of the contrary example': "no, because it is impossible for anyone who despises the Jaina scriptures to be loved by the gods and deserve honour"; 7) *dṛṣṭānta*, '[positive] example': "ascetics take food from householders because they cannot cook for fear of killing insects"; 8) *āśaṅkā*, 'objection': "but the sins of the householders should fall on the ascetics, since it is for them that they cook"; 9) *āśaṅkāpratiṣedha*, 'confutation of the objection': "no, because ascetics visit houses without warning and so it is not specially for them that the food has been cooked"; 10) *naigamana*, 'conclusion': "non-violence is consequently the highest virtue".[5]

---

[5] A different articulation with ten members is found in Ratnaprabha's commentary on the *Pramāṇanayatattvālokālaṅkāra* ('Ornament to the illustration of the true nature of the means of knowledge and of partial views') by Vādideva Sūri (twelfth century) (p. 222).

Buddhism

In the boundless sea of Buddhist doctrines, worked out on the basis of the Buddha's teachings over the roughly seventeen centuries of Buddhist presence on Indian soil, a consolidated doxographic tradition has identified as the most characteristic and representative those belonging to four schools: the Sarvāstivādin (Vaibhāṣika), the Sautrāntika, the Mādhyamika and the Yogācāra. For our necessarily succinct overview, we thus adopt the selection made by the *Sarvadarśanasaṃgraha* of Mādhava, followed by the *Sarvasiddhāntasaṃgraha* erroneously ascribed to Śaṅkara and also found in the ample and informed commentary that Guṇaratna devoted to the founder of the doxographic genre, the *Ṣaḍdarśanasamuccaya* by the Jain Haribhadra.[1] Besides the example of these illustrious precedents, presenting only these four schools is justified by the particular relevance of their doctrines in a prevalently ontological-logical-epistemological scenario, such as that provided in this volume. Lastly, an account will be given of the not easily classifiable work of Dignāga and Dharmakīrti, cardinal figures of the so-called logical-epistemological schools of Buddhism, who played a considerable role in the new developments in Indian thought as a whole.

The basis of all the various branches of Buddhism is a compact set of doctrines whose devising dates back to the founder himself. As often repeated in the Buddha's discourses, the aim of his teaching is to identify a path midway between the nihilism of those who restrict the subject to the brief event of the physical body (*ucchedavādin*, 'supporters of destruction') and the eternalism of those that conceive of it as an autonomous and permanent substance (*śāsvatavādin*, 'supporters of eternity'). Whatever it contains, both on the subject's and on the object's side, experience shares three general features

[1] See also the later *Sarvamatasaṃgraha* (Mejor 2007: 264).

(*lakṣaṇa*): frustration (*duḥkha*), impermanence (*anitya*) and absence-of-self (*anātman*). This last-mentioned does not refer solely to the non-existence of an 'I' substance acting as substrate and possessor with regard to the flow of mental and cognitive states.[2] It also concerns — in the widest sense of insubstantiality — the fluid objects of such states, which ordinary experience marked by an anguished 'thirst' (*tṛṣṇā*) tries to immobilise as 'things'. The Buddha teaches how to disentangle these knots and, first and foremost, break down the redundant edifice of the personal ego into five basic aggregations (*skandha*): form-matter (*rūpa*), sentiments (*vedanā*), perceptions (*saṃjñā*), impulses (*saṃskāra*) and consciousness (*vijñāna*). What causes these states are the twelve fields of the senses (*āyatana*): eyes, visible objects; ears, sounds; nose, smells; tongue, tastes; body, tangible objects; mind and mental objects. Thus, eighteen elements (*dhātu*) can be classified: the six organs of sense, the six objects of sense and the six sensorial consciousnesses.

Indeed, the 'Four Noble Truths' assert the existence of a state of frustration, that thirst is its cause, that it is possible to eliminate it by attaining *nirvāṇa*, and that an eightfold path leads to it, outlined by the Buddha. The first of these eight steps consists of achieving 'right vision' by investigating the state of things. Just before his 'awakening', the Buddha achieved global vision in which the single elements identified in his analysis of experience composed a sort of twelve-spoked wheel, in which the precedent is connected to the subsequent by a relationship of direct causality. The wheel of 'dependent causation' or 'conditioned co-production' (*pratītyasamutpāda*), described so many times in the texts — the source *par excellence* is the *Āryaśālistambhasūtra*, poised between the Hīnayāna ('Lesser Vehicle') and Mahāyāna ('Greater Vehicle') — as well as being the protagonist

---

2 However, at least one school within the Buddhist tradition, the Sāṃmitīyas, upheld the existence of the individual person, arousing the vehement reaction of their correligionaries. The criticism of the *pudgalavāda* ('personalism') has been very recently studied in Eltschinger 2010, focusing on the relevant passage of the *Mahāyānasūtrālaṃkāra* and its *Bhāṣya*.

of Buddhist iconography, begins with nescience and ends with old age and death, including in a rigorous chain all the phases of the world of experience. Although it probably arose to account for the trajectory of human experience for meditative purposes, it soon became the model of interpretation for all the real, affirming its unsubstantial nature by demonstrating the inter-dependence of all its elements, and showing, in the last analysis, its illusory nature, since knowledge itself is never free from the subtle pollution of desire and nescience.

The Abhidharma Schools. The Sarvāstivādins

Of the three 'baskets' (*piṭaka*) into which the texts of the Buddhist canon are divided, the Abhidharma is the most directly related to philosophical reflection. Whereas the Sūtra-piṭaka comprises the discourses ascribed to the Buddha himself and the Vinaya-piṭaka deals with monastic order, the Abhidharma is a first attempt to extract some kind of homogeneous content from the dialogue and narrative texts of the *sūtra*s — often poorly defined, also as a result of the Buddha's deliberate refusal to produce 'philosophical' texts — for didactic purposes, if nothing else.[3] The term *abhidharma*, according to one of the interpretations given by Buddhist authors, means 'approach, guide to Dharma [the Doctrine]', or also — according to another possible meaning of the preverb *abhi-*, 'super-*dharma*', signifying that the doctrine organised and clarified in the Abhidharma is superior to the very pronouncements of the Buddha. This claim, or else the excessive proliferation and appreciation of such literature, led to the reaction of the Sautrāntika school which, as its name states, preached a return to the *sūtra*s that alone preserve the Master's words. Although the Buddhist schools do not agree on the status to be attributed to the Abhidharmapiṭaka, an ancient tradition dates it back

[3] On the literature and philosophy of the various Abhidharma schools, see Frauwallner 1995, Cox 1995.

at least to one of the Buddha's direct disciples, Śāriputra, invited to make this compilation by the Master himself. The foundation of the abhidharmic texts are the so-called *mātṛkās*, or 'matrices', traditional lists of subjects for debate or memoranda for practice, sorts of extremely succinct catechism, various hypothetical reconstructions of which have been put forward. Besides providing elaborations based on the different *mātṛkās*, the Abhidharma also discusses the various criteria to be followed in their interpretation, proclaiming the first germ of that doctrine of double truth that would later produce such a large following in the schools of Mahāyāna Buddhism, for which any contradiction found between original texts depends on their different aims, i.e. whether to present absolute truth, or various provisional levels of truth, according to didactic requirements and the type of listener. Of the Abhidharmapiṭakas accepted by the various schools (the division within the Buddhist community, later traditionally split into eighteen schools, began immediately after the Buddha's death), only those of the Theravādins and Sarvāstivādins have come down to us in their entirety. The former, written in Pāli[4] toward the beginning of the Common Era, comprises seven canonical books. Of these stand out for their importance the *Dhammasaṅgani* ('Enumeration of Factors') and the *Kathavātthu* ('Subjects of Debate'), around which a great amount of exegetic literature has been written over the centuries. While this literature is confined to Sri Lanka, whence it spread to south-east Asia, the Abhidharma of the Sarvāstivādins, in Sanskrit, prevailed throughout Indian

[4] Pāli, the language of ancient Buddhism, and Ardhamāgadhī, the language of ancient Jainism, have several common features: both are forms of an eastern Prakrit, i.e. Māgadhī; both are presented in deliberate antagonism to Sanskrit, used by brahmanical culture; both exhibit a 'popular' aspect that in actual fact does not reflect their status as substantially artificial languages, neither more nor less literary than the Sanskrit they oppose. Pāli, a language with not a few extremely archaic features linking it directly to Vedic — but to a species of that multiform linguistic reality that differs from the one from which Sanskrit developed — has even been spoken of as an 'artificial' language (or at least as being strongly standardised) since it contains, in a wholly 'unnatural' manner, features peculiar to both western and eastern Prakrits (cf. Hinuber 1982).

Buddhism, constituting the doctrinal basis, or point of reference for the schools of the Lesser Vehicle and, at least in part, also for those of the Greater Vehicle.

The Sarvāstivādin school branched out, as early as the reign of Aśoka, from the central corps of the Buddhist community, represented by the Sthāviras ('Elders'). After the third Council, the school moved from Pāṭaliputra to Mathurā (second century B.C.E.) and then finally settled in Kashmir, where it prospered for several centuries, a branch of it spreading to Gandhāra and Bactria. Its Abhidharma canon has many parallels with that of the Theravādins, also consisting of seven texts — a central text, the *Jñānaprasthāna*, and six satellite texts, defined as its feet (*pāda*). The *Jñānaprasthāna* ('Arrangement of Knowledge'), composed toward the end of the first century B.C.E. by Kātyāyanīputra, and thus the most recent of the seven, was the subject of a monumental commentary, the *Mahāvibhāṣā* ('Great Analytical Explanation'). This encyclopaedic text, which has come down to us, like almost all the Sarvāstivādin Abhidharma, only in its Chinese version, soon took on such an important central role for this school that its followers were named Vaibhāṣikas ('Followers of the *[Mahā]vibhāṣā*'). According to a reliable tradition, it was drafted in the first half of the second century C.E., under the impulsion of the famous King Kaniṣka, by the hand of anonymous compilers who attributed its original composition to the Buddha himself. The enormous amount of heterogeneous material contained in the *Mahāvibhāṣā* was resumed, elaborated and coordinated in what was to become the most prestigious synthesis of the Sarvāstivādin school, the *Abhidharmakośa* ('Treasure of the Abhidharma') by Vasubandhu (circa fourth-fifth century).[5] In point of fact, Vasubhandu's summary was not without innovations and criticisms, accentuated in the *Bhāṣya* in which he himself commented on it, where the point of view assumed is decidedly that of the Sautrāntikas. This exposed him to criticism from Saṅghabhadra in

[5] Cf. the monumental work by L. de la Vallée Poussin (1923-31).

the *Nyāyānusāraśāstra*, of which only the Chinese translation has survived, which firmly restates the Sarvāstivādin standpoints. Vasubandhu's work was in turn the subject of major commentaries, including those by Guṇamati, Sthiramati and Yaśomitra (only the last-mentioned has survived in its original Sanskrit).

Abhidharma literature focuses wholly on identifying and classifying the ultimate components of the real, called *dharma*.[6] Their intent to proceed with a complete cataloguing of the existing associates the Buddhist schools of the Abhidharma with two ancient Brahmanic systems: Vaiśeṣika and Sāṃkhya. The results and, to some extent, the motives of the latter, however, are very different. Vaiśeṣika produces a 'horizontal' kind of cataloguing, photographing — thanks to the unexplicited employment of parameters borrowed from language — a spatialised and objectified world, emptied of all dynamism and temporal tension. Sāṃkhya, on the other hand, views the existing world as a phase in a continually evolving process, in which matter, the psychic and the intellectual develop from the same root. While Vaiśeṣika and Sāṃkhya substantially proceed with the cataloguing of objects, the Buddhist Abhidharma focuses attention rather on the interaction between objects and states of mind, i.e. on the world of experience rather than on the world *tout court*. To a Buddhist eye, a world made of things that confront a knowing and acting subject appears to be the outcome of a tacit failed attempt to check what, on closer examination, is none other than an incessant flow. The recourse to analysis is motivated by a soteriological concern, because only when the apparent solidity of the objects is broken down is the way to emancipation possible. Parallel to the crushing of the object is the de-substantialisation and de-personalisation of the subject, restricted to the flow of momentary mental states. In the systematization of the *Abhidharmakośa*, the number of these elementary principles or factors, not conceived as being isolated from each other, but on the contrary,

---

6 For a review of the various meanings and interpretations of this key term in Buddhist thought, cf. Cox 2004: 543-547; on the ontology of the Sarvāstivādins, cf. Williams 1981, Cox 2004.

all — except three [7] — closely interdependent, is established as 75, divided into five groups (the Theravādins list 82, the Yogācāras even reach 100). The first group (*rūpa*, 'matter') comprises the five sensory organs and non-conceptualised matter (*avijñapti*); the second group comprises just the mind; the third group comprises the 46 mental functions; the fourth, the 14 powers not linked to the mind; the fifth, the 3 non-conditioned *dharma*s. Without going into the highly intricate questions dealt with by Buddhist scholastics (the very number of *dharma*s can vary significantly from school to school and even from text to text within the same school), we should note the disproportion existing between what belongs to the domain of matter (eleven *dharma*s) and what is, in one way or another, related to the mind. This may suggest that all this sort of classification arose in a meditative context and set out as its first aim that of feeding and directing practice. The very chain of twelve causations concerns an essentially ethical and religious process.

Given such premises, the relationship of causality constitutes a favourite subject for debate in all Abhidharma schools. Once more the classic arrangement is as provided by the *Abhidharmakośa*, known as the doctrine of six causes and four conditions (as well as five effects). While the four conditions already appear on a list of twenty-four indicated in the Theravādin Abhidharma, the six causes seems to be a peculiarly Sarvāstivādin conception. The four types of condition are: the 'object' condition (*ālambana-pratyaya*; e.g. the object in the act of perception); the 'immediately preceding' (*samanantara-pratyaya*; the mental state that immediately precedes cognition); the 'predominant' (*adhipati-pratyaya*; what is most directly decisive for the nature of the effect, such as the organ of sight for visual sensation); the 'causal' (*hetu-pratyaya*; every contribution to the realisation of the effect, such as light in the case in question). The first of the six causes is the 'generic' cause (*kāraṇa-hetu*; each *dharma* in the universe

[7] The three non-conditioned *dharma*s: space (*ākāśa*), cessation deriving from reflection (*pratisaṃkhyānirodha*) and not deriving from reflection (*apratisaṃkhyānirodha*).

is in some way involved, even distantly, in every relationship of causality, e.g. by not obstructing it). Then follows the 'co-existing' cause (*sahabhū-hetu*; conditioning due to the *dharma*s produced in the same instant as those directly involved in the causation process); the 'homogeneous' (*sabhāga-hetu*; responsible for producing an effect of the same type or quality); the 'associated' (*samprayukta-hetu*; this refers to the concomitance of mental states only, e.g. the pleasure connected to certain sensations); the 'omni-pervasive' (*sarvatraga-hetu*; the negative influence exercised by the various contaminations of the mind); the 'maturation' [of the *karma*] (*vipāka-hetu*; the possibility of producing effects connotated by a positive or negative karmic coefficient).

The attention paid by the Sarvāstivādins to the relationship of causality led them to formulate a doctrine from which they later derived their own denomination (*sarvam asti*, 'everything exists'). All Buddhist schools concur in presenting causality as a temporal concomitance of events, without ever saying, contrary to common opinion, that something 'generates' something else (the Buddhist formulation, on the other hand, is: *tasmin sati idaṃ bhavati*, 'that being there, this comes into being'). On their side, the Sarvāstivādins note that, in order to account for causality, the theory of reality has to be reformulated in appropriate terms as impermanent and in continual flux, which some schools, such as the Sautrāntika, understand in terms of the 'instantaneity' of the *dharma*s. For the Sarvāstivādins — in contrast on this crucial point to other Abhidharmic schools, and in particular to the Dārṣṭāntika — a *dharma* has to extend its existence in some way throughout the three times (past, present and future) — even though only its present existence is to be considered as ultimately real. If it were not so, causes and effects, being present at different moments, would owe their status respectively to something that is not yet or that is no longer. As far as the doctrine of instantaneity is concerned, that too has to be reformulated: a *dharma* does not perish at the moment it is born, but passes through four distinct phases: birth, duration, decay and destruction. These four moments are themselves considered as *dharma*s and are included in the set of 14 'forces unconnected with the mind', according to the *Abhidharmakośa* system. The first place on that rather heterogeneous list is given to a fairly problematic entity, *prāpti* (lit. 'acquisition'), to which the Sarvāstivādins cling in an attempt to avoid risking the total shipwreck of the unity of the subject, brought about by the continuous rise and fall of the *dharmas*. *Prāpti* represents the *dharma*s 'belonging' in some impalpable way to a *continuum* (*santāna*) which, albeit not a 'person', at least makes sense of the notion of moral responsibility and karmic retribution. This solution did not suit their Sautrāntika cousins, who preferred to understand the *continuum* as a true substrate (*āśraya*) containing 'seeds' (*bīja*), corresponding to the psycho-physical complex in continual evolution, and to tendencies or impregnations (*vāsanā*) deposited by previous experiences.

The Sautrāntika School

The Sautrāntika school — 'those who appeal to the *sūtra*s as the ultimate authority' — arose around the fourth century C.E., probably within the Sarvāstivādins in Gandhāra, triggered by a rejection of the excessively scholastic and 'realistic' bent then being assumed by the Abhidharma tradition. Although not radical, doctrinal differences are considerable, opening the way for the more extreme positions of Yogācāra. The only explicit Sautrāntika work (or with strong tendencies) to have come down to us is the commentary (*Bhāṣya*) by Vasubandhu on his own *Abhidharmakośa*; another major source is the commentary by Yaśomitra on the same work by Vasubandhu. For the rest, we must refer to the frequent debates on their doctrines in other works, by Buddhist and Brahmanic or Jaina authors, who treat them as important interlocutors. According to Abhidharmic tradition, the founder of the school and the first of its 'suns' was Kumāralābha, of whom only a few quotations have survived. Sautrāntika masters, such as Bhadanta Śubhagupta,[8] are mentioned and their doctrines criticised by Śāntarakṣita and Kamalaśīla in the *Tattvasaṃgraha* and in the related *Pañjikā*. Also recognizable as Sautrāntika are the concepts that Dignāga and more particularly Dharmakīrti accept, as least as confined to the sphere of empiric reality. On the ontological side, the Sautrāntikas share with the Sarvāstivādins a belief in the external object, but do not conceive of its instantaneity in the same way. Each *dharma* lasts just an instant and perishes as soon as it comes into being, without there necessarily being a cause, but simply because such is its intrinsic nature. We can follow the elaborate logical justification given by the Sautrāntikas for this conception in the form presented in a valuable manual of Buddhist epistemology and logic, the *Bauddhatarkabhāṣā* ('Manual of Logic according to the Buddhists'), composed by Mokṣākaragupta in the eleventh-twelfth century (pp. 19-20; Kajiyama 1966: 87-88). Experience — says Mokṣākaragupta — shows us that things, such as a jar, are destroyed by contact with a hammer. If this destruction occurs because such is the nature of things, then they should be destroyed from the very moment of their birth, since their own nature exists, as such, right from the start. Indeed, if the jar's own nature were not such, then not even a hammer could destroy it. If the nature of a thing were to make it last not for one, but two instants, at the second it should last for another instant, i.e. a third, and so on. If one should object that a thing, by its nature, could be destined to last, but that it is forced to perish by another thing that is incompatible with it, such as a hammer, to that person we should answer that, if the thing were to perish, we cannot say that by nature it was permanent. Thus, a thing must be already produced by its cause as perishable, since an imperishable thing could never be connected with perishing. If, on conclusion, it is perishable by nature, then it can but perish at the first instant in which it comes into being.

---

8 In fact, Śubhagupta's affiliation is not free from doubts, since he also shows Vaibhāṣika features (but, unlike the Vaibhāṣikas, he is clearly a *sākāravādin*; see below pp. 164-165).

Impermanence and instantaneity do not consequently render the thing less 'real', but rather constitute the very condition of its reality. Only what is impermanent can produce effects, and causal efficiency is taken by the Sautrāntikas — and by thinkers who later continued to find inspiration in their doctrines, such as Dharmakīrti — as the very criterion for establishing whether a thing is real.[9] This revision of the concept of the transitory nature of the *dharma*s necessarily involves a rethinking of how they are known, since in the instant in which the object has laid the conditions of the cognitive act by its presence, it already no longer exists. This and other considerations lead the Sautrāntikas to dissociate from the Sarvāstivādins when they affirm that the agglomerates of atoms constituting objects enter directly into the field of perception. It is not the external object that is present in our knowing, but its mental image (*ākāra*) which it has deposited there prior to disappearing. When the vedāntin Mādhava — two or three centuries after Mokṣākaragupta, probably influenced by the presentation provided by the *Bauddhatarkabhāṣā* — as we have seen, restricted the group of Buddhist positions, stated above, for inclusion in his doxographic work to the Vaibhāṣikas, Sautrāntikas, Mādhyamikas and Yogācāras — for the Sautrāntikas he uses the already current definition of *bāhyārthānumeyatvavāda* ('doctrine of the [sole] inferability'] of the external object'). Whereas in normal inference, indeed, the fire inferred from the smoke is only occasionally found outside the range of perception (but it was perceived in the past and will again be perceived in future), the Sautrāntikas consider the mental image as a sufficient pointer to establish the existence of an external object as the only possible cause, although this object is destined to remain inaccessible to perception and to being solely perpetually inferable (*nityānumeya*). As recounted by an anonymous passage in

---

9 This is the so-called *sattvānumāna* ('inference of real existence') (cf. Mimaki 1976, Yoshimizu 1999) which, in the Dharmakīrti formulation states, "Whatever exists can only be instantaneous, since its being permanent would clash with its capacity to produce effects, which is, of course, the distinctive feature of real existence (*vastutvam*)" (*Hetubindu*, p. 4, according to the reconstruction of Steinkellner 1967: I, 37).

the *Bauddhatarkabhāṣā* (p. 36), one may continue to speak of 'perceiving' an external object, but only in a metaphorical sense (*bhāktam syād arthavedanam*).

Other conceptions with a Sautrāntika hallmark will be dealt with below, as integrated into the logical-epistemological thought of Dignāga and Dharmakīrti.

The Mādhyamika School

In defining the position of the four main Buddhist schools on the object and its knowability, the *Sarvadarśanasaṃgraha* — while attributing to the Vaibhāṣikas and Sautrāntikas belief in the reality of an external object that is directly perceptible for the former and only inferable for the latter — calls the Mādhyamikas supporters of the 'vacuity' of everything (*sarvaśūnyatva*). The concept of vacuity, found right from the earliest canonical works in reference to the absence of self, is taken by the Mādhyamikas (or Madhyamakas, 'Followers of the Middle Way') in its most extreme sense as the absence of an 'own nature' (*svabhāva*), not limited to the fictitious entities ('things') of conventional reality, but extending to the very *dharma*s into which the Abhidharma schools broke things down, considering them as ultimate reality.

The founder of the Mādhyamika school is Nāgārjuna (about 150-200 C.E.),[10] who in turn borrows from the teaching of the Prajñāpāramitā ('Perfection of Wisdom'), centered on the figure of the *bodhisattva* who, although aware of universal vacuity, devotes himself to rescuing creatures. Nāgārjuna's main work is the *Mūlamadhyamakakārikā* ('Fundamental Strophes on the Middle Way'), consisting of twenty-seven chapters and totalling 448 verses, devoted mainly to demonstrating the internal contradictions of the Abhidharma

[10] Fundamental on the development of the literary *corpus* of the Mādhyamikas in India is Seyfort Ruegg 1981.

doctrines, such as causal conditions, the twelve fields of the senses, the five aggregates, the eighteen elements, as well as of general notions common to the various realist schools, such as those of action/agent, being/non-being, cause/effect. It also contains chapters devoted to the Buddha, to *nirvāṇa*, and to the Four Noble Truths. Eight commentaries were composed on this work, the first of which, the *Akutobhaya* ('[Commentary] that fears nothing'), attributed by some to Nāgārjuna himself, is more likely to be several decades later. Of the other commentaries, the most significant are those of Buddhapālita (ca. 470-540), Bhāviveka or Bhavya (ca. 500-570) and Candrakīrti (ca. 600-650), the only one that has come down to us in the original Sanskrit. Another important work by Nāgārjuna is the *Vigrahavyāvartanī* ('Exterminator of Dissents'), which has survived in Sanskrit together with a brief self-commentary, in which Nāgārjuna answers the perplexities raised by his *opus magnum*, and in particular the central question as to whether his critique of all philosophical standpoints should itself be considered a position.

Many other works are ascribed to this thinker (cf. Lindtner 1987), on the authenticity of which a considerable variety of opinions exists. The situation is further complicated by the certain existence of other Buddhist authors of the same name in the centuries that follow. Among the works that can most probably be attributed to the Mādhyamika master are the *Yuktiṣaṣṭikā* ('Sixty Strophes on Reasoning'),[11] the *Śūnyatāsaptati* 'Seventy Strophes on Vacuity' and the *Vaidalyaprakaraṇa* ('Treatise on Pulverization [of adverse doctrines]'). A direct disciple of Nāgārjuna, and closely following his thought, is Āryadeva (ca. 170-270), the author of the *Catuḥśataka* ('Four Centuries'; cf. Lang 1986) and the *Śataśāstra* ('One Hundred Teachings'). Some centuries after Nāgārjuna, the Mādhyamikas split into two schools, which in Tibet were known as Prāsaṅgika and Svātantrika (the

[11] Of this important small work, only a few verses have survived in the original Sanskrit, thanks to quotations in other works. The Tibetan version of the *Yuktiṣaṣṭikā* together with its commentary by Candrakīrti have been aptly studied and translated by C. Scherrer-Schaub (1991).

denomination *svatantra* had however already been used by Candrakīrti). According to the former, headed by Buddhapālita and Candrakīrti, Nāgārjuna had no intention of holding his own theories, but only of reducing to absurdity (*prasaṅga*) those of his opponents. On the other hand, according to the Svātantrika school, founded by Bhāviveka, he was in fact setting out independent (*svatantra*) arguments.[12] The final period saw the formation of syncretic schools that fused the teaching of Nāgārjuna with that of the Yogācāras and Buddhist logicians, of whom the most illustrious were Śāntarakṣita (ca. 725-784) and his disciple Kamalaśīla. Among the most significant works, beside the commentaries on the *Madhyamakakārikā*, we should mention the *Madhyamakahṛdaya* ('The Heart of the Middle Way') by Bhāviveka with the author's (?) commentary *Tarkajvalā* ('Flame of Reasoning'), valuable for its doxographic references, and the *Madhyamakāvatāra* ('Introduction to the Middle Way') (and author's commentary) by Candrakīrti, which enjoyed great popularity in Tibet. Besides its merit as an accessible general introduction to the often impervious text of the *Madhyamakakārikā*, the *Madhyamakāvatāra* also develops themes only just hinted at by the root-text, such as the criticism of causality and the permanence of the self, at the same time highlighting the spiritual significance of Madhyamaka by outlining the ten stages of the progressive path of the bodhisattva toward perfect enlightenment. These are presented in one of the most ancient and famous Mahāyāna *sūtra*s, the *Daśabhūmikasūtra*.

The central affirmation of Mādhyamika doctrine is that all things lack a nature of their own (*svabhāva*), since they depend on each other for their production. This mutual conditioning to which all things are subject means that none can possess a definite and unchanging nature, and hence that none 'is' in any final analysis. The highly restrictive sense in which Nāgārjuna understands the concept

[12] On the centuries-old dispute between the Prāsaṅgikas and the Svātantrikas — which started in India at the very dawn of Mādhyamika and, when Buddhism disappeared in India, continued in Tibet — there exists a vast literature (cf. Seyfort Ruegg 1986, Yotsuya 1999, Seyfort Ruegg 2000: 105-232).

of *svabhāva* is explained in the 15th chapter of the *Madhyamaka-kārikā*. As Candrakīrti notes in his commentary (pp. 113-115), in Buddhism, the term *svabhāva* is found to have three different meanings: as the essential property of a thing (e.g. heat, for fire); as the essential characteristic of a single *dharma* (absolute particularity, *svalakṣaṇa*); as subsisting independently from another.[13] Understood in this last sense, Nāgārjuna's *svabhāva* — Candrakīrti is still speaking (*ibid.*) — means: nature not subject to change in the past, present and future; innate, not produced; of which it cannot be said that it comes into being not having existed before, or that it is dependent on causes and conditions. Measured thus, no reality can survive such criticism and each is thus equally 'empty'. "That which is conditioned co-production, for us is vacuity. The term 'vacuity' is to be understood in a metaphorical sense: the Middle Way is none other but this" (XXIV.18).

The Mādhyamika thinker is aware that by espousing the doctrine of vacuity he lays himself open to easy criticism. "Vacuity, say the Victors, is the elimination of all doctrines (*dṛṣṭi*); those for whom vacuity is a doctrine, they have been called incurable" (XIII.8). As Nāgārjuna himself explains in the *Vigrahavyāvartanī* (kār. 29; Bhattacharya 1971: 237-238), he does not intend to replace the doctrines whose inner contradiction he exposes with another doctrine of his own.[14] Any thesis (*pratijñā*) — whether positive or negative

---

[13] On the meaning of *svabhāva* in Mādhyamika, see recently Tillemans 2007; on the usage and meanings of this crucial term, in particular as regards the Sarvāstivādins, cf. Cox 2004: 558-578; cf. too the remarks by Steinkellner 1971: 179-211, focusing on the values of *svabhāva* in the logical and ontological conceptions of Dharmakīrti.

[14] This should not be understood to mean that Mādhyamika has no worldview (*darśana*). In his commentary on the *Madhyamakakārikā* (XVIII.5, XXIV.13), Candrakīrti is not afraid to affirm the existence of a *śūnyatā-darśana* (cf. also his *Yuktiṣaṣṭikā-vṛtti*, *ad kār.* 30; Scherrer-Schaub 1991: 237), which, as we have seen, consists precisely of not accepting any dogmatic assertion (*dṛṣṭi*), any 'thesis' (*pakṣa*, *pratijñā*) that would involve, either directly or indirectly, the affirmation of something as being endowed with inherent and absolute existence. Cf. Williams 1991:199-200; Seyfort Ruegg 2000: 133-136.

— that aims at establishing the existence of any kind of entity or *dharma* with its own specific nature is headed for some kind of implosion. Mādhyamika does not merely await the shipwreck of every theory without playing its own hand, however.[15] Its actual standpoint is to deny the sustainability of any unconditional 'assertion', attributing indistinctly to all the real a status of relative truth, even including the level of *dravyasat* ('existing substantially, existing really and truly'; the *dharmas*), which the Sarvāstivādins had conceived of in opposition to the level of *prajñaptisat* ('existing by convention'; cf. Cox 2004: 568-560).[16] This 'convention' was more particularly a linguistic one, and the Mādhyamikas were well aware of the central role of language and its *alter ego* — discursive thought — in building 'covering reality' (*saṃvṛti-satya*), in contrast to 'absolute reality' (*paramārtha-satya*). This division does not, however, open the way to a nihilistic view (*ucchedavāda*); as the *Madhyamakakārikā* (XXIV.10ab) says, "Absolute reality cannot be taught if first one has not based oneself on the practical order of things (*vyavahāram anāśritya*)" (practical reality, Candrakīrti remarks in p. 216, is the means, absolute reality the goal). Once this level is reached, all division ceases and one realises that *saṃsāra* coincides with *nirvāṇa*.

The *Madhyamakakārikā* shows the incongruity of any kind of doctrine or concept whose premises lead to unacceptable consequences (*prasaṅga*, '*reductio ad absurdum*'),[17] or considers them in terms of a dilemma (it is, it is not) or tetralemma (it is, it is not, it is and it is not, it neither is nor is not),[18] already found in the discourses of the

---

[15] On the meaning to be attributed to the non-acceptance of any theory, expressed in ambiguous terms by Nāgārjuna, both subsequent Mādhyamika thinkers and modern scholars have different opinions; cf. Seyfort Ruegg 1986, 2000: 105-232; cf. also Oetke 2003.

[16] On how the opposition *dravyasat*/*prajñaptisat* should be understood, cf. Williams 1980: 1-14.

[17] On this dialectic process, used in all Indian philosophy, but brought by the Mādhyamika to its most extreme form, cf. Seyfort Ruegg 2000: 136-138, 2002: 41.

[18] On the tetralemma (*catuṣkoṭi*) an ample bibliography exists; see, first and foremost, Seyfort Ruegg 1977; and, more recently, Westerhoff 2006.

Buddha. Buddhapālita, according to whom Mādhyamika never presents any theories of its own, transforms all the dilemmas and tetralemmas into *prasaṅga*s, in which the opponent's theses destroy themselves, whereas the Svātantrika Bhāviveka translates them all into normal assertive inferences. Tson kha pa (cf. Ruegg 1986; 2000: 195-199) later attempted to compose these views, which correspond to two possible ways of understanding the thought of Nāgārjuna. To understand the absence of 'own' nature (or non-substantiality) and vacuity, both positive determination (of negation) and negative determination (of 'own' nature) have to rise simultaneously in the same continuum of thought, since it is a characteristic of thought to define by exclusion (*pariccheda-vyavaccheda*). It is apparent that, between Tson kha pa and Nāgārjuna, the great season of the Buddhist logical-epistemological school has intervened.

The Yogācāra School

If the Vasubandhu mentioned previously and the Vasubandhu, champion of the school of Yogācāra ('in which Yoga is practiced') — also known as *vijñānavāda* ('school advocating the [sole reality of] consciousness'), *citta-mātra* ('only consciousness') or *vijñapti-mātra* ('only representation') — are effectively the same person, then we are faced with the very incarnation of a unitary trip from the realism of the Sarvāstivādins (with the *Abhidharmakośa*) to the phenomenalism of the Sautrāntikas (with the *Abhidharmakośa-bhāṣya*) up to the total reflux of the object into consciousness. Seen from this perspective, the Mādhyamika phase appears as a kind of blind alley — an insuperable peak, from which one can only turn back to the main road. This latter is represented by the meditative context in which Buddhist philosophy may have developed,[19] founded

[19] This is the position held by L. Schmithausen in several publications, starting from Schmithausen 1973; this assumption is strongly criticised in Franco 2009.

on the centrality of the mind as compared to the object, a mind and object that Nāgārjuna had equally suspended in the common absence of any 'own nature'. The rise of Yogācāra occurred — beside possibly in a meditative context — within the general unrealistic or anti-realistic tone that characterises the earliest Mahāyāna scriptures, with their unbridled multiplication of space and time, reaching an almost total fantastical dematerialisation of the ordinary world. The term *cittamātra*[20] appears in ancient texts, such as the *Pratyutpannabuddha-saṃmukhāvasthitasamādhi-sūtra* ('Sūtra of the *samādhi* of direct encounter with the Buddha of the present'),[21] translated into Chinese in 179 C.E., and the slightly more recent *Daśabhūmikasūtra* ('*Sūtra* of the Ten Stages'). The first *sūtra*s to present Yogācāra doctrines in a fairly systematic manner are the *Yogācārabhūmiśāstra* ('Treatise on the Stages of Yogācāra') and the *Saṃdhinirmocana-sūtra* ('*Sūtra* on the Untangling of Knots [in the sense of 'complete explanation of recondite meanings]'; ca. third-fourth century C.E.). The latter refers to precisely this line of development in speaking of three successive motions of the wheel of Dharma, the last and final one of which (*nītārtha*) is the doctrine of 'sole representation'. Another important Mahāyāna *sūtra* with a significant number of Yogācāra-like philosophemes is the *Laṅkāvatāra-sūtra* ('*Sūtra* on the descent on Śrī Laṅka'). The school reached its final form between the fourth and fifth centuries, with the works of Āsaṅga (including the *Mahāyānasaṃgraha*, 'Synthesis of Mahāyāna') and of Vasubandhu (among which, the *Viṃsatikā*, 'Twenty verses', the *Triṃśikā*, 'Thirty verses', and the *Trisvabhāvanirdeśa*, 'Teaching of the Three Natures'), based on a more recent set of scriptures, also commented on by them, attributed to Bodhisattva Maitreya. According to Tibetan tradition,

[20] Included in the famous formula *cittamātram idaṃ yad idaṃ traidhātukam*: "All this universe, formed of the three spheres, is nothing but consciousness". It is interesting to note how the Mādhyamika Candrakīrti in his *Madhyamakāvatāra* interprets this formula, as it occurs in the *Daśabhūmika-sūtra*, seeking to limit its ontological importance (Schmithausen 2005: 10).

[21] Cf. the English translation by G. Harrison, based on the Tibetan version (1990: 42).

Āsaṅga, discouraged at the fruitlessness of his meditations, stopped at the side of the road to rescue a wounded dog, when Maitreya finally became manifest to him and conveyed to him five of his works, three of which are amongst the cornerstones of Yogācāra: the *Mahāyānasūtrālaṃkāra* ('Ornament of the Mahāyāna *sūtras*'), the *Madhyāntavibhāga* ('Discrimination between the Middle and Extremes') and the *Dharmadharmatāvibhāga* ('Discrimination between the *Dharmas* and their Essence').

Two doctrines, packed with implications and developments on which we cannot linger here, form the core of classical Yogācāra: the three natures and eight consciousnesses. The whole world of experience is constituted by the evolution of consciousness (*vijñānapariṇāma*) in eight forms. The first six correspond to the five types of sensorial cognition plus mental cognition, already known in the earliest stages of Buddhism, while in the seventh emerges the aspect of subjectivity. The eighth, introduced by Yogācāra, is the 'consciousness deposit' (*ālayavijñāna*),[22] acting as a latent and unconscious substrate for the others, and providing them with an apparent object-content through the ripening of 'seeds' deposited in previous existences. The coordination and interdependence of the infinite karmic seeds deposited in it produce the illusion of an external reality shared by various minds. The 'consciousness deposit' would run the risk of resembling the Sāṃkhya *prakṛti* were it not for the fact of its being, like all the other consciousnesses, instantaneous (instants, each generating the next, creating the illusion of continuity). Of the three natures mentioned above, this continually rising and dissolving consciousness constitutes the middle one ('dependent' nature, *paratantra*). Since it consists of the continual flow of entities reciprocally conditioned by causal relations, it forms as it were an ontological substrate for the other two. The world of external objects, projected by discursive thought and language, forms the 'mentally constructed' nature (*parikalpita*). According to the definition given

[22] On the genesis and development of the complex doctrine of the *ālayavijñāna*, see the exhaustive study by L. Schmithausen (1987).

in the *Saṃdhinirmocana-sūtra* (VI.4), *parikalpita* nature coincides with "the names and conventions that establish their own nature and the differences of the *dharma*s for the purpose of their empirical designation". Once these deceptive projective mechanisms have been laid bare, the consciousness deposit, progressively freed from the impurities that afflict it, starting from the split between subject and object, reaches the stage of 'perfectly achieved' nature (*pariniṣpanna*). This radical turning point opening the door to liberation is called the 'revulsion of the substrate' (*āśrayaparāvṛtti*).

The Yogācāra position with regard to the reality of external objects appears not to be univocal. In any case, it is unclear whether, or up to what point, the affirmation that knowing is exercised only with regard to images already contained in the consciousness implies the ontological negation of all external reality. One of the texts most quoted on the question, providing a picture of possible ambiguities, is a short treatise by Dignāga, the *Ālambanaparīkṣā* ('Investigation on the support [of cognitions]'). Verse 6ac states in an apparently unequivocal manner, "Knowable internal reality that appears to be external, that is the object [...]" (*yad antarjñeyaṃ rūpaṃ bahirvad avabhāsate | so 'rthaḥ...*). Dignāga reaches this conclusion after asking what conditions the object of cognition must satisfy: it must be able to cause cognition (and thus be a 'real' thing) and have the same form that appears in it (and therefore be extended and not of a subtle nature). None of the objects put forward by the realist schools (the single atom, their aggregate or their agglomeration) can match these requirements. The necessary conclusion reached establishes the nature of the object that appears in the consciousness, but says nothing about whether or not it may also have external existence. A similar interpretation can be given to the principle formulated by Dharmakīrti in a famous passage of his *Pramāṇaviniścaya* (I.55ab): "By virtue of the invariability of their always being perceived in association, the non-difference is established between the colour light-blue and its cognition", matched by a verse of Prajñākaragupta's: "If light-blue is perceived, how is it then possible to say it is external?

If, on the other hand, it is not perceived, how can one say [even more so] that it is external?"[23] (Other aspects of Yogācāra epistemology are dealt with in the following section). It is difficult, however, to believe that Yogācāra thought in its totality can be read only as a kind of epistemological 'idealism', so repeated and — at least apparently — unequivocal are statements on the non-existence of the external object found as much in the *sūtra*s as in the commentaries.[24]

The Logical-Epistemologic School

The so-called logical-epistemologic school — or *pramāṇa* school — of Buddhism has long been seen as a foreign body that has penetrated a major spiritual tradition under the influence of contemporary Brahmanic philosophy, passively imitating its increasingly marked orientation toward these themes. Just recently, however, it has been claimed (Steinkellner 1982, Franco 1997, Eltschinger 2010) that such motifs were rooted in Buddhism itself and their soteriological significance rendered explicit. It should also be said that we should not wonder if such themes also found favour among Buddhists, since from every point of view Buddhism belongs to the central stream of Indian philosophy. Brahmanic logic and epistemology were profoundly renewed by their encounter-clash with the new Buddhist doctrines which, even when opposed, were always recognised as possessing great cultural prestige.

[23] The verse, from the *Pramāṇavārttikālaṃkāra* (p. 366, v. 718), is quoted by Mokṣākaragupta in the *Bauddhatarkabhāṣā* (p. 35). On inference based on the principle of 'restriction based on simultaneous perception', cf. Iwata 1991.

[24] Cf. Schmithausen 2005, taking into account a crucial passage of the monumental work by the Chinese pilgrim Xuanzang (*Ch'eng wei shih lun*, an elaborate commentary on Vasubandhu's *Vijñaptimātratāsiddhi*) and entirely devoted to a detailed critique of its interpretation in terms of admitting the external and independent existence of matter.

At the beginning of the great season of Buddhism's logical-epistemological school, we again find the name of Vasubandhu, already encountered as the author of Sarvāstivāda-Sautrāntika and Yogācāra works. The first reasoned distancing from the logical and epistemologic tradition expressed by Brahmanic culture (and first and foremost by the Nyāya) occurs in two works, the *Vādavidhi* and the *Vādavidhāna* (both titles can be translated as 'Norms of Philosophical Debate'), which have survived in their entirety only in Tibetan translation. Besides dealing with the ways of validating and confuting arguments — the aim of both works —, the *Vādavidhi* adds themes relating to the nature of the means of knowledge. Vasubandhu allows only two: perception and inference (van Bijlert 1989: 45-54). The former is defined as knowledge that derives solely from the object, including both perception of external objects by means of the senses and introspective knowledge of feelings and emotions. As the author himself seeks to clarify, this definition aims at excluding erroneous sensorial knowledge (owing to defects of the senses, etc.), conceptual knowledge (the result of mental constructs overlying pure data) and inferential knowledge. The definition of inference is just as rigorous and to a certain extent innovative, especially in not being satisfied, unlike Nyāya, with the generic notion of 'relation' (*saṃbandha*; cf. *Nyāyabhāṣya* p. 12) between *probans* and *probandum*: "Inference is the perception of an object inseparably connected (*nāntarīyaka*°) [with another object] by him who knows this [inseparable connection]" (Frauwallner 1957: 138). Vasubandhu also distances himself from Brahmanic tradition in his formalization of inference, reducing the five Nyāya members to three: thesis (*pratijñā*), expounding of the logical reason (*hetu*), and example (*dṛṣṭānta*). The object of inference (*anumeya*) is a specific property of the *locus* (the fire vis-à-vis the mountain), while the element to be demonstrated (*sādhya*) is the connection between the two. The logical reason consists in indicating the presence in the *locus* of an element linked to the object of inference by a relationship of invariable concomitance. This in turn is defined as the fact that element A is present in the presence of B and absent when B is absent. The example presents situations well-known to common experience in which such a presence-presence and absence-absence occurs.

Dignāga

If Vasubandhu can be considered the precursor of the logical school of Buddhism, its unquestioned founder is Dignāga (ca. 480-550; cf. Frauwallner 1959) who, according to Tibetan sources, was the disciple of Vasubandhu.[25] Of the many works ascribed to him (amongst which the *Ālambanaparīkṣā*, 'Investigation of the Support [of cognition]', the *Traikālyaparīkṣā*, 'Investigation of the Three Times', the *Hetumukha*, 'Introduction to Logical Reason', the *Prajñā-pāramitāsaṃgrahakārikā*, 'Stanzas summarising the Perfection of Wisdom', the *Hetucakraḍamaru*, 'The Drum of the Wheel of Logical Reasons' and the *Vādavidhāna-ṭīkā*, 'Commentary on the Norms of Philosophical Debate' [by Vasubandhu]), very few of the Sanskrit originals have come down to us. Several attempts have been made — with varying success — to reconstruct them from Tibetan translations (in some cases, however, only the Chinese translation is available).

The last of his works is the famous *Pramāṇasamuccaya* ('Synthesis of the Means of Right Knowledge'), *summa* of Dignāga's conceptions in the field of logic and epistemology, on which the author also provided a brief commentary (*vṛtti*). For both, there are complete Tibetan translations, while of the Sanskrit originals we have only fragments from many authors who have quoted from them over the centuries. Of great importance is the very recent discovery in China of two Sanskrit manuscripts of the major commentary by Jinendrabuddhi on the *Pramāṇasamuccaya*, the *Viśālāmalavatī*; its edition and translation is currently under way, directed by Ernst

[25] To the testimony of Bu-ston and Tāranātha should also be added that of the Jaina Siṃhasūri (Hattori 1968: 1-3).

Steinkellner.[26] The point of departure of the *Pramāṇasamuccaya* is the statement that only two means of knowledge are admissible — perception and inference — and that each has its exclusive field of application, respectively the particular and the universal (I.2a-c). This is already a break with tradition, in particular Nyāya tradition, which maintains rather the applicability of various means of knowledge to the same object (*pramāṇasamplava*). What has been rendered as 'particular' (*svalakṣaṇa*) literally means 'peculiar character [i.e., different from any other]'. According to Dharmakīrti (the term is not defined by Dignāga), *svalakṣaṇa* is capable of causal efficiency (*arthakriyā*); is different from any other object; cannot be expressed in words, and is not known in the presence of signs differing from itself (*Pramāṇavārttika*, 'Gloss on the Means of Right Knowledge', III.1-2); moreover, according to its nearness or distance, it determines a difference in the form that appears in cognition (*Nyāyabindu*, 'Drops of Logic' I. 13). As further clarified by Mokṣākaragupta, *svalakṣaṇa* is real, unique, determined by space, time and form that belong to it alone. By way of example, he mentions a specific jar, capable of containing water, characterised by definite time, space and form, not diversified in its multiple properties, differing from whatever belongs to its own or a different class. In a narrow sense, on the other hand, *svalakṣaṇa* is absolute undivided reality, an instant (*kṣaṇa*). Perception is defined as a cognitive act exempt from conceptual elaboration (*kalpanā*); in the same verse of the *Pramāṇasamuccaya* (I.3), *kalpanā* is in turn defined as the 'application of a proper name, of a name indicating a class, etc.' This latter definition, which actually lends itself to various interpretations (and translations), refers anyhow to the requirement that any element belonging to the

[26] For the time being, only the critical (and diplomatic) edition of the first chapter has been published (Steinkellner, Krasser, Lasic 2005). This exemplary work is accompanied by a reconstruction of the Sanskrit text of the first chapter of the *Pramāṇasamuccaya* (and *vṛtti*), taken from the commentary (in which the original text is reproduced only partially) and with the aid of the two Tibetan translations, by E. Steinkellner (2005). Pind 2009 provides the restored Sanskrit text of the fifth chapter along with a thoroughly annotated translation.

sphere of conceptualisation/ verbalization be absent from perception. In resuming Dignāga's definition, Dharmakīrti specifies that perception must be 'non-erroneous' (*abhrānta*)[27] — i.e. not conditioned by any dysfunction of the senses — and makes his characterisation of *kalpanā* more nuanced and comprehensive, taking it to be 'a cognition associated with a linguistic expression' (*Pramāṇaviniścaya* I.4, pp. 7-8; cf. Vetter 1966: 40-41), or, even more subtly, 'a cognition in which what is manifested is susceptible to being associated with a linguistic expression' (*Nyāyabindu* I.5). For Dignāga, perception includes not only sensorial perceptions, but also mental awareness of perceptions and emotions and the supra-normal perception of the yogin.[28]

The universal, the object of the other means of knowledge (inference), is conceived of in solely negative terms. Against the materialization and reification of the universal proposed by the realist Brahmanic systems, for Dignāga its content is merely the 'exclusion of what is other' (*anya-apoha*). The earliest formulation of the theory of *apoha* is found in the *Nyāyamukha* and in the *Pramāṇasamuccaya* (Chapter V), although its application is apparently still limited to the inferential process and the denotation of words. "The word expresses things as being qualified by the negation of other meanings" (*śabdo 'rthāntaranivṛttiviśiṣṭān eva bhāvān āha*) and "[The word] expresses its meaning by excluding all other [meanings]" (*svārtham anyāpohena bhāṣate*): so we read in two fragments by Dignāga that have survived as quotations.[29] The application of this concept was later extended by Dharmakīrti to all fields in which universals operate, i.e. in a wider sense to the content of discursive thought (*Pramāṇavārttika* I.134).

---

[27] Mention of this feature of valid perception can already be found in an early Mahāyāna scripture, the *Yogācārabhūmi* (cf. Yao 2004: 59).

[28] The issue as to whether Dignāga conceived of three or four kinds of perception is unsettled (cf. Hattori 1968: 27, 92-94; Franco 1993; Yao 2004), while it is clear that for Dharmakīrti they are four (*Nyāyabindu* I.7 *tat [pratyakṣaṃ] caturvidham*).

[29] The first passage comes from the self-commentary on the *Pramāṇasamuccaya* V.36d (Pind 2009: A15); the second is from the *Pramāṇasamuccaya* V.1cd (Pind 2009: A1). On the development of *apoha* in the work of Dignāga, see Frauwallner 1959: 99-106; Pind 2009: 43-62.

Thus, language and discursive thought do not express universals present in an undivided manner in single particulars, as the realists affirm, but only a 'difference' (*bheda*) by excluding what is other, i.e. all those things that are united by the fact of having different effects with respect to the thing in question. The intrinsic (and ineffable) nature of the thing constitutes its 'difference', while the exclusion of what is other (potentially) constitutes its 'common' dimension (cf. *Pramāṇavārttika* I.180ab). Exclusion of the other, however, shares all the essential characteristics of the universal it intends to replace: unity, permanence and complete presence in each of the particulars. The word thus applies to that difference in which the exclusion of the other has caused the appearance of a 'common' structure. As clarified by Dharmakīrti and later Jinendrabuddhi, it is not a matter of two distinct operations, since denoting the meaning of a word in itself involves the exclusion of other meanings, precisely because its own meaning is the 'difference' (*Pramāṇavārttika-svavṛtti* p. 63). However, adds Dharmakīrti (*Pramāṇavārttika* I.128), difference should not be taken as a real entity (*vastu*) — as exclusion is not, either — but only as a relative term. Something effectively real might be 'form' (*rūpa*), but the object of a word is not 'form', but 'difference'. Almost all debates among subsequent Buddhist thinkers, seeking to reformulate the *apoha* theory in the light of Nyāya and Mīmāṃsā critiques, turn on these points and polarize on three distinct (albeit not antithetic) positions: "the word expresses only exclusion" (Dignāga and Dharmakīrti); "the word expresses firstly a positive entity and only secondly, by implication, exclusion of the other" (Śāntarakṣita and Kamalaśīla); "the word expresses a positive entity qualified by exclusion of the other (Jñānaśrīmitra and Ratnakīrti). The power of the word as source and transmission of knowledge is thus drastically limited. The thing, states Dignāga (*Pramāṇasamuccaya* V.12ab; Pind 2009: A5), owing to its many aspects, can never be expressed fully by one word. The latter's function, according to Dharmakīrti (*Pramāṇavārttika-svavṛtti*, pp. 62, 64), is merely to denote a certain portion of the thing by excluding what is other from it. This, however, does not mean that the thing has 'parts', but only that it appears to be associated with various causes of error concerning its nature. The task of a word is merely that of removing one of such causes.

Operating with the universals thus conceived is the second of the two means of knowledge, inference, whose definition is given in *Pramāṇasamuccaya* II.1: "Inference is of two kinds [inference for oneself and inference for others]. Inference for oneself knows an object by means of a triple sign" (Katsura 1983, Oetke 1994). The 'sign' (*liṅga*) is property 'A' present in the *locus*, which serves to establish another property 'B' in the same *locus*. For this to occur, three conditions must be fulfilled: 'A' must be present in 'B'; it must be present in cases in which 'B' is present; it must be absent in cases in which 'B' is absent (*Pramāṇasamuccaya* II.5cd; cf. Randle 1926: 22-23). The concept of invariable concomitance is closely linked to the notion of 'pervasion': the extension of class 'B' must be greater than (or at least equal to) that of class 'A'. The resulting knowledge will thus be of a general kind, without providing 'B' with any specific characteristic. This does not mean, as noted later on by other exponents of the Buddhist logical school, such as Dharmottara and Arcaṭa, that inference is exhausted in abstract play. On the contrary, whoever uses it in ordinary reality is mostly the particular it aims at. Its usefulness consists of making it possible, by means of argument where solely conceptual abstractions occur, to establish the existence, e.g. of a 'particular' fire, which at that moment cannot be perceived, and to act accordingly.

Inference for others (cf. van Bijlert 1989: 70-80) serves for an external presentation of the contents of this internal inferential process (*svadṛṣṭārthaprakāśana*), first by convincingly formalizing the 'triple sign' (*trirūpaliṅgākhyāna*), which is articulated in the 'triple logical reason' (*hetu*). The first step consists of stating what has to be demonstrated (*sādhyanirdeśa*), which notion may include the property to be inferred, the *locus* of such property and the connection between the two, always bearing in mind — as recognised by Dignāga himself in a passage handed down in many quotations — that the differentiation between property and the possessor of the property is merely a conceptual fiction, without any basis in reality, used only instrumentally (Randle 1926: 51). The central moment is represented by stating the logical reason, which assumes a choice of nine possible combinations between the property to be demonstrated, the related property actually visible that serves to establish its existence, and the related positive and negative examples. This is known as the 'wheel of nine logical reasons' (*hetucakra*) which, together with the 'triple sign' theory, constitutes the unmistakable mark of Dignāga's doctrine, even though this latter theory, at least, definitely existed before him.

It now remains for us to assess the ontological assumptions of this sophisticated theory of knowledge: not an easy task, which becomes, if possible, even more delicate with regard to the work of Dignāga's successor, the great Dharmakīrti, in which an intentional basic ambiguity is still further accentuated. Major clues to a solution can be deduced from the way both thinkers define the relationship between the knowing process, in which only the two *pramāṇa*s deemed valid act, and acquired knowledge (*pramā*). The final position of Dignāga (*Pramāṇasamuccaya* I.8cd-10) and Dharmakīrti (*Pramāṇavārttika* III.366-367) is that there is no real differentiation between the two moments, *pramāṇa-pramā*. The object of knowledge appearing to the consciousness (*prameya*) is none other than consciousness itself presented in the form of the object (*viṣayābhāsa*); *pramāṇa* is cognition in the form of subject (*svābhāsa*). As *Pramāsamuccaya-vṛtti* p. 4 (ad I.9a) says, "Cognition arises having two manifestations (*dvyābhāsam*): it contains the manifestation of itself and that of the object. The self-awareness of both manifestations constitutes the result [of cognition]." [30] The 'apprehending cognition' part assumes the form of the 'apprehended object' part;

[30] In the various formulations of this doctrine by Dignāga himself and his followers, we can find a fluctation in terminology which does not affect their overall meaning (*sva*°, *grāhaka*°; *viṣaya*°, *artha*°, *grāhya*°; °*ābhāsa*, °*ākāra*). The only real difference is given by the Sautrāntika or Vijñānavāda framework: while for the former the image is projected onto consciousness by an only inferable (*nityānumeya*) external object, for the latter the image arises from consciousness itself. See also recently Chu 2006.

the cognitive process consists precisely in the conformity or likeness (*sārūpya*) between the two.[31] Thus, acquired knowledge is the moment of the self-awareness (*svasaṃvitti*) of cognition. The distinction between *pramāṇa* and *pramā* is merely the result of the analytical consideration of a reality that in itself is unitary, and the hypostatization of the result is rather a differentiation of roles within the same unique reality. From another point of view, even the attempt to attribute distinct functions (*vyāpāra*) to the elements appearing in the cognition process cannot but be rejected in the light of the basic consideration that all *dharma*s are instantaneous (*Pramāṇasamuccaya-vṛtti*, ibid.: *nirvyāpārās tu sarvadharmāḥ*).

While the soteriological value of logical arguments had already been admitted by early Yogācāra scriptures, Dignāga particularly develops epistemological issues, which Dharmakīrti will qualify with a strong apologetical concern (cf. Eltschinger 2010b: 400).

See also Excursus II, III, IV.

Dharmakīrti

Dharmakīrti (ca. 600-660; H. Krasser's on-going research tends to put his *floruit* back by several decades) is indeed a singular figure, and wholly atypical in the Indian scenario, where the single author tends to remain in the shade. A verse attributed to him paints a haughty and contemptuous picture, full of awareness of his intellectual superiority, as also of his being without real interlocutors. His treatises are not composed for teaching purposes (in any case no one would ever understand them), but only for pleasure, to pass the time, aware that "[my work] will be absorbed in my person and with it will perish, just as a river disappears into the ocean".[32] But Dharmakīrti

[31] This conception, upheld by Dignāga and Dharmakīrti — and, more generally, by Sautrāntikas and Vijñānavādins (along with Sāṃkhya and Vedānta) — is known as *sākāravāda*. The *nirākāravāda* is followed by Vaibhāṣikas (and Nyāya-Vaiśeṣikas, Mīmāṃsakas and Jainas); cf. Kajiyama 1989.

[32] Quoted above, Chapter 1, Note 13. Tibetan tradition gives a vivid portrayal of his peculiar mix of bitterness and pride. In Tāranātha's narration, Dharmakīrti, as

was indeed mistaken about the fate of his work, in view of the immense prestige it has enjoyed for centuries among followers and opponents, and of its remaining, after the disappearance of Buddhism in India, as an object of veneration and study in Tibet down to our own time. Certainly, reading him is arduous, owing both to his intrinsic complexity and to his unmistakably concentrated style, to the extent that no one has yet attempted to produce a complete translation of his works. Of the works ascribed to him — the so-called 'seven jewels' (in actual fact, if his self-commentaries are included, they number nine), all surviving in Tibetan translations — until recently only the main one, the *Pramāṇavārttika*, and another two (the already-mentioned *Nyāyabindu* and the *Vādanyāya* ('Method of Philosophical Debate') were available in the Sanskrit original; almost complete, through quotations, is also the short work *Sambandhaparīkṣā* ('Investigation on Relationship'). The Sanskrit manuscripts of a further two works (the *Pramāṇaviniścaya*, 'Ascertainment of the Means of Knowledge', and the *Hetubindu*, 'Drops of Logical Reason') have recently been discovered in China and are currently being edited by a team of scholars under the auspices of the Austrian Academy of Science. On the first chapter of the *Pramāṇavārttika*, devoted to inference-for-oneself (*svārthānumāna*), Dharmakīrti also composed a highly important commentary (*vṛtti*). According to Frauwallner (1954), the first chapter and self-commentary constitute his first work, and were only subsequently incorporated in his *magnum opus*, devoted — at least as a starting point — to a critical examination of Dignāga's doctrines.[33]

---

soon as he had finished his *magnum opus*, showed it to a gathering of learned pandits, but they were far from appreciating it. As a mark of contempt, they tied the palm-leaf manuscript to the tail of a dog. In running about the village streets, the dog scattered the leaves here and there, at which, Dharmakīrti, undaunted, commented, "Just as the dog runs through the streets, so my work will run throughout the vast world" (cf. Stcherbatsky 1930-32: I, p. 36).

[33] On the historical and social background of Dharmakīrti's work, see recently Eltschinger 2010c: 432-433.

His fundamental ambiguity, mentioned earlier, has rendered problematic any attempt — in any case, rather futile — at defining at all costs his affiliation to any single school. In actual fact, Dharmakīrti bestrides two trends: phenomenalistic-type realism, similar to that of the Sautrāntikas, and 'idealistic' absolutism of the Yogācāra sort. The former corresponds to the level of relative truth, the latter to the level of absolute reality. His main works are distributed over these two trends, the *Pramāṇaviniścaya* and the *Nyāyabindu*, closely inter-connected, mainly belonging to the former and the *Pramāṇavārttika* (in particular Chapter 3, devoted to perception) to the latter. When Dharmakīrti states in the *Nyāyabindu* (I.14) that the ultimately real corresponds to the 'particular' (*svalakṣaṇa*), he might thus be restricting his statement to the level of ordinary reality. On the other hand, it seems inevitable that anyone aiming at investigating the nature of the means of knowledge must accept to cling, at least provisionally, to the only perspective in which they are authorised to operate. Objects that are true in an absolute sense (*pāramārthika*; as compared to the substantial unreality of the universals), meaning the *svalakṣaṇa*s, as one reads in the *Pramāṇavārttika* (I.87), do not unite to form a class, nor are they divisible in substance and quality. If this occurs, it is due exclusively to the intervention of discursive thought. Although the sole reliable means of knowledge is thus perception, in which the particular is reflected in its own unicity entirely and without fragmentation, its content however is destined to remain unattainable and incommunicable, and consequently incapable of entering the circuit of human experience, unless 'translated' by discursive thought (*anumāna*, 'inference', in the widest sense) which, although ultimately 'false', does serve to make the content of perception in some way usable and to remove causes of error.[34] However, although absolute

[34] Generally speaking, this act of ascertainment (*niścaya*) — or, to use a broader term, of conceptual elaboration (*vikalpa*) — operates on the content of perception, which would be destined by its very nature to remain in the reign of *nirvikalpa*, that is, over and above the sphere of ordinary reality (*vyavahāra*). In order to give a picture of the contrast-interaction between the *vikalpa* and *nirvikalpa* dimensions of human knowledge, Abhinavagupta (*Īśvarapratyabhijñā-vivṛtivimarśinī* vol. II p. 15) resorts

otherness lies between the thing and its mental image (*sāmānya* 'universal'), there is nevertheless an undeniable coordination between the two, the one being the cause of the other. Furthermore, from what Dharmakīrti says in the *Nyāyabindu*, it is clear that the two objects of knowledge (*prameya*), of which Dignāga also speaks, are not two distinct entities, but only two different ways in which the sole existing entity (the particular) is grasped by two different means of knowledge. But what makes a means of knowledge valid? The definition given by Dharmakīrti (*Pramāṇavārttika* II.1ac) introduces a criterion that is totally absent in Dignāga: not deluding the (pragmatic) expectations of the knower (*avisaṃvādana*), i.e. assuring its effective action (*arthakriyā*).[35] After few verses, to this criterion he adds (as an alternative?) a second (*Pramāṇavārttika* II.5c), well-known moreover to Brahmanic schools: that of making manifest an object that has not previously been known (*ajñātārthaprakāśa*).[36]

Dharmakīrti also provides a fundamental contribution to the doctrine of inference, lingering to analyse the ultimate foundation of logical reason. Only two relations can aspire to the qualification of 'essential connection' (*svabhāvapratibandha*)[37] between two things,

---

to a nice simile. The *vikalpa* is just like the doorkeeper of the dancing hall who helps the poor villager in his desire to leave this too lofty place where he has accidentally found himself, and return to the more modest reality of his village, where he is accustomed to live; likewise, the *vikalpa* helps the human subject leave the very 'uncomfortable' plane of pure perception and return to ordinary life where he can at least make some use of the wealth (less bright, of course) of *nirvikalpa* perception.

35 On the concept of *arthakriyā* (already indicated in the *Nyāyabhāṣya*) in its various meanings, see in particular Nagatomi 1967-68, Mikogami 1979, Kano 1991.

36 According to Franco's analysis (1997: 45-66; criticised in Oetke 1999 and 1999a), in actual fact, Dharmakīrti deliberately abstained from giving a personal and univocal definition of *pramāṇa*. The passage in *Pramāṇavārttika* II.1-7 is translated and carefully examined in van Bijlert 1989: 115-180; see also Katsura 1984: 219-220. The various interpretations of the two (?) definitions given by Buddhist tradition, and particularly the Tibetan, are studied in Dreyfus 1991; for a thorough investigation of the question in the wider scenario of the work of Dharmakīrti and his main commentators, see Krasser 2001: 184-195; on Dharmottara's interpretation, see Krasser 1995: 247-249. It is likely the second definition is specially aimed at his Mīmāṃsā opponents.

37 On the possible interpretations of this problematic concept, see Steinkellner 1984.

or rather — since we are dealing with inference — between two concepts: causality (*tadutpatti*) and identity (*tādātmya*); cf. Steinkellner 1971. The sole inferences to be deemed valid are thus those based on an essential property (*svabhāva*) — "this is a tree because it is an oak", in which the two concepts are co-extensive, since the former implicitly embraces the latter and both refer to the same 'thing', and on effect (*kārya*) — "here there is fire because there is smoke". On the other hand, inference that starts from the cause (*hetusāmagrī*, 'totality of causes') to arrive at the effect is deemed to belong to the first type, since causal efficiency constitutes the very nature of the thing.[38] Subsistence of the cause-effect relationship must first be established by means of a concatenation of a certain number of perceptions and non-perceptions of the two entities in question (Dharmakīrti appears to require a total of five of them,[39] as against the three for subsequent thinkers). Lastly, Dharmakīrti recognises a third type of logical reason — non-perception — even though he ends up considering it as a special case of identity (Iwata 1991: 86-88): "Here there is no pot, because there is no perception of it". Perception of the absence of the pot, says Dharmottara in his commentary on the *Nyāyabindu* (pp. 122-123), although in itself distinct from that of the empty surface, has however an 'essential connection' with it, just as determined knowledge is tied to direct perception and represents its successive stage: the same cognitive act embraces both. In several of his works, Dharmakīrti returns to this major addition as compared to Dignāga and enriches it with remarks and new classifications (four types are indicated in the *Pramāṇavārttika*, eight in his self-commentary on

[38] On *svabhāvahetu* (and more generally speaking the meaning of the crucial term *svabhāva*, 'essential nature, etc.' in Dharmakīrti's works), see in particular Steinkellner 1974, 1996 and Iwata 1991; cf. also Torella 2002: 179-180.

[39] Indeed, this is the interpretation by Dharmottara in the *Pramāṇaviniścaya-ṭīkā*, by Mādhava in the *Sarvadarśanasaṃgraha* and Abhinavagupta in the *Īśvarapratyabhijñā-vivṛtivimarśinī*, whereas Śākyamati, Karṇakagomin and Arcaṭa recognise only three as essential (Steinkellner 1967: II, 97 n. 49). The debate between the two standpoints is reconstructed in Kajiyama 1963.

Pramāṇavārttika I, ten in the *Pramāṇaviniścaya* and eleven in the *Nyāyabindu*). In order to pass legitimately from the positive perception of something (here: the empty space) to knowledge of the absence of the thing that one expected to see, at least two requisites have to be fulfilled: 1) both things must possess an equal capacity for arousing a certain cognition so as to be presumably associated in the same cognitive act; 2) all conditions making any vision possible both from the side of the object and of the subject must occur (the thing must not be invisible by nature, the sensorial faculties must not be impaired, etc.). As also specified in the various classifications, beside the primary — 'direct' — form of determining such absence, there are various other indirect forms, such as perception of something that is contrary to what is expected; or perception of the effect of what is contrary to it, and so on.[40]

Dharmakīrti's choice of giving a positive content — anchored first of all in the reality of things and not, as in Dignāga's conception, only of a formal order — to the relationship between *probans* and *probandum*, identifying its only three possible means as identity, causality and non-perception, is not without consequence. It involves a substantial increase both in terms of rigour and simplification, rendering ultimately superfluous any recourse to negative concordance (*vyatireka*) between *probans* and *probandum*, and limiting the use of exemplification (*dṛṣṭānta*) just to cases in which the *probandum* is not known to the interlocutor (cf. p. 182; see also van Bijlert 1989: 107).

Lastly, it should be noted that neither Dignāga nor Dharmakīrti (although with reservations) rejects the inclusion of authoritative testimony among the mens of valid knowledge, first and foremost that of the Buddha, but they include it in the wider context of inference. In fact, it would not be impossible to read all the prestigious production of Buddhist logic as an interminable gloss on

---

[40] On non-perception, cf. Steinkellner 1967: II, 21-28, Torella 2002: 139-144; Kellner, 2001, 2003. A highly interesting critical re-reading of the Buddhist position on non-perception by non-dualist Śivaite philosophers is provided in Torella 2007a.

the epithet *pramāṇabhūta* ('who is/ is like/ has become a means of valid knowledge'; in fact, several different translations would be possible), with which Dignāga salutes the Buddha in the initial verse of the *Pramāṇasamuccaya*.[41]

See also Excursus II, III, IV.

[41] "After rendering homage to him who is/ has become/ is like a means of right knowledge, to him who strove for the good of the world (*jagaddhitaiṣin*), to the Instructor (*śāstṛ*), to the Well-Gone (*sugata*), to the Saviour (*tāyin*) [...]". The attention of Buddhist philosophers dwells at length on each of these crucial epithets; cf. first and foremost the second chapter of the *Pramāṇavārttika* (Pramāṇasiddhi), to the exegesis of which, in turn, first the Indian and then the Tibetan tradition was to devote itself for centuries. On the meaning to be attributed to the expression *pramāṇabhūta* we now possess an ample (and discordant) literature (cf. in particular, Seyfort Ruegg 1995, Franco 1997: 16-17, Krasser 2001).

Excursus

I. The Form of the Texts

In the various branches of traditional knowledge, the 'original' text tends to be very succinct, making it difficult or sometimes impossible to understand without interpretative support, presumably provided in the beginning by the oral teaching of a master. Any attempt at directly accessing a *sūtra* without the help of traditional exegesis — states the Jaina Dharmasāgara (seventeenth century) — is like trying to open the lock of an adamantine casket with your teeth (Dundas 1996a : 84). The term *sūtra* used to designate this type of text (Renou 1963) always seems to refer to a more articulated presentation, of which the *sūtra* expounds only the fundamental points, thus also facilitating — thanks to its brevity — easier memorization. This is what the commentators refer to when they speak of 'thread' (the literal meaning of *sūtra*), which unites the pearls on a necklace, i.e. the various parts of a complex teaching. Another interpretation of the term sets it against the background of the great Indo-European metaphor of the text as a 'web' (whether cloth or a spider's web), of which the *sūtra* constitutes, of course, a 'thread'. The Jain tradition (Dundas 1996a: 84) adds its own variations on the theme, advancing decidedly into the sphere — so dear to Indians in a wider sense — of 'creative etymology', making *sūtra* derive from the root *sūc-* ('to indicate'; i.e. the *sūtra* does not signify directly, but 'suggests, alludes to'),[1] or else from the root *sup-* ('to sleep'; the *sūtra*, by its very nature, is destined to remain in a state of lethargy, until 'awoken' by a commentary). The most widespread translation of *sūtra* is 'aphorism' (the term may be used either to

[1] The same etymology is proposed by the *Yuktidīpikā* (p. 3).

denominate a single 'aphorism' or the corpus of aphorisms forming the work). According to one of the traditional definitions of its main features — found, for example, in the most important commentary on the *Sāṃkhya-kārikā*, the *Yuktidīpikā* (p. 3), in the commentary by Madhva on *Brahmasūtra* I.119, etc. — the *sūtra* must comprise a limited number of syllables (*alpākṣara*), it must be free from doubt (*asandigdha*),[2] contain the gist of a teaching (*sāravat*), be of general significance (*viśvatomukha*), be without repetitions (*astobha*) and free from defects (*anavadya*).[3]

The ideal model of the *sūtra*, even though not the most ancient in absolute terms, is given by the Grammar of Pāṇini (*Aṣṭādhyāyī*, fifth-fourth century B.C.E.), governed by iron rules of expository economy aimed at the greatest possible generalization, its accessibility further complicated by the use of a specific metalanguage, as well as the necessary application of metarules (*paribhāṣā*). Fortunately, besides this unsurpassable model (indeed, any farther along the path of conciseness of a *sūtra* like the one concluding the *Aṣṭādhyāyī* — *a a iti*,[4] one would encounter only silence), this kind of literature presents a considerably varied range of levels of conciseness and ellipsis, which always make its intrinsic intelligibility as an independent text somewhat problematic. Later on, besides the *sūtra*, originally in prose, we have the *kārikā*, a kind of versified *sūtra*, as a rule much less hermetic and more usable even for independent reading, i.e. not mediated by a commentary.

---

2 This requirement seems to clash with the polysemy of the *sūtra*, but, I would say, only apparently so. Indeed, the *sūtra* is not required to be banally ambiguous, but to shine in perfect autonomy, leaving its interpreter to turn first to one then to another of the sparkles which, like a facetted stone, it emanates in its perfection.

3 For a similar list of characteristics current in the Jaina tradition, cf. Balbir 1987.

4 Lit. "*a* is *a*". That is to say: "The short *a* phoneme which, in order to avoid clashes in formulating phonological rules, has been herein artificially considered as being produced by an 'open' articulatory effort, may return, at the end of the work, to its original nature as a 'closed' vowel". Indeed, in Sanskrit the short *a* is not to be considered merely as the short counterpart of a long *a* — as occurs in the case of all other vowels — since between the two phonemes there is also a difference in timbre: open for the long *a*; closed for the short *a*.

The *sūtra*'s primary support consists of a simple and brief kind of commentary (*vṛtti*) that paraphrases the text, filling in the ellipses and focalizing on the argumentation process along broad lines. It seems likely that every *sūtra* was initially accompanied by a *vṛtti* (even Pāṇini's Grammar seems to have had an oral *vṛtti*, which has not come down to us).

Although the *vṛtti* has a relatively modest, albeit fundamental, scope, the *vārttika* on the other hand — which we might translate as 'gloss' — is a commentary with a much more ambitious intent, viewing the text critically with a considerable margin of independence. It is presented in the form of short nominal sentences in prose, of a terseness as refined as the habitual simplicity of the *vṛtti* (some of the *vṛtti*s are, however, extremely arduous, a conspicuous example of which is the *vṛtti* on the first chapter of Bhartṛhari's *Vākyapadīya*). The *vārttika* can also be in verse form, and as such is called *śloka-vārttika*, 'gloss composed in *śloka* (a thirty-two syllable verse, widely used in all kinds of literature)'. Two illustrious examples are provided by Kumārila (*Mīmāṃsā-ślokavārttika*) and Abhinavagupta (*Mālinī-ślokavārttika*). According to the classic definition given by Nāgeśa, the *vārttika* formulates hypotheses about what may be unspoken (*anukta*) or expressed in an unsatisfactory manner (*durukta*) in the original text (cf. *Nyāyakośa*, p. 741). Of the various kinds of commentary, it is certainly the least systematic, usually presented in the form of sporadic notes on parts of the original text that have given rise to the glossarist-commentator's critical reaction.

The *bhāṣya* is a wide-ranging commentary which, in some of the specimens that have come down to us, incorporates *vārttika*s either by previous authors or composed by the author of the *bhāṣya* itself. The commentary on the original text is sometimes direct, but more often with the intermediation of one or more *vārttika*s, raising preliminary problems to be solved and ideas for further reflection. In the form in which these commentaries have come down to us, it is not always easy to distinguish between the three levels of *sūtra-vārttika-bhāṣya*, and in particular to identify the level of the *vārttika*s, which tend to remain embedded in the body of the text. Often, their peculiar form — a highly synthetic nominal sentence, relatively out of context — is the only clue to discovering them. Texts in which a careful analysis reveals such structures are, by way of example, the *Nyāyabhāṣya* ('Commentary on the *Nyāya[sūtra]*') by Vātsyāyana Pakṣilasvāmin (fifth century C.E.), the *Tattvārthavārttika* ('Gloss on the [*sūtra* on the] meaning of true reality') by Akalaṅka (seventh-eighth century C.E.), the *Yuktidīpikā* ('Illuminator of reasoning'; seventh-eighth century C.E.), the most far-reaching and important commentary on the *Sāṃkhyakārikā* (cf. Bronkhorst 1991). According to the definition given by Patañjali, the author of the *bhāṣya* par excellence (on the *Aṣṭādhyāyī* by Pāṇini jointly with the *vārttika*s by Kātyāyana): "*Bhāṣya* specialists define it as the commentary that elucidates the meaning of the *sūtra* by means of words that conform to the *sūtra*, and then goes on to elucidate the words themselves" (cf. *Nyāyakośa*, p. 627). It is worth noting that the Indian cultural and scientific world often appears to make no difference between a *sūtra* and a certain commentary belonging to one of the above-mentioned categories, deemed particularly exemplary or prestigious, and considers them as a unitary text and, in a certain way, as an inseparable entity. Among the most significant examples, belonging to various traditions, we should mention the *Yogasūtra* with the *bhāṣya* by Vyāsa, the *Vākyapadīya* with the *vṛtti* (probably by Bhartṛhari himself), the Jaina *Tattvārthādhigamasūtra* ('Aphorisms on comprehending the meaning of true reality') with the *bhāṣya* by Umāsvāti, the Buddhist *Madhyāntavibhāga* ('Discrimination between the middle and the extremes') with the *bhāṣya* by Vasubandhu, the *Arthaśāstra* ('Treatise on the useful') with the *bhāṣya* by Viṣṇugupta (cf. Bronkhorst 1991).

There are also commentaries of a more generic kind, less ascribable to a specific model, providing a detailed interpretation of the original text, often supported by an abundance of quotations from works deemed authoritative, discussions on alternative theses and sometimes even lengthy digressions that may form a treatise within the treatise. The most current denominations are *ṭīkā*, meaning precisely 'extensive commentary', *vivṛti* ('disclosure'), *vimarśinī* ('reflection'), *vyākhyā* ('explanation'), etc. Frequent, too, are titles with metaphorical intent: *pradīpa* ('torch'), *prakāśa* ('light'), *candrikā* or *kaumudī* ('moonbeam'). Commentaries of this kind are expected — as stated in the *Parāśara-purāṇa* ('Antiquities of the sage Parāśara') — to provide word-divisions, an explanation of their meaning, an analysis of compounds, sentence construction, the formulation of objections and their subsequent solution.

In this play of interpretations, amplifications and cross-references — often commentaries explain previous commentaries, destined to be commented on in turn — the original text of the *sūtra*, as a rule restricted to a few lines or at the most a few pages, to our eyes risks being totally suffocated beneath the weight of thousands and thousands of pages of commentary. This is not the case, however, since each *sūtra* is explicitly endowed with an irreplaceable role as a sign of a continuing tradition, a role made possible by its very form as an 'embryo' text. By virtue of the inexhaustible wealth of meaning attributed to it, it can constitute either the point of departure or of arrival, one of the characteristic requisites of the *sūtra* being precisely that of being polysemic (*bahvartha*). The ambiguity thus assumed by the *sūtra* is consequently not viewed as a defect, but on the contrary as one of its essential requirements as a *sūtra*. The basic material for this planned ambiguity is provided by the Sanskrit language, with its 'natural' polysemy, which so much struck the learned al-Bīrūnī in his extraordinary description of India in the eleventh century.[5]

[5] "[...] the language has an enormous range [...] calling one and the same thing by various names, both original and derived, and using one and the same word for a variety of subjects [...]. For nobody could distinguish between the various meanings of a word unless he understood the context in which it occured [...]" (Sachau 1910: 17-8). The polysemy of Sanskrit is, moreover, all the more accentuated in the prakrits, as a result of their phonological simplification: the Jain Dharmasāgara (Dundas 1996a: 100) mentions the case of the prakrit term *saro* in a Jaina *sūtra*, which could indifferently correspond to the Sanskrit *śara* ('arrow'), *saras* ('lake') and *svara* ('sonority') (and the commentator is called upon to extract from the

Disputes may of course arise concerning the legitimacy of the various ways of tackling it, which are mainly of two kinds: according to the first, maintained by Kumārila, whatever is derived from a *sūtra* must in one way or another be present in the letter of the same, and of all these various expositions the *sūtra* must strictly remain the 'matrix' (*yoni*). For the second, on the other hand, the author of the *sūtra* is not bound to indicate in the letter of the text what can be derived from the text by implication (this is the opinion, by way of example, of Vācaspati Miśra).[6]

A highly interesting exemplification of how an Indian author perceived the dynamics of text-commentaries is provided by the shrewd remarks of Abhinavagupta (tenth-eleventh century B.C.E.) concerning the textual corpus of the Tantric school of the Pratyabhijñā 'Recognition [of the Lord]' (*Īśvarapratyabhijñā-vivṛtivimarśinī*, vol. I, p. 16). The author of the root-text, the *Īśvarapratyabhijñā-kārikā* or °*sūtra* ('Verses on the recognition of the Lord') is Utpaladeva, who simultaneously composed the original text together with a short *vṛtti* to make it intelligible, and later on a lengthy commentary (*ṭīkā* or *vivṛti*) in which he develops the various implications of the doctrine

---

context as many as three different, equally reliable, overall meanings!). Another Jaina author, Samayasundara (end of the seventeenth century; cf. Dundas 1996b: 153), reacts to the accusation of excessive polysemy in *ardhamāgadhī*, by asserting that Sanskrit is just as bad: using highly sophisticated methods of interpretation, he demonstrates that, from an innocent Sanskrit phrase such as *rājāno dadate saukhyam* ("kings dispense happiness"), it is possible to derive something like 800,000 different meanings.

6 The same attitude is found in the *Yuktidīpikā* (see the articulated argument on the concept of *liṅga*, 'index', which the unknown author develops on pp. 4-6). A kind of *liṅga* raised to the second power is the concept of *jñāpaka*, 'revealer'. Besides presenting the more or less obvious *liṅga*s, the root-text is here and there interposed with 'revealers', meaning minor inexplicable anomalies to be taken as occult messages that the text launches at its interpreters: when the *sūtra*, which by definition is without defects (*anavadya*), presents incongruities, it is because it wishes to indicate obscurely something that for one reason or another it deems cannot be formulated openly. Hunting for *jñāpaka*s is a favourite sport for the followers of the *śāstra* of grammar, but not only for them: thanks to this expedient, the possibilities of manipulating the original text become practically limitless.

and disputes with rival schools. According to Abhinavagupta, a preliminary distinction must be made between two categories of potential 'listener-readers': those who are drawn to this teaching after adhering to other doctrines in the past, and those who for the first time wonder about the nature of reality. The latter must first tackle the aphorisms-short commentary (*sūtra-vṛtti*) together, which will prepare them for the final moment, the study of the *sūtra*s alone. The former, on the other hand, must begin with the long commentary (*ṭīkā*), which will prepare them for the aphorisms-short commentary corpus, before finally approaching the root-text (the *sūtra*), which thus does not come at the beginning, but the end. Abhinavagupta also mentions a subsequent moment, in which even the *sūtra*s themselves are surpassed by reaching the very core of the doctrine, beyond any formulation in words, identifying with the mind of their author. To explain the reciprocal relations of the various layers of the text united with its commentaries, Abhinavagupta also uses another model, drawn from philosophical-linguistic speculation, which identifies four distinct levels in the all-pervasive reality of language. In order of increasing ontological dignity and progressive rarefaction, these are: the articulated and hearable language of everyday worldly commerce (Vaikharī, 'Corporeal [Voice]'); the articulated but unhearable language of inner discourse (Madhyamā, 'Median [Voice]'; the language that henceforth compresses any actual differentiation and articulation, coinciding with intuition, etc. (Paśyantī, 'Seeing [Voice]'), and lastly Parā ('Supreme [Voice]'), wholly undifferentiated word-consciousness that transcends the other three and also acts as their necessary substrate. The level of the *ṭīkā* thus belongs to the Corporeal Voice, the level of the *sūtra-vṛtti* corpus to the Median, culminating in the *sūtra*s alone at the Seeing level. At the level of the Supreme Voice, it is clearly no longer possible to speak of 'texts'.

II. Logic

Unlike Western thought, where logic's field of action appears much wider, defining the nature of the logic peculiar to Indian thought essentially amounts to defining the nature of inference. Indeed, Indian philosophers have systematically made use of 'linked reasoning', particularly in establishing the principles of the necessary connection between a given property in a certain entity and another property of the same entity, momentarily or permanently inaccessible to direct perception, so as to go back to one from the other. The Sanskrit term commonly translated as 'inference', *anumāna*, tells us only that we are dealing with knowledge (*-māna*) that is not primary, but comes behind (*anu-*) something else — as a rule, direct perception — which has occurred previously and from which it proceeds for further development, i.e. reaching where perception alone does not, or assessing the validity of the perception itself, since Indian thought as a whole, surprisingly for those who blame it for excessive abstractness and vagueness, is unanimous in assigning epistemological primacy to direct perception. As Abhinavagupta strongly affirms in the *Abhinavabhāratī* (vol. I, p. 281), even though, regarding a certain object, various indirect means of knowledge might be available — such as authoritative testimony or inference — knowledge does not come to its definitive resting point (*na viśrāmyati*) but after direct perception. The source of Abhinavagupta is a passage from *Nyāyabhāṣya* (p. 9), dealing with the possibility of applying different means of knowledge to the same object. In these cases, knowledge acquired through authoritative testimony then seeks confirmation in inference, and the latter in direct perception. Only with direct perception the wish for knowledge is at last fulfilled, and ceases (*jijñāsā nivartate*), since all knowledge culminates in direct perception (*sā ceyaṃ pramitiḥ pratyakṣaparā*).

Western logic, beginning from Aristotle, started by distinguishing inductive from deductive inference, the former proceeding from the particular to the universal and the latter from the universal to the particular. Whereas for the former the path is always problematic and risky, but capable of producing a real increase in knowledge, for the latter it is much more linear, albeit susceptible to tautology. For deduction, a risk still more insidious than tautology is to lose itself in the correctness of the method used to draw conclusions, which may be formally correct, but factually wrong. As a first approximation, we should note that generally speaking Indian inference tends not to allow any such duplicity of evaluation: inference is 'correct' only if confirmed as so being by reality.

In the earliest stages of Indian logic, represented in particular by the great medical schools, early Nyāya and Vaiśeṣika up to the fifth century C.E., inductive inference clearly predominates (Katsura 2000, Tillemans 2004), the burden of proof being placed on the accumulation of examples, thus leading to results that always risk being invalidated by a contrary example (which is the objection of the Lokāyatas). This is what is known in Western thought as probable inference or inference by analogy, at one end of which we have the limit case of the induction of a general truth reached by examining the totality of particular cases.

Like Western thought, in India too the form most employed — and also with greater cognitive relevance — is induction of the ampliative kind, which leads to an increase (albeit not absolutely certain) of knowledge by recourse to a limited number of examples, selected for their particular significance. A quality leap is marked by the introduction in Nyāya of the criterion of agreement and difference (*anvaya-vyatireka*), which represents the passing from a mere accumulation of examples to the coordinated employment of positive and negative examples. An interesting Western parallel is the so-called 'Mills' method' (cf. Matilal 1999: 17-18), elaborated in the second half of the nineteenth century by the English philosopher for inductive inference: the method of agreement; the method of difference; the joint method of agreement and difference; the method of remainders and the method of concomitant variation.

A further step, also within the confines of reasoning of an inductive kind, is taken by Dignāga's doctrine known as the 'triplicity of logical reason' (*liṅgatrairūpya*): property 'A', to be demonstrated, must be present in property 'B', occurring in the same substrate; it must be present in those cases in which 'B' is present and absent in those cases in which 'B' is absent. This is linked with the introduction of the concept of 'pervasion', called upon to replace and make more precise the previous generic notions of 'relation', 'co-presence', 'concomitance', etc. The extension of class 'B' must be greater than (or at least equal to) class 'A'. The ideal trajectory of inductive reasoning may be said to end with the work of Dharmakīrti (600-660 C.E.). Dharmakīrti, deeming that Dignāga's reform was incomplete, reformulated the 'triplicity of logical reason' in more restrictive terms. In particular, also unsatisfied by his master's attempt, Īśvarasena, with the intent of making logical reason more consistent (the introduction of the clause of not noticing an invalidation by contrary cases; *adarśanamātreṇa*, 'by virtue of mere non-seeing'), restricts admissible logical reasons to just three types, their validity being first established as intrinsically and factually existent (principle of causality, principle of identity and absence of perception). The path of reasoning is thus inverted from inductive to substantially deductive, as shown by the loss in importance — for the first time — of examples.[7] Although the positive example may still appear, albeit reduced from an element of proof to a rhetorical artifice or additional information for the simple-minded, the negative example no longer has any *raison d'être*. The relevance — or lack of it — of the example is also referred to by the notions of 'external pervasion' (*bahirvyāpti*) or 'internal pervasion' (*antarvyāpti*), used by medieval scholasticism as one of the classification criteria for inference theories. External pervasion has to be proven 'from the outside', i.e. through examples,

---

[7] An extensive investigation into the role of the example in Indian logic is provided by the recent volume edited by Katsura and Steinkellner 2004.

while internal pervasion is proven 'a priori' within the subject of inference itself (*pakṣa*). The Buddhist Ratnākaraśānti, in upholding the latter position with his *Antarvyāptisamarthana* ('Demonstration of Internal Pervasion'; cf. Kajiyama 1999), accepted also by the Jains, does not realise that all its presuppositions were already contained in Dharmakīrti's work (Bhattacharya 1986). In Dharmakīrti, the leap from induction to deduction remains however imperfect: deductive reasoning is, for example, guaranteed by the causality relationship, but what can guarantee the guarantor beyond any doubt except recourse, yet again, to a (problematic) induction? [8]

[8] On the criteria for establishing a causality relationship, cf. p. 169.

III. Knowledge and Truth

In the field of epistemology, Mīmāṃsā is linked to the doctrine of the intrinsic validity of all knowledge,[9] the obvious motivations for which have already been mentioned. It is first presented by Kumārila in Chapter II of his *Ślokavārttika*, developing the implications of an argument put forward by Śabara in his *Bhāṣya* on *Mīmāṃsāsūtra* I.1.2 — not by chance, in response to an adversary who was not willing to admit that *dharma* is revealed by Vedic injunction (*codanā*). The validity of cognition cannot depend on other cognition, because in such a case a third cognition would be required to validate the second, and so on, with infinite regression. Furthermore, all cognition arises with an innate force of conviction as to its validity, without which the sphere of ordinary experience would become impossible (all cognition would be held up perennially awaiting confirmation). That certain cognition is not valid is, of course, possible, but such an occurrence would be as it were a sporadic incident en route owing to well-understood causes that jam the mechanism of the cognitive act, such as, for example, a disease of the visual organ, or a contradictory experience in similar circumstances, which would therefore require arbitration to establish which of the two is right.

The question of the intrinsic or extrinsic validity/invalidity of cognition, inaugurated as it appears by Mīmāṃsā, later became a recurrent argument in Indian philosophy, frequently utilised in doxographic works as a principle for classifying the various schools of thought. Indeed, the most famous of these works, the *Sarvadarśanasaṃgraha* (p. 557), quotes an anonymous verse summarising the status of the question: "Sāṃkhya followers maintain that both the validity (*pramāṇatva*) and invalidity (*apramāṇatva*) of cognition are intrinsic

[9] A thorough assessment of Mīmāṃsā position can be found in Taber 1992.

(*svataḥ*), whereas Nyāya followers deem it to be extrinsic (*parataḥ*). For the Buddhists, the latter is intrinsic, while the former is extrinsic. Followers of the Veda [i.e. the Mīmāṃsakas] on the other hand assert that validity is intrinsic and invalidity extrinsic" (Hattori 1997: 361).

This theme is of central relevance to Indian epistemology and deserves further elucidation. Of these positions, the least known is the first, according to which what makes cognition true or false are the very conditions under which it is produced; validity and invalidity thus belong to cognition from the start, are evident in themselves and do not need to be ascertained from the outside. Such a position is in line with the philosophic assumptions of Sāṃkhya, but there is no extant Sāṃkhya text that explicitly mentions it. The Nyāya position on the other hand is well known, from both ancient and recent Nyāya works (Navyanyāya), which in defending it train their guns mainly at the Mīmāṃsaka position. All cognition consists of the manifestation of an object (*arthaprakāśa*), which depends on a determined ensemble of causes. Its validity or invalidity, consisting mainly of its agreement or disagreement with the object, depends on the occurrence of the special positive (*guṇa*) or negative (*doṣa*) conditions of its causes (*kāraṇa*), which are added to the general conditions operating in all cognition (e.g. in sensory perception, the sense coming into contact with the object constitutes the general condition; excessive distance, darkness or a sight defect constitute the special conditions, in this case negative and consequently invalidating the cognition). Ascertainment of validity or invalidity is an inferential act that always occurs subsequent to the achievement of the related cognition — founded on capacity to obtain the expected results from the object thus known. Even the position that the quoted verse attributes to the Buddhists is not supported by the texts: the great masters of the logical-epistemological school, Dignāga and Dharmakīrti do not even touch on the question. Śāntarakṣita (eighth century), in responding to the critique of Kumārila in the section of the *Tattvasaṃgraha* devoted to the investigation of intrinsic validity (*svataḥprāmāṇyaparīkṣā*), indicates that the Buddhists do not identify with any of the positions outlined, because all of them indistinctly show excessive standardisation.[10] For Buddhists, all cognition, even when false, is self-revealing, but this self-revelation concerns only the cognitive act, not its content. Congruity with reality is ascertained only later, by verifying causal efficiency (*arthakriyā*), i.e. the capacity of the object as known to produce expected effects. This however does not apply to some types of cognition, which have to be considered 'intrinsically' valid: introspective cognition of the various mental states; the cognition of the yogin; cognition in which causal efficiency is manifest; inference and cognition that come from repeated practice (that of the jeweller recognizing at first glance the quality of gold or precious stones).

The various theories on ascertaining the validity of cognition are interwoven with various conceptions concerning the ways in which cognition is revealed, i.e. whether awareness of the cognitive act that has taken place depends in turn on a subsequent mental operation, or whether each cognitive act possesses an intrinsic power of self-revelation. The four possible combinations are consequently as follows (Mohanty 1966): self-revelation and intrinsic validation (Vedānta and Prābhākara Mīmāṃsā), hetero-revelation and intrinsic validation (Bhāṭṭa Mīmāṃsā), self-revelation and extrinsic validation (most Buddhist schools), hetero-revelation and extrinsic validation (Nyāya-Vaiśeṣika).

It remains to be established however what the 'validity' or 'truth' of cognition consists of for the various schools. This, indeed, is a changing concept and is not always stated openly, which includes, variously blended by each school, the criteria of 'non-contradiction by other cognitions' (*abādhitatva*), the 'novelty of the acquisition' (*anadhigatatva*), 'congruity with the true nature of the object' (*yāthārthya*) and 'successful employability in practical reality' (*pravṛttisāmarthya*).

[10] The final position is clearly explained by the commentator Kamalaśīla in the summary *excursus* that concludes the chapter (p. 981; quoted in Hattori 1997: 368).

All Indian philosophies have, at the same time, investigated the nature of error, and in particular error in perception.[11] The classical positions are denominated technically using a nominal compound whose final element is the word *khyāti* ('perception, appearing [in cognition]'), with reference to the standard example of mother-of-pearl mistaken for silver (or else, particularly appreciated by Vedānta thinkers, the rope mistaken for a snake). For Nyāya, Vaiśeṣika and Yoga, error is *viparītakhyāti* ('inverted perception') or *anyathākhyāti* ('perception in terms different [from the real]') (some characteristics of mother-of-pearl, observed inattentively, recall similar characteristics seen in the past as belonging to silver; the silver believed to be seen is thus not totally inexistent, but present in the memory and existent elsewhere). For Mīmāṃsā, on the other hand, it is *akhyāti* ('non-perception') (the two components of mistaken perception — perception and memory — are valid in themselves, although in the case in point they are limited to general characteristics. The defect lies in the mind, which has improperly mixed them up, but this would not have happened had their specific characteristics also been surveyed. No true and proper perception of silver has thus, in actual fact, ever taken place). As affirmed by the Prābhākara school, in any final analysis, error does not concern cognition but practical action and the verbalization it triggers; wrong action and verbalization have their roots in the non-recognition of the difference between what is the object of perception and what is the object of memory (the standpoint of the other major Mīmāṃsaka school — that of the followers of Kumārila — on the other hand, presents elements that bring it closer to the *anyathākhyāti* of Nyāya). For Yogācāra Buddhists, perceptive error is a case of *ātmakhyāti* ('perception of something that exists [only] internally'); for the Mādhyamikas however it is a question of *asatkhyāti* ('perception of something non-existent'; to which the Nyāya objection is that mere non-existence could not

[11] See, in particular, the study by L. Schmithausen (1965), which accompanies his translation of the *Vibhramaviveka* by Maṇḍana Miśra; cf. also Matilal 1986: 180-220; more recently, Rao 1998.

generate any kind of cognition, not even of the erroneous kind). The late Sāṃkhya work known as the *Sāṃkhyasūtra* ('Aphorisms on Sāṃkhya'), conventionally attributed to Kapila, speaks of *sadasatkhyāti* ('perception of something existing and of something not existing'; V. 56). The commentator Aniruddha (*Sāṃkhyasūtravṛtti*, p. 106) states that in the erroneous statement "this is silver" the 'this' component remains true as such, whereas it is only the identification with silver that is subsequently invalidated. According to Vijñānabhikṣu however, it is the silver that exists/does not exist: it exists in that it can be found in a jeweller's window, for example; it does not exist in perception whose real object is mother-of-pearl. The Advaita Vedānta of Śaṅkara speaks of *anirvacanīyakhyāti* ('perception of something indefinable'): indeed, the silver cannot be said either to exist (since otherwise there would be no error), or not to exist (because it could not trigger any cognition at all). Its status is thus that of labile existence lasting until a subsequent cognition corrects the error. According to the Viśiṣṭādvaita ('Advaita with qualifications') of Rāmānuja, every erroneous perception is always *satkhyāti* ('perception of something that exists'): silver actually exists in mother-of-pearl (after all, everything is in everything), but only in a minute quantity. The error consists of misunderstanding the proportions and proceeding accordingly with disappointing results. This conception is not unlike the one ascribed by Jayanta (*Nyāyamañjarī* vol. I, pp. 478-479) to a not-otherwise-identified Mīmāṃsaka, dismissed as *ajña* ('insipient'); Jayanta defines it as *alaukikakhyāti* ('perception of a non-ordinary object'). In this case the silver perceived in the mother-of-pearl is considered only as a special type of silver as compared to silver commonly understood. For Abhinavagupta (based on Utpaladeva), error is in fact an 'imperfect' cognition (*apūrṇakhyāti*): the reflective awareness (*vimarśa*) 'silver' in the presence of the mother-of-pearl is in itself valid, but the *vimarśa*'s natural tendency to last comes to be later blocked by a further awareness which contradicts it.

IV. Linguistic Speculations

By placing a text as the supreme and sole source of knowledge, at least in the sphere of *dharma*, Mīmāṃsā cannot fail to make language itself the subject of a prolonged and in-depth investigation. The central questions posed by Mīmāṃsā, together with the whole of India's philosophic and linguistic tradition, are as follows: what is it that makes a sound a word; what is indicated by the word; what is its relationship with its meaning; what is a sentence; what are its relations with its component words; and, more generally, can language be a vehicle of knowledge, i.e. how reliable is its 'reproduction' of the real?

In the spectrum of answers that Indian thought has elaborated over more than two thousand years, those of Mīmāṃsā belong, according to expectations, to the more obstinately 'positive' side. If the axioms of Vaiśeṣika also include concordance of language (as well as thought) and things, for its own part Mīmāṃsā does not attribute such concordance to any convention, whether or not established by the Lord, but deems it to be spontaneous and eternal, just as spontaneous and immutable (*autpattika*; *Mīmāṃsāsūtra* I.1.5) is the relationship between signifier and signified. In the classic systematisation of Vaiśeṣika, little or nothing is said about the matter, but this silence itself indicates that, since the problem is not even felt to be such, Vaiśeṣika thinkers take the correspondence of words and things for granted. This is not so for the system's root-text, the *Vaiśeṣikasūtra*, which states peremptorily that there is no intrinsic relationship between word and meaning (VII.2.19: *śabdārthāv asambaddhau*), and that if the pronouncing of a word is followed by understanding of its meaning, this is merely the fruit of convention. The motivation for this resolute statement is a direct result of Vaiśeṣika ontology, which, considering sound only in its physical dimension, classifies it as a quality (of the substance ether).

As a quality, any kind of relationship can only refer to a substance and hence not to the quality 'sound'. There exists a special kind of relationship known as inherence (*samavāya*), which could indeed bind a substance to a quality, but such a connection would be immutable and necessary. This would in fact imply that anyone could know the meaning of all words without any need for learning them, which clashes with common experience. Furthermore, if we are dealing with an intrinsic connection — the Nyāya philosophers add — then the word 'sword' should cut, or the word 'fire' burn. Consequently, by exclusion, the principle of convention is accepted. However, as the Naiyāyikas say later on, any convention made by man would be unstable and contradictory by nature, whereas language has to be first and foremost a constant reality shared by all. The only option left, as Jayanta affirms, is to attribute this convention to the Lord, who establishes it anew at the start of every cosmic era, just as each time he recreates the Veda. Man too has the power to establish conventions, but only within a limited space, such as the creation of sectoral languages or the coining of technical terms. The conventional nature of language is accepted, albeit with various nuances, by all other schools of thought in India, the only difference being that those who, like Buddhism, tend to disparage the cognitive significance of language, accordingly accentuate the element of arbitrariness and substantial unreality in this convention.

On their side, the Grammarians [12] accept as a basis the position stated by the first *vārttika* of Kātyāyana, with its indeed highly ambiguous formulation.[13] According to this, the relationship between word and meaning is *siddha* ('established'?, 'permanent'?, 'fixed'?), to which is added the notion, found also in the *Yogasūtra* (III.17), of 'superimposition' or '[mistaken] identification' (*adhyāsa*), governing linguistic use, representable as a triangle at whose vertex stand word,

[12] For a succinct and penetrating overview of the Grammarians' linguistic thoughts and doctrines, see Cardona 2002; Staal 1972 provides an extensive presentation of studies on the classical grammatical tradition.

[13] Not more ambiguous, however, than the *autpattika* of the Mīmāṃsakas.

(conceptual) meaning and a possible external referent, which co-imply and refer to each other. To this, the Grammarians add a fourth element, the form itself of the word conveyed by the word together with its meaning. "Just as light has two powers", we read in a famous verse of Bhartṛhari's *Vākyapadīya* (fifth century C.E.), "that of being perceived and allowing perception, similarly these two powers have been separately established for all words" (I. 56).

The Grammarians however seem only to look on without taking any stand on another centuries-old dispute: what is the subject of the denotation of the word. In the highly pregnant premise (*paśpaśā*) to his *Mahābhāṣya*, Patañjali lists four elements one after the other, each of which could constitute an answer to this question: individual substance (*dravya*), action (*kriyā*), quality (*guṇa*) and generic or universal configuration (*ākṛti*). Bhartṛhari, in the second section of the *Vākyapadīya* (vv. 119 *et seq.*), examines no less than twelve possible alternatives. The responses of the different philosophy schools polarized, with various solutions, on the particular/universal alternative, two positions that had already been stated by two ancient grammarians — Vyāḍi and Vājapyāyana respectively — prior to Patañjali. Mīmāṃsā obviously embraces the 'universal' option without any compromise, the only one that conforms to the axiom of word permanence. It does not deny that in everyday experience language is employed to indicate single things, but this is achieved through its power of 'indirect' meaning (*lakṣaṇā*). On the other hand, according to late testimonies, Sāṃkhya, starting from the same observation of what is shown by everyday experience, accepts the opposite theory that the word designates only the individual. The *Nyāyasūtra* (and commentaries), after weighing up these and other intermediate theories, concludes, in a manner not wholly dissimilar from the Grammarians, that they are all right to a certain extent and that the word has the power of designating the individual, the general conformation shared by the different members of a class, and the underlying universal (solely the speaker's intention makes one or the other of these meanings prevail on one occasion or the other).[14] In accordance with their own theory of knowledge, the thinkers of the logical-epistemological school of Buddhism provide a variation on the theory of meaning as universal. Each word designates only one of the infinite aspects composing the artificial unity of the object, each aspect being merely a conceptual abstraction whose sole content is the negation of what is otherwise (for the Buddhist theory of the concept of *apoha* 'exclusion', cf. pp. 161-162).

The most strenuous opponents of such a de-substantialisation of language, which endangers the whole structure built on the absolute reality of the word of the Veda, are the Mīmāṃsakas, and in particular Kumārila. To their belief in an eternal and permanent word, followers of Nyāya, who share the same realistic option, but not to such extremes, tempered as it is by healthy 'common sense', reply that one merely has to look around to see that every pronunciation of a word is a contingent fact, produced by the combination of very definite causes. The Mīmāṃsakas insist that word — or rather its component phonemes — is, in itself, omnipresent and eternal and it is merely its manifestation, by means of the process of phonation, that is a contingent fact. At this point, the Grammarians come in, later on finding an unexpected ally in the Mīmāṃsaka (or former Mīmāṃsaka) Maṇḍana Miśra, with their theory of *sphoṭa* (lit. 'flowering, eruption'). They agree to the 'revealer' function attributed to sounds, albeit the signifying element manifested by them does not coincide with a simple grouping of phonemes, but with an undivided structure (of which the phonemes form, as it were, the body), which is the only true vehicle of meaning. This process clearly has two sides (speaker-listener). The triangle mentioned above thus undergoes further complications. Here, we can only mention a further solution to the problem of verbal signification, provided by one of the most profound and versatile thinkers of India, the Tantric master Abhinavagupta. With the intention of providing an apparently impo-

---

[14] Cf. the Solomonic position of the *Nyāyasūtra* II.2.65: *vyaktyākṛtijātayas tu padārthaḥ*, "Word meaning covers the individual, the general configuration and the universal".

ssible bridge between the Mīmāṃsakas and the Grammarians, at the same time staking his post firmly in the sacred Śivaite scriptures that consider phonemes as divine entities in which the Supreme Consciousness is articulated and from which its dynamism is drawn, Abhinavagupta deems that phonemes are the only true vehicles of meaning. The phenomenon of verbal signification thus remains substantially a mystery, a miracle that is repeated every day, for the realisation of which, on each occasion, the phonemes of daily language have to let themselves be 'embraced by the divine phonemes'.[15]

In thus defining what the word is, Indian theorists vacillate between criteria of a formal and of a semantic order. According to Pāṇini's definition, echoed in the root-text of the Nyāya system (II.2.57), what turns a sound into a word is the presence of a nominal or verbal ending (I.4.14: *suptiṅantaṃ padam*), which does not exclude the indeclinables, to which a 'zero' suffix is attributed. Later Nyāya, on the other hand, invokes the criterion of meaning, which may be simple or complex (complex is when the word contains several elements that have meaning, e.g. in the verb *pacati* ("he cooks"), the segments *pac-a-ti* express 'root', 'thematic vowel of the present' and 'personal ending' respectively. In passing, it should be remembered that identification of the morpheme concept is an exclusive acquisition of Indian linguistics. Central to all subsequent speculation is, even in its intrinsic ambiguity, the definition which, after various attempts deemed unsatisfactory, Patañjali reaches in his *Paśpaśā*: "Speech is that which, when pronounced, gives rise [for example, in the case of 'cow'] to the notion of the animal having a dewlap, tail, hump, hooves and horns".

Indian linguistic speculation does not stop at defining the status of the word. Almost all schools agree that communication does not consist of words, but of sentences. Even the notion of the sentence reveals problems, however. The first two verses of the most pene-

[15] Abhinavagupta takes this expression from a famous śivaite text, the *Mālinī-vijayottara-tantra* ('Further Tantra on the Victory of the Garlanded One'). The complex context in which Abhinavagupta's position should be read is reconstructed in Torella 2004.

trating and influential investigation into the nature of the sentence, the second chapter of the *Vākyapadīya* ('Of the sentence and word') by Bhartṛhari, present as many as eight different positions. "About the sentence there exists among the learned a wide variety of opinions. Indeed, it is identified from time to time with the verb, with the agglomerate [of words], with the universal inherent in the agglomerate [of words], with the single word lacking parts [with the word seen as a single unity without parts], with the succession [of words], with the unification that takes place in the mind, with the first word, with each word taken separately and requiring the others" (II.1.1-2). The two positions on which the debate has tended to polarize are firstly the one affirming the exclusive centrality of the verb, starting from the truly ambiguous formulation of Kātyāyana: *ekatiṅ [vākyam]* ('the sentence consists of [or else: contains] a single verb') (*vārttika* X ad P. II.1.1; cf. Joshi 1968: 108-119), and that of the Nyāya followers, for whom, on the contrary, the presence of the verb is not essential. For an ensemble of words — whether nouns or verbs, as in the accommodating definition given by the most prestigious lexicon of classical India, the *Amarakośa* — to give rise to a sentence, three conditions have to be satisfied:[16] expectation (*ākāṅkṣā*, i.e. no feeling of suspension should be given, caused by any lack of elements to complete the overall meaning), syntactic-semantic compatibility (*yogyatā*; e.g. 'the fire is cold' does not constitute a sentence in the strictest sense) and proximity (*āsatti*; no component of a sentence may be distant from the others and mixed with components of another sentence). Of these three requirements (to which a fourth is sometimes added: *tātparya*, meaning the speaker's intention), it is the first that is deemed absolutely essential, whereas the second is of only limited importance to the sentence (which does not necessarily have to express the real) and the third has a purely ancillary value. The linguistic speculation of Mīmāṃsā — always starting from its main preoccupation, the exegesis of Vedic injunctions (i.e. sentences) — identifies

[16] This doctrine comes to light in the Mīmāṃsaka context, but is rapidly and widely accepted by the other schools.

a further level to the problem: although the sentence is composed of words, how can the single words closed in their respective meaning release that necessary relational element on which the new organism thus created is based? Yet again, Kumārila and Prabhākara split, providing two contrary doctrines, on which on countless occasions thinkers not adhering to Mīmāṃsā will also take their stand. Kumārila puts a decided emphasis on words that individually denote the meaning that is proper to them, then developing the relational element that binds them in the unity of the sentence and consequently satisfying the three mentioned requirements. Prabhākara does not deny that words possess an individual power of denotation, but this is conditioned by the structure of the sentence, which is clearly of a superior order with respect to the words. These doctrines, the subject of innumerable and often highly refined attacks and defences, are known respectively as *abhihitānvaya* ('connection of meanings already denoted by the single words') and *anvitābhidhāna* ('denotation of meanings already connected in the sentence') (Kunjunni Rāja 1963: 191-227). Whereas for Kumārila words construct the sentence, for Prabhākara it is rather the sentence that constructs the words, i.e. creates the binding frame of reference, only within which can the individual word 'signify'.[17] On Prabhākara's side we find the Grammarians, even though it would seem difficult to reduce the position of Bhartṛhari to the sole 'sentence' option; on Kumārila's side, albeit not without distinction, are ranked the followers of Nyāya. The latter, however, are alone in judging the content expressed by the sentence: for them, it consists essentially of connecting a subject (*uddeśya*) to a predicate (*vidheya*). In the resulting ideal nominal sentence, the verb is limited to a copula that in Sanskrit is as a rule unexpressed. Grammarians and Mīmāṃsakas (particularly the Prabhākara school)

[17] The gloss by Śālikanātha on the *magnum opus* by Prabhākara is categorical: when the *Mīmāṃsāsūtra* I.1.5 (quoted above) states that the relationship between meaning and word is spontaneous and innate (*autpattika*), in actual fact it refers to the relation between meaning and sentence, since the word alone expresses 'no' meaning. It does so only when it is included in a sentence (Jha 1942: 115).

object that far from being an ancillary element, the verb is the very soul of the phrase, the pivot on which all the elements turn. Although opinions are divided about what, in its turn, the essence of the verb may be — an impulse to action (*bhāvanā*), as the Mīmāṃsakas hold, their mind bent on their initial concern centering on the injunctions of the Vedic texts —, what is certain is that a sentence containing only static and already 'established' elements (*siddhapadārtha*) would not provide any new knowledge as compared to perception and inference.

Among the great historical civilisations, India has devoted the most constant and penetrating attention to language. The linguistic and grammatical thought of Western classical antiquity pales when faced with the acquisitions of the cognate Indian traditions in terms of the most lucid scientific observation of linguistic facts in the various domains (from phonetics to phonology, morphology and semantics). The fact that Western linguistics managed to leave behind the impasse into which it had fallen is largely due to the shock caused by the discovery, starting from the second half of the eighteenth century, of Indian treatises focusing on Sanskrit.

On the philosophical-linguistic side, one of the central intuitions of the Grammarians is the inextricable link between consciousness and language, seen as two sides of the same coin. This aspect, with antecedents in Vedic literature, culminates in the work of the great grammarian-philosopher Bhartṛhari (fifth century), and from there even penetrates the speculations of Tantrism, which sees supreme power (*śakti*) as supreme consciousness and supreme word. Esoteric speculations on speech continue however to maintain a subtle, but firm anchorage in 'scientific' grammatical tradition. In Tantric texts — as more generally in the philosophical and religious literature of all schools — we frequently encounter doctrines and positions that are merely transpositions of linguistic doctrines (cf. Torella, 1987, 1998, 1999c, 2001, 2004).

Appendices

1. Orality and Writing

> "They do not allow the Veda to be committed to writing, because it is recited according to certain modulations, and they therefore avoid the use of the pen, since it is liable to cause some errors, and may occasion an addition or a defect in the written text. In consequence it has happened that they have several times forgotten the Veda and lost it."

The speaker is the Arab traveller al-Bīrūnī, a perceptive observer of eleventh century India.[1] 'They' are clearly the brahmins. We may take al-Bīrūnī's notes as our starting point for our reflections on the status of writing and manuscripts in India, aware that we are entering a territory that is contradictory and still insufficiently studied.

Although it is apparent that in India all knowledge tends to be structured as a text — starting from the sound-form of the Absolute itself, condensed into the 'text' *par excellence*, the Veda —, those familiar with Indian culture would protest against any apparently contiguous attribution to India of a culture of the 'book', in the meaning used to define the three major monotheistic religions as 'religions of the book'. An equivalent of our 'learned, knowledgeable' is the ancient expression, used throughout India's plurimillennial culture, *bahuśruta* — lit. 'he who has much listened, heard', rather than the non-existent 'he who has much read'.[2] On the contrary,

---

[1] The last to draw attention to this famous passage was J. Bronkhorst in a recent article (Bronkhorst 2002: 799). The passages by al-Bīrūnī are quoted in the classical translation by E. Sachau. For the above passage, see Sachau 1910: vol. I, 125-126.

[2] A similar lack of reference to reading in defining a 'learned' man can be found, for example, in classical Greece. The word *grammatikós*, used only from the fourth century B.C.E., indicates merely someone who can read (and also teach reading, whence the later substantial equivalence with our 'school-master'), without

Nārada includes recourse to books as one of the six *obstacles* to knowledge.[3] "What has been learned relying on books", says the same sage, "and not from direct contact with the teacher, is incapable of shining in the midst of the assembly, like a woman's bastard son".[4]

The essentially oral nature of knowledge (but, as we shall see, especially of Brahmanic knowledge) is confirmed by the fact that India was able to do without writing for over one thousand years of its history, if we choose the earliest factual epigraphic evidence to date its introduction (with the Emperor Aśoka in the mid-third century B.C.E.), rather than uncertain speculation.[5] Even the very structure

---

involving any wider connotation of a 'man of culture'. This differs from the Romans who, more accustomed to deriving knowledge from written texts (first and foremost Greek texts), introduce a clear opposition *litteratus/illitteratus*, substantially equivalent to our learned/unlearned (cf. Havelock 1982: 40-42).

[3] The other five obstacles are: gambling, passion for the theatre, women, laziness and somnolence. The passage is quoted in the *Smṛticandrikā* ('Moonbeam on Tradition'; cf. Kane 1974: 349, n. 844), which attributes it to the mythical sage Nārada. The verse does not appear however in the most famous work linked to his name, the *Nāradasmṛti*, or at least in the text provided in the critical edition by R. Larivière (1989). It should be borne in mind, however, that many verses in the Dharmaśāstra literature are attributed to Nārada, who is considered the authority *par excellence* in this branch of knowledge.

[4] This verse too recurs in the *Smṛticandrikā*, a vast compilation of texts of the *smṛti* genre (Kane 1974: 348, n. 2).

[5] That writing may have been introduced in India in earlier times is, on principle, not impossible, but all things considered is culturally irrelevant. The Near-Eastern civilisations show that the invention of writing may for centuries remain a 'dead letter' — to make a pun — to the extent to which, owing to its intrinsic complexity (e.g. excessive number of signs) and considerable margin of ambiguity, it necessitates recourse to a specialist for both active and passive purposes, while being restricted to highly specific ends. As Havelock has emphasised (1973: 97), the invention of the alphabet is quite different from literacy, if it is true that in Greece — where the much greater simplicity of the writing system (overtaken however in simplicity and accuracy by the Indian) as compared to previous Semitic results gave rise to a highly advantageous situation — at least three centuries passed between the two moments. (Cf. Yunis 2003: 4: "Greek life and society were indeed developing, but they did so, as they had previously, primarily without writing"). The procedures and cultural consequences of introducing writing in the Greek world have been the subject, after the fundamental work of Havelock, of many specific studies that enrich (and, at least in part, render problematic) the over-terse lines of its architecture (see, among the most noteworthy recent contributions, Yunis 2003, already mentioned.).

of the language sciences, which from time immemorial assist Vedic knowledge and qualitatively rank so highly that they cannot be compared to the vacillating and confused Graeco-Latin language sciences, assumes an object made up of sounds (not letters!), whence the very imperfect equivalence of the Sanskrit term *vyākaraṇa* with the 'grammar' of the classical world (*grammatikḗ* [*téchnē*], *grammatica*) which indeed dealt first and foremost with *grámmata*, 'letters'.[6]

However, let us continue with al-Bīrūnī's highly interesting text:

> This is the reason why, not long before our time [around the year 1000], Vasukra, a native of Kashmir, a famous brahmin, did on his own account undertake the task of explaining the Veda and committing it to writing. He took upon himself a task from which everybody else would have recoiled, but he carried it out because he was afraid that the Veda might be forgotten and entirely vanish from the memory of men, since he observed that the characters of men grew worse and worse, and that they did not care much for virtue, nor even for duty. (cf. Sachau 1910: I, 126-127)

Writing was thus attained out of painful necessity, but without the manuscript ever really replacing oral instruction. Living knowledge coagulates in the written text, like blood on a sheet of paper, or on a leaf. I refer to the legend of the transmission of one of the cornerstones of grammatical literature, the *Mahābhaṣya* ('Great Commentary') that Patañjali devoted to the *sūtra*s of Pāṇini and the *vārttika*s of Kātyāyana. Gauḍapāda, in the shape of a demon avid for human flesh, the ultimate repository of Patañjali's teaching, is ready to recite

[6] Even in the Sanskrit vocabulary, at least one term with the same ambiguity managed to insinuate itself: *akṣara* (originally 'indestructible'), which can mean 'phoneme', 'syllable' or 'grapheme'. On the other hand, Aristotle also appears to use *grámma* to refer to the phoneme, not merely to its graphic representation (Havelock 1982: 48). A separate question, albeit worthy at least of a mention, is whether the breakdown of language into minimal units of sound (the phonemes) is, as it were, not a primary operation, but usually linked to preparatory work for the construction of writing (at least this is what the Greek example would suggest).

it, but only once and without interruptions, to Candraśarman, the only one to have demonstrated his suitability by answering a difficult grammatical question that had cost the life of all his predecessors. Fearing to forget the Great Commentary,[7] Candraśarman transcribed it word by word, using as support the leaves of a tree and, as ink, his own blood. A very similar example comes from the most celebrated *Kathāsaritsāgara* ('Ocean of the Rivers of Stories'), a masterpiece of Indian narrative, in the eighth 'wave' of the first book, which narrates the antecedents that will gradually lead to the *Kathāsaritsāgara* text in its current form.

> On the invitation of Guṇāḍhya, Kanakabhūti thus narrated in his own tongue that divine story that comprises seven stories, while Guṇāḍhya, using the same tongue [*paiśācī*], in seven years wrote it down, enclosing it in seven hundred thousand *grantha*s [verses of 32 syllables]. So that the Vidyādharas [heavenly spirits] should not take his composition away, for lack of ink that great poet wrote it in the forest with his own blood.

But King Satavāhana, to whom the text was presented, was anything but delighted. Too long, composed in an inferior dialect, and what's more, written in blood! The story continues with the author deciding to get rid of his despised work, sorrowfully burning the leaves one by one, but not without reading them for one last time to the wild animals, who listen, their eyes full of tears, until... Another example of writing in blood is recorded in the *Rājataraṅgiṇī* ('Wave of the Kings') by Kalhaṇa (IV.575-577), connected with the supreme act of affectionate devotion of a minister who immolates himself to save his king.[8]

---

[7] According to one of the final verses (v. 485) of the second section of Bhartṛhari's *Vākyapadīya*, the subject of many conflicting interpretations, the (oral) tradition of the science of grammar (or rather, in particular, of the Great Commentary) had been discontinued, but survived, in the south of India, only in written form. Thus writing alone is insufficient to make a tradition live, but at the same time can prevent its total disappearance.

[8] I wish to thank Fabrizia Baldissera for pointing this out to me.

Even within the esoteric and consequently markedly oral universe of Tantrism, which only allows transmission of knowledge 'from mouth to ear', there is room for writing down, according to the testimony of the Śaiva Madhurāja. Coming from distant Tamil Nadu to meet the great Abhinavagupta, he leaves us four verses that provide a snapshot of a teaching session of a master to his disciples. In an atmosphere of great elegance and refined detachment more suited to a Renaissance prince than a bony ascetic, the master speaks, his discourse blended, from time to time, with the notes of the lute he holds in his hands. His disciples, starting from the chief of these, Kṣemarāja, seated at his feet, listen intently, but they are also portrayed in the act of taking notes in writing of what the master is saying.[9] Beside this 'vital' aspect of writing, a support for the always irreplaceable oral teaching, India is also familiar with a deadly, sinister aspect, which Charles Malamoud has highlighted, most effectively albeit a little too exclusively, in one of his fine essays (*Noirceur de l'écriture*, 2002: 127-149).

> [...] writing is dangerous. Its dangers do not lie merely in its deficiencies: they also come from the link established between the act of writing and writing, on the one hand, and royal power on the other, since its model is the inexorable royalty of Yama and, by extension, the power of the creditor and of the scribe at his service. [...] Writing, a line of writing, becomes the metaphor for the insuperable limits fixed by fate, time or death [...]. What is fearsome in writing is not that it is a dead letter, but that it is death-bringing [...] [10]

---

[9] v. 2 *āsīnaḥ kṣemarājaprabhṛtibhir akhilaiḥ sevitaḥ śiṣyavargaiḥ pādopānte niṣaṇṇair avahitahṛdayair uktam uktaṃ likhadbhiḥ [...]*. The verses of Madhurāja, known as *Dhyanaślokāḥ*, have been edited and translated by K.Ch. Pandey 1963: 21-22, 738.

[10] "[...] l'écriture est redoutable. Ses dangers ne tiennent pas seulement à ses insuffisances; ils proviennent aussi du lien qui s'est instauré entre le geste d'écrire et l'écrit, d'une part, et le pouvoir royal, d'autre part, en tant qu'il a pour model l'inexorable royauté de Yama et, par extension, le pouvoir du créancier et du scribe qui est à son service. [...] L'écriture, la ligne d'écriture, devient la métaphore

Brahmanic texts say little about reading and writing, with reluctance as it were, giving the impression of a marginal and underrated reality. Even myth neglects writing,[11] while on the contrary it holds speech in the highest esteem, even raising it to the rank of a creatrix deity (Vāc). Even in this case, however, as in many other examples of the presentation of socio-cultural or religious facts and conduct on the part of the prescriptive texts produced by the Brahmanic élite, one suspects that in actual fact things were rather different from the way they are presented by Brahmanic wishful thinking, in an attempt to keep them under their own control.

Providing us with clues for reflection is, by way of example, the dialogue and polemic nature of much of the philosophical literature of classical India. Starting from the idea that knowledge is only transmitted in a direct line, by direct contact with the master and always within a specific tradition, one may wonder how a single author can be so well-informed about the positions of the rival schools he criticises, since it is highly improbable that he learned about them

des limites infranchissables fixées par le destin, le temps ou la mort [...]. Ce qui effraie dans l'écriture ce n'est pas qu'elle soit lettre morte, c'est qu'elle soit mortifère [...]" (Malamoud 2002: 142). F. Baldissera (1999-2000: 154-159) has also dwelt effectively on the sinister aspect of writing in an article referring particularly to a few passages of the *Narmamālā* by Kṣemendra: p. 155, v. 16, "To him whose ink and pen are like the goddess Kālī who destroys everything [...]"; p. 156, v. 29, "Kālī melted into liquid and is still present in the guise of ink. Just as the Gaṅgā bestows Heaven, this liquid bestows hell." The blackness that may characterise the world of writing in India may have its antithesis, as we have seen above, in the red of the blood of the person who decides to produce the writing using the most intimate and most precious of his vital fluids. Writing is thus also the will to live (or even, as in the passage of the *Rājataraṅgiṇī* quoted above, to offer life generously), to survive, refusal of the deadly human drift toward oblivion. It seems therefore that it is not so much writing in itself that is vituperated as a certain application of it, of which the substance used for writing becomes the emblem (here, the blackness of the ink). Auspicious substances may also be used however, such as saffron, or sandalwood paste, their light colour reflecting, on the contrary, the ethically or ritually pure context in which the writing takes place (F. Baldissera, personal communication).

[11] The invention of writing is attributed to the god Brahmā, concerned that everything slipped rapidly from man's memory (cf. the passage from the *Nāradasmṛti*, quoted above).

from any direct frequentation of the rival masters. A solution might be sought in a phenomenon that is highly characteristic of Indian culture, encountered from the very earliest times, which should certainly not be undervalued: the custom of public debate (*śāstrārtha*) on philosophical, religious, or even scientific themes (Solomon 1976-78: 833-875). Convened by the sovereign, scholars belonging to the most disparate schools presented their doctrines and attempted to overcome those of their adversaries, sometimes placing even their own lives at stake. The frequency, as well as the level, of these philosophical jousts doubtless rendered them a valuable occasion for divulging knowledge outside the circles that had produced it. This, however, does not seem sufficient to explain the often vast knowledge of opponents' positions, nor do the frequent textual quotations, largely found in the philosophical literature (Bronkhorst 2002: 812-820). Although it is likely that the follower of a certain school was bound to memorise his 'own' texts, it is less probable that he exercised his art of memory on texts that he did not agree with, or even despised. Moreover, although this could be held of authors focusing on a specific rival school, what should we say of those who practised the doxographic genre, which requires a very wide range of textual competence, often — as in the *Sarvadarśanasaṃgraha* — providing accurate literal quotations? The only plausible answer is that manuscripts circulated much more widely than the prescriptive texts would have us believe, as also confirmed by the enormous quantity of Indian manuscripts that have come down to us, despite the perishability of their material (birch bark, palm-leaves and paper), exposed to the perils of the climate and all kinds of insects and other voracious creatures (including mankind).

Laboriously, and at a relatively late period, the manuscript was finally fully accepted on the Indian cultural scene. An unequivocal testimony to the end of its quarantine is provided by a lapidary phrase by the learned Nīlakaṇṭha in his *Dānamayūkha* (sixteenth century): "Thus, the gift of knowledge may occur in three different ways: through the gift of manuscripts, the gift of divine images, and teaching" (*evaṃ trividhaṃ vidyādānam — pustakadānaṃ pratimādānam adhyāpanaṃ ceti*; quoted in Sarma 1991: 20).[12] However, for some centuries testimonies had already been appearing of the regular and widespread use of writing. Rājaśekhara (tenth century) in the *Kāvyamīmāṃsā* ('Investigation into Ornate Literature') includes a scribe and writing necessities as an essential part of the poet's equipment,[13] rules are established for copyists, techniques and materials are codified;[14] the quality of the inks of the ultra-oral India are praised throughout Asia.

That there is something behind this over-exhibited discrediting of written texts in the Brahmanic tradition can be intuited from the considerably different attitude of two other major Indian traditions, which, it should be emphasised once again, spring from the same humus and share many of the cultural and spiritual assumptions of Brahmanic tradition: Buddhism and Jainism. Even the followers of the Buddha and Mahāvīra are convinced of the centrality of a direct relationship with a master, but this does not render them quite so suspicious of manuscripts, whose role is important in the propagation of the Dharma, which the Jains but more especially the Buddhists consider as their prime task. Manuscripts can travel, reach remote outposts, act as a potential store of wisdom while awaiting a reader who can make them live, or a teacher who recites and comments on

---

[12] The gift of knowledge (*vidyādāna*) is increasingly associated with the offering of a manuscript and with the cult dedicated to it. Sometimes the sacred texts themselves define the criteria with which they must be transferred to manuscript form, on how the material support must be prepared, what writing must be used, what style (see the passages of the *Śivadharmottara* collected in Ganesan-Barois 2003: 256).

[13] In this connection, see Chapter X (*kavicaryā rājacaryā ca*, 'Conduct of the Poet and Conduct of the King'); Stchoupak-Renou 1946: 144-162. Among the multitude of evidence of the regular use of manuscripts for the diffusion of — in this case philosophical — works, see, for example, the episode quoted above (p. 165, n. 32) concerning Dharmakīrti (of course, a Buddhist) and his just completed *Pramāṇavārttika*.

[14] As far as I know, this is most fully dealt with by the *Kṛtyakalpataru*, a late compilation of normative texts, which refer back to secondary (and later) scriptures, such as the *Devīkālottara-āgama* and the *Nandi-purāṇa* (Sarma 1991).

them, or simply remain, as a cult object, a dumb witness to the teaching of the Buddha or Mahāvīra. Although a pan-Indian saying, found in all Sanskrit manuals for beginners, warns that "Knowledge written in a book is neither more nor less than wealth in another's hands",[15] the importance of manuscripts, if only for utilitarian purposes, was gradually accepted even by the Brahmanic world. Within certain limits, the manuscript ensures the work's survival ("Since in man's mind everything is cancelled within six months, in ancient times the Lord created letters to write down on leaves", says a frequently quoted anonymous verse).[16] "Within certain limits" means that, given the perishability of its material support, the work survives only if it is periodically re-copied, and this only occurs if the work is still topical in the present (and, may we add, in the orality of the present?). A parallel history of Indian literature could be its lost works, sometimes of enormous intrinsic — or, we might say, historical — importance, which nonetheless were rapidly eclipsed by more compact and less problematic works. A typical example is the great *Saṃgraha* by Vyāḍi, an important work of grammatical literature (prior to the *Mahābhāṣya*): of its one hundred thousand verses dealing with, according to the testimony of Bhartṛhari's *Mahābhāṣya-ṭīkā*, 14,000 different subjects, all that has survived are a few meagre quotations. The torrent, i.e. the manuscript, says Kālidāsa's *Raghuvaṃśa*, is even so a way of entering the sea of learning proper[17] which, first and foremost, remains oral. In the end, remarks Abhinavagupta, even a letter must possess some special power, seeing that it is able to trigger for us the phoneme it represents:

---

[15] Transposed to modern times, it makes one think of the illusory sense of 'possession' that for example the entire Pāli canon contained on the slim surface of a CD-Rom can give...

[16] The verse appears in various digests, such as the *Vyavahāranirṇaya* and the *Vyavahāraprakāśa* (cf. Murthy 1996: 18, n. 15; Salomon 1998: 8, n. 3).

[17] *Raghuvaṃśa* III.28: *liper yathāvad grahaṇena vāṅmayaṃ nadīmukheneva samudram āviśet* (quoted in Murthy 1996: 18, n. 16).

> We know that some things have particular excellence, such as those, among statues, with four arms, three eyes, fat, thin, etc., and among substances, wine, alcoholic beverages and so on. By all these things we are made to reach the real level to which they refer; and the same occurs with written phonemes, which allow the reader to reach the true phonemes.
>
> (*Paratriṃśikāvivaraṇa* p. 268; cf. Gnoli 1985: 153)

Although, we may imagine, intimately convinced as he was of the primacy of orality, Abhinavagupta would not be ready to underwrite the verdict of *anṛta* ('unreal, false') that Śaṅkara, a couple of centuries earlier, had pronounced against letters — and this not only for the different ontological option that makes him exclude any radical unreality or falseness of the manifest world. Beside its basic 'reality', the grapheme has, says Abhinavagupta, its own special 'excellence' (*utkarṣabhāgitvam*). Within the Vedāntic tradition, it was Rāmānuja who replied to Śaṅkara directly, contesting the unreal nature of writing: it is exactly because writing is itself real that it leads to recognition of the real sound (Malamoud 2002: 128). If we wish to let a third voice be heard, that of Abhinavagupta, in the debate outlined by Malamoud, we could contribute a verse from the *Mālinīvijayavārttika* ('Gloss on the Victory of the Garlanded One'; II.122):

> Just as children, thanks to letters, are introduced vividly to the reality of phonemes, in the same way men of weak intellect are able to penetrate by degrees, thanks to the various means [ritual and Yoga practices, etc], to supreme reality.

Let us, however, return for a moment to the verse just quoted ("Since in man's mind everything is cancelled..."). It is frequently associated with another verse: "If Brahmā had not created writing — the best of eyes —, the progress of the things of this world would not have been so satisfactory". Now, both verses are associated with the name of the sage Nārada and are usually taken to testify to the increasing value of writing in the Indian world (Murthy 1996: 12; Salomon 1998: 8, n. 3), except that, as we have seen, Nārada is also considered the author of the two pitiless condemnations of the written text given above (p. 198). The contradiction only becomes apparent if we identify the context in which the said verses appear. I have only been able to do so for the first of the initial couple, but the result is already rather significant. It was quoted by Asahāya in commenting on verse I.65 of the *Nāradasmṛti*, which examines the proofs accepted in jurisprudence: "The written document, direct witnesses and effective possession". The commentary opens with the praise of writing (*likhitapraśaṃsā*), adducing the said verse for the purpose. At this point, we cannot but notice a considerable imbalance in appraisal: writing is accepted and even praised (by the same brahmins on whom almost all the literature of the Dharmaśāstra depends) for practical and administrative ends, to which the 'victims' may associate those deadly nuances highlighted by Malamoud; it is condemned and even derided (by the brahmins), if taken as a source of higher 'knowledge'.

Brahmanic resistance to writing, in this second dimension, was for long centuries insuperable solely with regard to the Veda which, as al-Bīrūnī also noted, was given a written form only many centuries after the outset of the Common Era (well-known are the hostile reactions of more traditionalist environments to the printing of the *editio princeps* of the *Ṛgveda* by Max Müller). At the same time, in the case of the Veda, there existed — and still survives — an extraordinary memorization technique ensuring — *pace* al-Bīrūnī — their transmission from generation to generation in the most perfect manner and much more reliable than any writing.

Contradictory as it is, the data so far presented necessitates some attempt at interpretation. Certainly, India has never assigned any position of absolute prestige to the manuscript, or to writing in general (an indirect proof is the almost complete absence of any calligraphic art, such as that expressed in Islamic civilisation),[18] always giving preference to the living word uttered by that god-on-earth, the teacher. The exaltation of orality, however, at the levels found in Brahmanic India, reveals that its nature is, as it were, not primary, i.e. instrumental to the grandiose and refined cultural and social control strategy put into effect by the Brahmanic élite. The brahmins, numerically overwhelmed by their (cultural) subjects, were bound to create a rigidly pyramidal structure, continually restating, through the need for oral — and hence personal — reception of Vedic knowledge, their irreplaceable function. Like toy Chinese boxes, orality too has its hierarchies in the end, if one considers that learning the Vedic texts is not necessarily accompanied by learning their meaning. While this is true of Vedic schools today, even many centuries prior to the Common Era various levels of incomprehension of meaning were spoken of, thus giving rise to a thousand-year debate as to whether or not the Veda had any meaning, in an absolute sense.[19]

Let us once more hear what al-Bīrūnī has to say on the subject:

> The brahmins recite the Veda without understanding its meaning, and in the same way they learn it by heart, the one receiving it from the other. Only a few of them learn its explanation, and still smaller is the number of those who master the contents of the Veda and their interpretation to such a degree as to be able to hold a theological disputation. The brahmins teach the Veda to the kshatriyas. The latter learn it, but are not allowed to teach it [...] (Sachau 1910: I, 125).

---

18 It seems impossible however to establish any strict connection between literacy and an increase in the value attributed to writing, on the one hand, and the presence of calligraphic art, on the other. As a rule, calligraphy makes the use of writing even more arduous and elitist (cf. Havelock 1982: 53-54).

19 This question was first raised at the time of Yāska (sixth-fifth century B.C.E.) in the *Nirukta*, the treatise that is the foundation of the science of etymology (or perhaps — still better — of semantic analysis). Yāska reports — and criticizes — the theory of Kautsa, maintaining the absolute lack of any meaning in the Veda (*Nirukta* I.15-16). The question is again raised by the *Mīmāṃsāsūtra* (I.2.31-39), around the first century B.C.E., is later developed by commentators and for centuries remains a *tópos* of fervent debate.

This deification of orality so as to hold on to a monopoly of knowledge is encountered with renewed force in the esoteric currents of Tantrism (cf. Padoux 1995). Nothing of any significance can come from solitary study of the manuscript texts or from reading the *mantra*s appearing in them: they lose their force, or — as Śaiva masters say literally — their 'virility' (*vīrya*).

> The basic rule of it [the rite] is as follows, that the mantric essence must not be revealed by the master to the disciple in writing, and that especially in our doctrines, which are superior to all others. The *mantras* are made of phonemes and these of consciousness. They may be transmitted to the disciple only if unseparated from the master's awareness. Written *mantras* however lack any force, being created by imagination [by us, and hence unreal]. Owing to convention [which obfuscates them], their [natural] radiance is not manifested by books.
>
> (*Tantrāloka* XXVI.20-23; cf. Gnoli 1999: 494-495)

This position, which we may term a principle, albeit remaining in the background, is the subject of distinctions and subtle nuances, which may demonstrate that we are progressively distancing ourselves from the crux of Brahmanic control. Furthermore, the texts in question belong to a time (ninth-tenth century C.E.) in which writing had already achieved its role in Indian civilisation. Immediately after bluntly stating the general principle (in the above text), on the basis of the authority of one of the main Trika scriptures, the *Siddhayogeśvarīmata*, Abhinavagupta half-closes the door to any solitary learning through a *tête-à-tête* between the pupil and the manuscript. This, he says, is not impossible, except that it requires a pupil endowed by god with special grace, which in extremely rare cases allows perfect masters to spring up, independently of any discipline or even any spiritual tradition. Not infrequently, moreover, sacred texts are revealed by God, already in written form, such as, for example, the already-mentioned *Śivasūtra*, 'discovered' by the sage Vasugupta following precise instructions given to him by Śiva in a dream, engraved on a rock-face of the Mahādeva mountain in Kashmir. The written letter thus has its own dignity, even its own power, which in certain cases goes well beyond a mere ancillary status to the sound it represents. An example of this can be found in the well-known ritual practice of the *mantranyāsa* the 'imposition of the *mantra*', consisting not only of its recitation, but of placing the written letters corresponding to the various parts of the pupil's body (Padoux 1980). Consequently I feel I cannot agree with what Malamoud says on the matter in the already quoted study:

> A token — negative though it be — of the little love felt for writing is [...] the absence of any reflection concerning the symbolism or aesthetics of the form of letters. [...] Especially lacking is any speculation on the evocative power of each letter as an object perceived by the eye [...]
> (Malamoud 1992: 143) [20]

The enigmatic passage of the *Tantrasadbhāva* (ancient Trika scripture, still unpublished, but available in manuscript form) quoted by Kṣemarāja in his commentary on the *Śivasūtra* shows a very different attitude, devoting itself to describing the gradual development of the grapheme A (Torella 1999b: 88-90). The grapheme A is identified with the supreme power Kuṇḍalinī. Śiva is in turn identified with the first phoneme, i.e. A: the supreme power constitutes the 'body' of Śiva, just as the grapheme A constitutes the 'body' of the phoneme A. Other details are added by the verse that in the manuscripts of the *Tantrasadbhāva* immediately follows the passage quoted by Kṣemarāja: "Raudrī is the head, Vāmā is the mouth, Ambikā is the arm, Jyeṣṭhā is the weapon. [...]", in other words, the four goddesses are made to match the four essential elements of graphic sign A (Torella 1999b: 88-89, n. 133). Yet again, phoneme E in *śaiva* esoteric speculation is called *trikoṇabīja* ('triangular seed') because reference

[20] "Un indice, négatif il est vrai, du peu d'amour pour l'écriture est [...] l'absence d'une réflexion qui porterait sur le symbolisme ou l'esthétique de la forme des lettres. [...] Surtout font défaut une spéculation sur le pouvoir évocateur de chaque lettre en tant qu'elle est un objet perçu par l'œil [...]"

is made to the shape of grapheme E in the script in which these Tantras were penned, the Kashmiri *śāradā*. Other examples could easily be found.

The different valuation of the manuscript by the followers of the Buddha and Mahāvīra (to which we have only been able to allude here)[21] matches the transition from the closed world of Brahmanism to the open one of the Buddhists and Jains, committed not to withholding knowledge for the purpose of power, but to spreading it as widely as possible, engaging in a work of proselytism that was intrinsically foreign to Brahmanism. The manuscript forms an integral part of such dynamics.[22]

---

[21] We should at least remember that the writing down of the Buddhist canon in the first century B.C.E. appears to have taken place, not as a natural development, but as the result of a terrible famine that devastated India at that time, giving rise to the fear that the Dharma might be forgotten. This attitude of great open-mindedness toward the manuscript, culminating in its sacralization as a source of spiritual merit first for the writer, then for the reader and preserver, was cultivated especially by Mahāyāna Buddhism, in which the universalistic inspiration and impetus toward proselytism became more marked than in primitive Buddhism.

[22] Consequently, as an epiphenomenon, the only manuscripts to develop some form of calligraphic art on the subcontinent were those of the Buddhists and Jains.

2. From the Sarvadarśanasaṃgraha: the Pratyabhijñā-Darśana [23]

Then there are other Śaivas who, dissatisfied with the system that we have just examined [24] (finding it untenable that it considers as causes inert realities, which lack any capacity to set up intentional relations — *apekṣā*), provide a different conception, maintaining that the creation of everything is due exclusively to the will of the Supreme Lord (*parameśvara*). The Supreme Lord — whose coinciding with the inner self is demonstrated by direct personal experience, by reason and by the Scriptures — has a simultaneous relation of identity and difference (*bhedābheda*) with the multiple forms of knowledge, of the knowable, etc.; He is absolutely free — freedom (*svātantrya*) meaning non-dependency on anything; He makes phenomenal realities appear within Himself, like reflections in a mirror.

These Śaivas, doing away with all the stock-in-trade of laborious efforts consisting of external and inner practices, breathing control and so on, propose a way to liberation or perfection of an inferior kind, accessible to everyone, consisting of a pure and simple act of 'recognition' (*pratyabhijñā*). They refer to the doctrine of Pratyabhijñā.

An expert on Pratyabhijñā said the following on the texts on which this school is based: "The corpus of authoritative texts of Pratyabhijñā comprises the five commentaries on the treatise, meaning the *sūtra*, the *vṛtti*, the *vivṛti* and the two *vimarśinīs*, the long one and the short".[25] The first verse [of the *Īśvarapratyabhijñā-kārikā*, ĪPK]

---

[23] Abridged version and without philological appendices of Torella 1979.

[24] The Śaivadarśana, which presents the doctrines of another school of Tantric Śaivism: the dualist Śaivasiddhānta.

[25] The verse is taken from the *Śāstraparāmarśa* (v. 4) by Madhurāja Yogin (cf. Pandey 1963:147). The treatise (*prakaraṇa*) is the *Śivadṛṣṭi* by Somānanda, which lays the basis of Pratyabhijñā. The *sūtra* is the *Īśvarapratyabhijñā-kārikā* (ĪPK) by

goes like this: "After having in some way (*kathaṃcid*) attained (*āsādya*) the status of servant (*dāsyam*) of the Supreme Lord and wishing to offer assistance (*upakāram*) also (*api*) to the whole of mankind (*janasya*), I shall make possible the awakening (*upapādayāmi*) of the recognition of the Lord (*tatpratyabhijñām*), which brings about the achievement of all success (*samastasampatsamavāptihetum*)" (cf. Torella 2002: 85).[26]

The word *kathaṃcit* ('in some way, in an indefinable way') means "thanks to devotion to the lotus-feet of a master united with Parameśvara himself". The word *āsādya* — in which *ā-* has the meaning of 'completely, perfectly' — means "having rendered [the status of servant of Maheśvara] freely, fully, accessible to one's direct experience". This indicates that the author, having personally known what was to be known, deems himself qualified to compose a text for others. If it were not so, such a work would be merely a deceit. The Blessed One, Maheśvara, is ultimately light-bliss-unbounded freedom; and it is only by virtue of a crumb of his sovereignty that [also other] entities such as Viṣṇu or Brahmā — charged to operate on the level of the great *māyā*, despite being by their own nature beyond *māyā* — are sovereign. By *dāsa* ('servant') is meant "him to whom all is granted (*dīyate*) by the Lord, according to his desires"; he is a receptacle of the essential freedom of the Supreme Lord — this is the meaning. The word *jana* ('man, mankind') indicates that there is no restriction regarding those to whom this teaching is directed, in the sense that no special qualification is required of followers. Indeed, all indistinctly obtain the supreme fruit, those in whom their own nature is manifest, since it is this very mani-

Utpaladeva, the *vṛtti* and the *vivṛti* (also known as *ṭīkā*) are the two commentaries on the ĪPK composed by Utpaladeva himself. The *laghu-vimarśinī* ('short consideration') is the commentary by Abhinavagupta on the ĪPK (*Īśvarapratyabhijñā-vimarśinī*, ĪPV) and the *bṛhad-vimarśinī* ('extended consideration') is his commentary on Utpaladeva's *vivṛti* (*Īśvarapratyabhijñā-vivṛtivimarśinī*, ĪPVV).

[26] Here I have kept to the most immediate meaning of the verse. Abhinavagupta's interpretation, given almost fully in the text, is, on the contrary, much more complex and contrived.

festation that, in its very self, is the absolute fruit. Thus teaches the blessed Somānandanātha, the master of the masters (*paramaguru*),[27] in the *Śivadṛṣṭi* (VII.5-6): "After knowing just once with firm understanding, thanks to a means of valid knowledge (*pramāṇa*), to revealed Scriptures or to the master's word, that the nature of Śiva [perceived within ourselves] extends to all, what need is there of bodily postures (*karaṇa*) or meditative realisation (*bhāvanā*)? Once gold has been known as such, tools (*karaṇa*) and careful observation (*bhāvanā*) should be abandoned".

The word *api*, letting it be understood that the speaker (Utpaladeva) henceforth conceives that he is in no way distinct from other men, denies that he, having attained fullness, can have any other scope than achieving the good of others. The good of others becomes the scope, because it responds exactly to the definition of 'scope'. "There is no divine curse", it has been said in this connection, "like that of having one's own good for one's scope and not the good of others". This is why Akṣapāda said, "The scope is the goal, in aiming at which one turns to action" [*Nyāyasūtra* I.1.24]. *upa-* [in *upakāram*] has the meaning of 'closeness'; the result aimed at is thus solely to lead mankind to a condition of 'closeness' with Parameśvara.[28] The word *samasta* ('all') means this: when the nature of Parameśvara is achieved, all obtainable perfections — which are actually none other than emanations from Parameśvara — are thereby obtained, just as by reaching Mount Rohaṇa [29] one comes into possession of all its gems. Once you have achieved the nature of Parameśvara, what else can you desire? As Utpaladeva says [*Śivastotrāvalī* XX.11], "Those who possess the riches of devotion, what more can they desire? And contrariwise, those who have little devotion, to what else should they aspire but that?"

---

[27] Abhinavagupta's teacher in Pratyabhijñā doctrine was Lakṣmaṇagupta, in turn the disciple of Utpaladeva, the disciple of Somānanda.

[28] To the word *upakāra* ('help') is thus artfully attributed the meaning of 'bringing (*-kāra*) close (*upa-*)'.

[29] Rohaṇa is the mythical mountain of gems.

Considering, as we have done so far, that the last two members of the compound *samasta-sampat-samavāpti-hetum* are linked by a genitive relationship, it indicates the scope; taken on the other hand as an attributive compound (*bahuvrīhi*), what is indicated is the means. In the latter case, the compound acquires the following meaning: "[recognition] which has as cause the achievement of a perfect understanding of the manifestation — i.e. of the revealing of its own true being to consciousness — of everything (*samasta*), i.e. of both external and inner realities, such as the colour blue, pleasure and so on". *Tatpratyabhijñām* means "recognition of that one", i.e. of Maheśvara; *pratyabhijñā* means "backward (*pratīpam*) knowing (*jñāna*) a thing while being in front of it (*ābhimukhyena*)". Indeed, in everyday experience recognition is the name given to knowing, which has as object something that is before us and takes place through joining together (*pratisaṃdhāna*), such as "this Caitra [who is here] is that person [whom I have met previously]". And similarly, in this context, there is, on the one hand, the Supreme Lord, endowed with infinite powers according to the authority of well-known Purāṇas and Śaiva scriptures, or by inference, and so on, and on the other, our own self made present to us [in all its fullness]: recognition is that knowledge that arises as a result of connecting the powers that are perceived in both, which makes us say, "But in actual fact I am none other than the Lord himself!"[30] It is this recognition that I 'cause to arise' (*upapādayāmi*). Here, the root *upapad-* means 'to arise'. So *upapādayāmi* [causative of *upapad*] means: "I (Utpaladeva) cause the recognition to arise — in

[30] To use Abhinavagupta's words (ĪPV, vol. I, p. 20), recognition is based on the connection (*anusaṃdhāna*, glossed by sub-commentator Bhāskarakaṇṭha as *ekīkaraṇa*, 'unification') of what is present now to our consciousness with something that has been known previously. Recognition — again according to Abhinavagupta — is knowing something on the occasion of its (re)-presentation before us: such knowledge is animated by going backward and 'connecting' a thing known previously and in the meantime forgotten with the same thing now. Recognition is an experience that, both for its vivid immediacy and because of the direct presence of its object, must be kept quite distinct from mere 'remembering'.

the sense that my activity as causal subject (*prayojaka*)[31] puts it in a condition to arise".[32]

If it is true, however, that the self shines in its essence as being identical to the Lord, what is the good of so much effort to demonstrate this recognition? The response to this observation is as follows: it is true that the self is permanently present as self-illuminating, but owing to the power of *māyā*, it manifests itself as such only in a partial manner. Recognition is consequently taught so that it can be displayed in all its fullness, and such recognition takes place once the self's peculiar powers have been brought to light, i.e. knowledge and action. The argument can be formulated as follows. The self has to be identified with Parameśvara, since it possesses the powers of knowledge and action; he who knows and acts with regard to a certain thing is lord with respect to that thing, just as in the case of the Lord, universally known, or a king. So the self is recognised as (potentially) omniscient and omnipotent and thus it is admissible to say "I am the Lord".

Here, recourse to the five-member syllogism is because the follower of Pratyabhijñā recognises as valid, within the sphere of

---

[31] *Prayojaka* (lit. 'he who prompts') is technically called the subject of the causative phrase, the one which 'prompts' the *prayojya*, 'he who is prompted', i.e. he whose action is prompted by the *prayojaka*. In this case, the *prayojaka* is Utpaladeva and the recognition that arises (because Utpaladeva in composing the ĪPK acted in this sense) is the *prayojya*. As Abhinavagupta makes clear, out of the three main meanings of the causative form, this causative is of the *samarthācaraṇa* type. On the many philosophical implications of the causative, cf. Torella 1987.

[32] Abhinavagupta's interpretation of this initial stanza of the ĪPK, which already appears complex in the summary made by the author of the *Sarvadarśana-saṃgraha*, is much more so in the original text. The linearity of its syntax is broken by a set of multiple references: single and compound words are analysed and understood in several different ways and are all utilised simultaneously. The outcome is so intricate that in the end even Abhinavagupta feels the need to summarise it (ĪPV, vol. I, p. 22): "Having myself in some way achieved the status of the Lord's servant and wishing, by making other men in some way achieve recognition of the Lord, to bring them to a condition of 'closeness' to Him — a condition that is the cause of obtaining all the perfections and consists of the status as the Lord's servant —, I cause recognition of the Lord to arise, which is achieved as a result of a perfect understanding of the manifestation of the universe."

māyā, the logical procedures of Nyāya. This has all been stated by Udayākara's son [Utpaladeva], "What intelligent being could ever deny or establish the Knower and Agent, the Self, Maheśvara, established from the beginning? [33] However, since He, though being directly perceived, is not discerned for what He is because of delusion, precisely for this reason, by bringing His powers to light, recognition of Him is shown. Indeed, the foundation of insentient realities rests on the living being; knowledge and action are considered the 'life' of living beings. Of these two powers, knowledge is self-established; action, when it is manifested through a body, also becomes cognizable by others. Thanks to it, knowledge in others can be guessed." [34] (ĪPK I.1.2-5; transl. Torella 2002: 85-87). "And this intuitive light (*pratibhā*),[35] influenced by the succession of all the various objects is the knowing subject, which is consciousness devoid of succession and limit, Maheśvara" (ĪPK I.7.1; transl. Torella 2002: 136). As Somānandanātha also says (*Śivadṛṣṭi* V.105cd), "I know as being Eternal-Śiva (Sadāśiva), Sadāśiva knows as being me".

---

[33] This is the recurrent theme of the non-applicability of the *pramāṇa*s to the supreme reality: that which is the source of all light cannot be illuminated, not even by the light of the *pramāṇa*s.

[34] The power of Action enters the range of the means of knowledge only when, at the level of *māyā*, it makes its abode in bodies to manifest itself through many empirical activities. In this way, it also reveals the co-presence of cognition (knowing is implicit in action). This does not mean that knowledge is seen as an object, because this would be in contradiction to the very nature of knowledge. In actual fact, knowledge is one, it rests on the 'I', and all the various knowers, on close examination, reveal that they are in reality one. The appearance of 'other' subjects is due solely to the intervention of limiting factors (*upādhi*), such as the body, etc. Saying that knowledge is 'guessed', thus means that it cannot become the 'object' of the *pramāṇa*s. The same can be said for action (cf. ĪPV, vol. I, pp. 45-49).

[35] The coming to light, the manifestation of the various objects, which the limited subject regards as separate and independent (objective) entities, has its centre of gravity in the 'I'. The very expression "the pot appears, is manifest" in itself means "the pot appears to... [someone]", implicitly referring to a knower who is the true protagonist of the sentence, while the 'pot' is to be seen only as the formal subject (cf. Bhāskarakaṇṭha, vol. I, p. 348). The multiplicity of objects delineated on the substrate of the 'light' aspect of Consciousness does not modify its essential nature, just as the reflections caught by a crystal do not sully its purity.

This is also stated at the end of the section on Knowledge (Jñānādhikāra) "On the basis of what has been said, without a unity of cognitions, ordinary worldy activity would not be possible. It is on the unity of light that the unity of the various cognitions is based and this unitary light is precisely the one knowing subject. This has been definitively established. And precisely this knowing subject is Maheśvara, insofar as He is characterised by indefectible reflective awareness. In fact, in God this awareness is pure knowledge and action." (ĪPK I.8.10-11; transl. Torella 2002: 152). These verses have been commented on by Abhinavagupta. That the whole body of objective reality derives its light from the majesty of the light of Consciousness is affirmed by the Revelation: "The All shines solely in relation to the shining of Him. This whole universe shines by virtue of His light".[36] Indeed, although the manifestation (lit. the 'light') of objective reality is differentiated, this is so because the light is variously coloured by the multiplicity of the objects, being distinguished as yellow 'light', blue 'light', and so on. In any absolute sense, however, the light, lacking any contractions in determined spatial-temporal forms, is in itself beyond all differentiation. And it is this very light that, having consciousness as its essence, constitutes the knower: "The self is consciousness", as we read in the *Śivasūtra* (I.1; cf. Torella 1999b: 51-55). He is absolute Lord, or in other words, he has consciousness (*cit*) as its essence, is unlimited reflective awareness, independent of any thing, solely permeated by beatitude. And this reflective awareness 'I' consists solely of pure, absolute knowledge-action: knowledge is its being light; action its creating the world by itself.[37] This is spoken of in the section devoted

---

[36] This is the second half of a verse from the *Kaṭha Upaniṣad* (II.2.15), which also recurs in the *Muṇḍaka* (II.2. 11) and in the *Śvetāśvatara* (VI. 14). The first half reads: "There the sun does not shine, nor the moon, nor the stars, neither do these lamps shine and not even this fire".

[37] Or, in the words of Abhinavagupta (ĪPV, vol. I, p. 338): "Knowledge is the 'light' aspect (*prakāśa*), action is the 'reflective awareness' aspect (*vimarśa*) whose essence is freedom with regard to knowledge itself: reflective awareness' is the interiorisation of light."

to Action (Kriyādhikāra): "And thus, His power being infinite, He makes those things manifest thanks to His volition: and this constitutes His activity, His being creator." (ĪPK II.4.1; transl. Torella 2002: 175). And also in the conclusion: "Therefore, causality, agency, action are nothing but the will of Him who wishes to appear in the form of the universe, in the various manifestations of jar, cloth and so on (II.4.21; transl. Torella 2002: 187).

As stated by the verse that says, "Also the relation of cause and effect conceived of as 'there being this, this other is produced' (*asmin satīdaṃ bhavati*) is not admissible for realities that are insentient and as such incapable of 'requiring' (*apekṣā°*)" (II.4.14; transl. Torella 2002: 183). A cause cannot be a non-sentient reality,[38] as neither can a conscious subject that is not the Lord Himself. As a consequence, what constitutes that activity that increasingly pours forth, or is the creator of all, is solely the will of the free and

[38] As we see in the ĪPK, Buddhists call causality the link that binds two entities, the second of which is produced when the first is present. This is the conception taught by the Buddha himself — and developed by the Abhidharma schools — with the formula *asmin sati idaṃ bhavati*, which means that the appearing of every reality is closely tied to the previous presence of another, without thereby investing the preceding reality with the status of efficient cause personally producing the rise of the other. This antecedent-consequent relationship — says the ĪPV — matches that of *prayojaka-prayojya* (cf. p. 216, n. 31): each of the two elements needs ('rests on') the other. As we see in the formulation of the causal relationship referred to in the stanza (*asmin sati idam asti*), in *asmin sati* ('this being here') there is a kind of forward imbalance, just as in *idam asti* ('this is produced') there is a backward imbalance. The relationship that ties the two elements of the causal relation together in this way is called *apekṣā*. What is consequently assumed is the possibility of entering into reciprocal relations, a possibility that is precluded to inert realities. This relational capacity belongs only to the sentient subject, of which it is the very essence. Only the subject is capable of connecting (*anusaṃdhāna*) with things and of connecting the things to each other on the basis of his own consciousness. Whatever is not sentient is excluded from such a dynamic, and is confined solely within itself; and how can what is confined solely within itself 'move' toward the other? In short, how can it bind itself in an *apekṣā* relationship with other entities? It follows that the causal relationship can only be actuated by the conscious subject, and in any final analysis all causality depends on and moves in the latter. These themes are analysed in Torella 2002: 183-184.

blessed Maheśvara, who desires to manifest Himself in the thousand forms of activity of becoming (birth, permanence, etc.) with all the various differentiations.

In support of the theory that the world was created by virtue only of will, a very clear example is provided: "The various things, jar, etc. — lasting and able to fulfil the functions that are proper to them — may also be produced by virtue of the volition of the yogins alone, without the need for clay or seed" (II.4.10; transl. Torella 2002: 179). If just the clay and so on were truly causes with regard to a pot [thus argues the Pratyabhijñā follower], then how should we explain that a pot may be also produced by the sole will of the yogin? To those who would reply saying that the pot or shoot, etc., produced by the clay or seed are one thing, and that these same entities produced by the will of the yogin are another, we should remark that all accept that different groups of factors produce different effects.[39] Then there are some who, deeming that a pot or other things cannot be produced without a material cause, maintain that the yogin brings together the single atoms, operating on them with his will. To them too, we should point out the implications of what they affirm, i.e. that by not admitting, as they do, that the cause-effect relationship in the case of the yogin may take different forms from the ordinary, then each of the factors that in everyday experience contribute to cause a certain thing — such as clay, a wheel, a stick, etc. for a pot, or the union of a man and woman, etc., for a body — are implicitly to be considered as equally necessary. Thus, we reply, can you explain the fact that a pot or a body is indeed made to exist immediately by the will of the yogin? Any aporia collapses, however, once we consider that what is manifested in these various forms is always and only the Blessed

[39] This last observation constitutes, for the first time, a substantial alteration of the ĪPV text, followed step by step so far. Abhinavagupta's conclusions are of a totally different kind: "Between the two sets of objects [those produced by ordinary means and those produced by the will of the yogin] there is no difference, since the subject does not take cognizance of them in a differentiated manner" (ĪPV vol. II, p. 154).

One, the Glorious, the Great God — the conscious being *par excellence* —, in his absolute freedom to conform to or transgress the laws of necessity.[40] This is why Vasugupta[41] said, "Praise be to the God of the trident, worthy of praise for His art, who, doing away with material causes and without any wall acting as substrate, projects the spectacle of the world".

In reply to those who ask how the inner self, while not being different from Parameśvara, comes to be involved in *saṃsāra*, in the section devoted to Revelation (Āgamādhikāra), we read: "This knower blinded by *māyā*, bound by *karma* is immersed in *saṃsāra*; but once Science (*vidyā*) has made him recognize his own nature as Lord, then, his essence being solely consciousness, he is called 'liberated'" (ĪPK III.2.2; transl. Torella 2002: 197). Those then who ask, since the knowable is essentially none other than the knower, what difference there is between the enslaved and the liberated being with regard to the knowable, will find an answer in the section devoted to the Summary of Principles (Tattvasaṃgrahādhikāra): "The liberated soul looks at 'common' cognizable reality as being undifferentiated from himself, like the Supreme Lord; the bound soul, on the contrary, looks at it as absolutely differentiated" (ĪPK IV.13; transl. Torella 2002: 217).[42]

But [someone may object] if the nature of the Supreme Lord is already innate in the self, then there is no point in trying to recognise it. The seed, even without being 'recognised', produces the

[40] If therefore this same necessity that governs everyday experience is not an absolute fact but, like all reality, is nothing but one of the ways in which the freedom of Consciousness is manifested, one need not wonder that those who move on a level beyond the world (the yogins) are, like the Lord, free to conform to it or transgress it.

[41] The author of the *Sarvadarśanasaṃgraha* believes he can identify the *pūrvaguru*, to which the ĪPV generically attributes this quotation, in Vasugupta. In actual fact, the verse quoted comes from the *Stavacintāmaṇi* (v. 9) by Bhaṭṭa Nārāyaṇa.

[42] Common reality (*sādhāraṇa*) is what is experienced by all subjects: 'common' since it is distinct from that experienced only by certain subjects under certain anomalous conditions (hallucinations, defects of the senses, etc.), which is thus termed *asādhāraṇa* (cf. ĪPV, vol. II, p. 265). The liberated subject will regard knowable reality as though it were his own body (ĪPK III.2.3, etc.).

shoot just the same; it suffices that all the concomitant causes are operative. That being so, why insist so much on recognition of the self? To this hypothetical objector, the Pratyabhijñā follower responds thus. Hear, then, this secret doctrine! There are two sorts of causal efficiency (*arthakriyā*): one — the one that makes the bud to shoot, etc. — is external; the other's essence is 'wondrous enjoyment' (*camatkāra*)[43] of rest in the self and is made of joy, etc. Of these two, the first does not depend on recognition, but the second does. He whose essence is wondrous enjoyment — "I am the Lord!" — produces supreme perfection or partial perfection [respectively] determining the attainment of liberation while alive, or supernatural powers: for this, recognition of one's own true nature must be sought.

But how can we maintain that this kind of causal efficiency, essentially founded on the knower, cannot occur without recognition and vice-versa? To this objection, we respond with an image. There is a fascinating young girl, increasingly enamored of a heroic character merely on hearing his many qualities praised; beside herself with passion and unable to bear the pain of separation from her beloved, she informs him of her state, sending him messages of love. But once she encounters him [without knowing who he is] as he passes fleetingly by, the sight of him, notwithstanding everything, does not penetrate her heart, because now that his qualities are not manifest he seems to be a man like any other. But when, thanks to the words of a go-between, she becomes aware of that man's celebrated qualities, she instantly enters a state of fullness. In the same way, the manifestation of the self, even though it shines constantly as Lord of all, does not determine any state of fullness

[43] The term, bound for great success in aesthetic speculation, is perhaps used for the first time in a pregnant sense by Utpaladeva himself. 'Wonder' is the modality of the enlightened subject, his taking cognizance of the self and of everything in a perpetual and infinite 'wondrous enjoyment', as opposed to the restricted and automatic nature of ordinary consciousness. Cf. Torella 2002: pp. 118-119 (with references to an essential bibliography on the subject).

until one is aware of its qualities. When, however, through the words of a master or by other means, awareness of the greatness of Maheśvara arises, characterised by omnipotence, omniscience, etc., the state of absolute fullness is immediately achieved. As is said in the Fourth Section (IV.2.2), "Just as the man beloved finally arrives after so many prayers in the presence of the listless girl, even standing in front of her gives her no pleasure until he is recognised for who he is, appearing up to that moment wholly similar to other men; so too for human beings, the Self, which is yet the Lord of the world, cannot manifest the glory that is its own until its qualities are brought to light. For this reason, the doctrine of the recognition of the Lord has here been expounded."

These themes have been amply developed by various masters, first of all Abhinavagupta. We, however, shall stop here for fear of digressing, since the present work is just a synthesis.

Bibliography

Texts

Abhinavagupta, *Abhinavabhāratī: Nāṭyaśāstra of Bharatamuni with the Commentary Abhinavabhāratī by Abhinavaguptācārya*, edited by R.S. Nagar, vols. I-IV, Delhi 1994.

——, *Īśvarapratyabhijñāvimarśinī*, edited by Mukund Ram Shastri, vols. I-II, Kashmir Series of Texts ans Studies XXII, XXXIII, Bombay 1918-1921.

——, *Īśvarapratyabhijñāvivṛtivimarśinī,* edited by Madhusudan Kaul Shastri, vols. I-III, Kashmir Series of Texts ans Studies LX, LXII, LXV, Bombay 1938-43.

——, *Mālinīvijayavārttikam*, edited with notes by Madhusudan Kaul Shastri, Kashmir Series of Texts ans Studies XXXI, Srinagar 1921.

——, *Parātriṃśikāvivaraṇa*, see Gnoli 1985.

——, *Tantrāloka with Commentary by Rājānaka Jayaratha*, edited with notes by Madhusudan Kaul Shastri, vols. I-XII, Kashmir Series of Texts ans Studies XXIII, XXVIII, XXX, XXXVI, XXXV, XXIX, XLI, XLVII, LIX, LII, LVII, LVIII, Allahabad-Srinagar-Bombay 1918-1938.

Aniruddha, *Sāṃkhyasūtravṛtti*, edited by Rāmaśaṅkara Bhaṭṭācārya, Varanasi 1964.

Bhartṛhari, *Vākyapadīya (mūlakārikās), Bhartṛharis Vākyapadīya*, edited by W. Rau, Abhandlungen für die Kunde des Morgenlandes, 42, Wiesbaden 1977.

Bhāsarvajña, *Nyāyabhūṣaṇam*, edited by Svāmī Yogīndrānanda, Ṣaḍdarśana-prakāśana-pratiṣṭhāna-granthamālā No.1, Varanasi 1968.

Bhāskarakaṇṭha, *Bhāskarī. A Commentary on the Īśvarapratyabhijñāvimarśinī of Abhinavagupta*, vols. I-II, ed. by K. A. S. Iyer and K. C. Pandey, The Princess of Wales Sarasvati Bhavana Texts Nos. 70 and 83, Allahabad 1938-50.

Brahmasūtra with Śaṅkara's *Bhāṣya* [and many of the other principal commentaries], edited by G.S. Sadhale, Delhi 1985.

Devasūri, *Pramāṇanayatattvālokālaṅkāra*, see Bhattacharya 1967.

Dharmakīrti, *Hetubindu*, see Steinkellner 1967.

——, *Nyāyabindu*, see Durveka Miśra, *Dharmottarapradīpa*.

——, *Pramāṇavārttika* with the Commentary *'Vṛtti'* of Acharya Manorathanandin, critically edited by Swami Dwarikadas Shastri, Varanasi 1968.

——, *Pramāṇavārttika* I : *Pramāṇavārttikam. The First Chapter with the Autocommentary*, text and critical notes by R. Gnoli, Serie Orientale Roma XXIII, IsMEO, Roma 1960.

——, *Pramāṇaviniścaya* I, II: *Pramāṇaviniścaya* chapters 1 and 2, critically edited by E. Steinkellner, Sanskrit Texts from the autonomous Tibetan region No. 2, Beijing-Vienna 2007.

Dharmottara, *Nyāyabinduṭīkā*, see Durveka Miśra, *Dharmottarapradīpa*.

Dignāga, *Ālambanaparīkṣā*, see Tola & Dragonetti 1982.

——, *Nyāyamukha*, see Tucci 1930.

——, *Pramāṇasamuccaya* I, see Steinkellner 2005, Hattori 1968; *Pramāṇasamuccaya* V, see Pind 2009.

Diogenes Laertius, *De clarorum philosophorum vitis*, see Hicks 1966.

Durveka Miśra, *Dharmottarapradīpa* [being a sub-commentary on Dharmottara's *Nyāyabinduṭīkā*, a commentary on Dharmakīrti's *Nyāyabindu*], edited by Pandita Dalsukhbhai Malvania, Kashiprasad Jayaswal Research Institute, Revised II Ed., Patna 1971.

Gaṅgeśa, *Tattvacintāmaṇi* [with several commentaries], edited by K.N. Tarkavagisa, Biblioteca Indica 98, 1884-1901 (repr. Varanasi 1990).

Haribhadra Sūri, *Ṣaḍdarśanasamuccaya with Guṇaratna's Tarka-rahasyadīpikā*, edited by L. Suali, Biblioteca Indica 167, Calcutta 1905-1914.

Jayanta Bhaṭṭa, *Nyāyamañjarī with the Commentary Granthibhaṅga by Cakradhara*, edited by Gaurinath Sastri, vols. I-III, Varanasi 1982-1984.

Jinendrabuddhi, *Viśālāmalavatī Pramāṇasamuccayaṭikā,* Chapter I. Part I: Critical Edition, by E. Steinkellner, H. Krasser, H. Lasic, China Tibetology Research Centre - Austrian Academy of Sciences, Beijing-Vienna 2005.

Kauṭilya, *Arthaśāstra with the Commentary Candrikā*, edited by N.S. Venkhatanathacharya, University of Mysore, Oriental Research Institute Series No. 158, Mysore 1986.

Kiraṇa-āgama [or *-tantra*], see Vivanti 1973, Goodall 1998.

Kṣemarāja, *Pratyabhijñāhṛdaya*, edited by J.Ch. Chatterjee, Kashmir Series of Texts and Studies III, Srinagar 1911.

Kumārila, *Ślokavārttikam* with the commentary *Nyāyaratnākara* of Śrī Pārthasāratimiśra, edited and revised by Swami Dwarikadas Shastri, Prācyabhārati Series-10, Varanasi 1978.

Mādhavācārya, *Sarvadarśanasaṃgraha*, edited by Uma Shankar Sharma, Vidyabhawan Sanskrit Granthamala 113, Varanasi 1978.

Madhyāntavibhāgaśāstra, containing the *Kārikās* of Maitreya, *Bhāṣya* of Vasubandhu and *Ṭīkā* by Sthiramati, critically edited by R.C. Pandey, Delhi 1972.

Mīmāṃsādarśana [...], edited by the paṇḍits of Anandashram, vols. I-VII, Anandashram Sanskrit Series No. 97, repr. Pune 1994 (I Ed. 1929-1943).

Mokṣākaragupta, *Tarkabhāṣā*, edited by Embar Krishnamacharyya, Gaekwad Oriental Series 94, Oriental Institute, Baroda 1942.

Nāgārjuna, *Madhyamakaśāstra with the Commentary Prasannapāda by Candrakīrti*, edited by Swami Dwarika Das Shastri, Bauddha Bharati Series 16, Varanasi 1983.

Nāradasmṛti, see Larivière 1989.

Nyāyasūtra, see Ruben 1928.

Nyāyasūtra and *Bhāṣya*: *Gautamīyanyāyadarśana with Bhāṣya of Vātsyāyana*, edited by A. Thakur, New Delhi 1997.

Nyāyakośa, or Dictionary of Technical Terms of Indian Philosophy, by M.M. Bhīmācārya Jhalakikar, revised and re-edited by V.S. Abhyankar, Bombay Sanskrit and Prakrit Series 49, Poona 1978.

Patañjali, *Vyākaraṇa-mahābhāṣya*, edited by F. Kielhorn, III ed., revised [...] by K.V. Abhyankar, vols. I-III, Poona 1962-1972.

Prajñākaragupta, *Pramāṇavārttikālaṃkāra*: *Pramāṇavārttikabhāṣyam or Vārttikālaṃkāraḥ, being a Commentary on Dharmakīrti's Pramāṇavārttika,* ed. by R. Saṅkṛtyāyana, Patna 1953.

Praśastapāda, *Padārthadharmasaṃgraha* with Śrīdhara's *Nyāya-kandalī*, edited by D.Jh. Sarma, Varanasi 1963.

Sāṃkhyakārikā, see Sharma 1933.

Śaṅkara, *Brahmasūtrabhāṣya*, see *Brahmasūtra*.

——, *Upadeśasāhasrī with Ānandagīri's Ṭīkā*, edited by S.S. Sastri, Advaita Grantha Ratna Manjusha No. 15, Varanasi 1978.

Śāntarakṣita, *Tattvasaṃgraha with the Commentary 'Pañjikā' of Kamalaśīla*, vols. I-II, critically edited by Swami Dwarikadas Shastri, Bauddha Bharati Series 1, Varanasi 1981.

Upaniṣads: *Ten principal Upaniṣads with Śāṅkarabhāṣya*, Delhi 1964.

Utpaladeva, *Īśvarapratyabhijñākārikā* and *vṛtti*, see Torella 2002.

Vācaspati Miśra, *Yogatattvavaiśāradī*: *Yogasūtra with Vyāsa's Bhāṣya, Vācaspati Miśra's Yogatattvavaiśāradī and Nāgeśa Bhaṭṭa's Vṛtti*, edited by R.S. Bodas and V.S. Abhyankar, Varanasi 1917.

Vaiśeṣikasūtra: *Vaiśeṣikasūtra of Kaṇāda with the Commentary of Candrānanda*, edited by Muni Sri Jambuvijayaji, GOS 136, Baroda 1961.

Vātsyāyana, *Kāmasūtra with the Commentary Jayamaṅgalā by Śrī Yaśodhara*, edited by P.N. Dvivedi, Varanasi 1999.

Vasubandhu, *Abhidharmakośabhāṣyam*, deciphered and edited by Prof. Prahlad Pradhan, revised with introduction and indices by Dr. Aruna Haldar, K.P. Jayaswal Research Institute, Patna 1975.

——, *Vijñaptimātratāsiddhi*, Deux traités de Vasubandhu. *Viṃśatikā* accompagnée d'une explication en prose et *Triṃśikā* avec le commentaire de Sthiramati, publié par Sylvain Lévi, Bibliothèque de l'École des Hautes Études, fasc. 245, Paris 1925.

Vijñānabhikṣu, *Sāṃkhyapravacanabhāṣya*, edited by Āśubodhavidyābhūṣaṇa and Nityabodhavidyāratna, Calcutta 1936.

Yāska, *Niruktam nighaṇṭhupāṭhasamupetaṃ durgācāryakṛtaṛjvarthākhyavṛttyā samavetam*, edited by R.G. Bhadkamkar, vols. I-II, Bombay Sanskrit and Prakrit Series Nos. LXXIII, LXXXV, Bombay 1918-1942.

Yuktidīpikā, critically edited by A. Wezler and Sh. Motegi, vol. I, Alt- und Neu-Indische Studien herausgegeben vom Institut für Kultur und Geschichte Indiens und Tibets an der Universität Hamburg, 44, Stuttgart 1998.

Studies and translations

Aklujkar, A. (2002-2003) "Where do lakṣaṇaika-cakṣuṣka and lakṣyaika-cakṣuṣka apply?", *Bulletin of the Deccan College*, 62-63 (= *Ashok R. Kelkar Felicitation Volume*), pp. 179-85.

—— (2009) "Veda revelation according to Bhartṛhari". In: Chaturvedi, M. (ed.), *Bhartṛhari: Language, Thought and Reality (Proceedings of the International Seminar, Delhi 12-14, 2003)*, Delhi, pp. 1-98.

Bakker, H. & Bisschop, P. (1999) "Mokṣadharma 187 and 239-241 reconsidered", *Asiatische Studien / Études Asiatiques*, 53, 3, pp. 459-472.

Balbir, N. (1987) "The perfect sūtra according to the Jainas", *Berliner Indologische Studien*, 3, pp. 3-21.

Balcerowicz, P. (2001) "Two Siddhasenas and the authorship of the *Nyāyāvatāra* and the *Saṃmati-tarka-prakaraṇa*", *Journal of Indian Philosophy*, 29, pp. 351-378.

Baldissera, F. (1993) *Somadeva, L'oceano dei fiumi dei racconti*, a cura di F. Baldissera, V. Mazzarino & M.P. Vivanti, 2 vols., Torino.

—— (1999-2000) "Sinister fluids: the evil juices of love, writing and religion", *Bulletin d'Études Indiennes*, 17-18, pp. 153-172.

Bandyopadhyay, N. (1979) "The Buddhist theory of relation between pramā and pramāṇa". *Journal of Indian Philosophy*, 7, pp. 43-78.

Bhattacharya, H.S. (1967) *Devasūri, Pramāṇanayatattvālokālaṅkāra*, rendered into English with commentary by H.S. Bhattacharya, Bombay.

Bhattacharya, K. (1971) *The Dialectical Method of Nāgārjuna: Vigrahavyāvartanī*, Delhi.

—— (1986) "Some thoughts on antarvyāpti, bahirvyāpti, and trairūpya". In: Matilal & Evans 1986 (eds.), pp. 89-105.

—— (2006) "On the language of Navya-nyāya: an experiment with precision through a natural language", *Journal of Indian Philosophy*, 34, pp. 5-13.

van Bijlert, V.A. (1989) *Epistemology and Spiritual Authority*, Wiener Studien zur Tibetologie und Buddhismuskunde, Heft 20, Wien.

Bouy, Ch. (2000) *Gauḍapāda. L'Āgamaśāstra, text, traduction et notes*, Collège de France, Paris.

Brockington, J. (1999) "Epic Sāṃkhya: texts, teachers, terminology", *Asiatische Studien / Études Asiatiques*, 53, 3, pp. 473-490.

Bronkhorst, J. (1985) "Patañjali and the Yogasūtras", *Studien zur Indologie und Iranistik*, 10, pp. 191-212.

—— (1990) "Vārttika", *Wiener Zeitschrift für die Kunde Südasiens*, 34, pp. 123-146.

—— (1992) "Quelques axiomes du vaiśeṣika", *Les Cahiers de Philosophie*, 14 ("L'Orient de la pensée"), pp. 95-110.

—— (1991) "Two literary conventions of classical India". Proceedings of the First International Conference on Bhartṛhari: University of Poona, January 6-8, 1992, in: *Asiatische Studien / Études Asiatiques*, 47.1, pp. 210-227.

—— (2002) "Literacy and rationality in ancient India", *Asiatische Studien / Études Asiatiques*, 56.4, pp. 797-831.

—— (2002/2003) "Uttaramīmāṃsā", *Cracow Indological Studies*, 4-5, pp. 113-120.

Bronner, Y. (2002) "What is new and what is navya: Sanskrit poetics on the eve of colonialism", *Journal of Indian Philosophy*, 30, pp. 441-462.

Cardona, G. (2002) "L'analisi linguistica come paradigma della scienza vedica". In: Torella 2002a, pp. 740-756.

—— (2007) "On the position of vyākaraṇa and Pāṇini". In: Preisendanz 2007 (ed.), pp. 693-710.

Chatterjee, S. (1950) *The Nyāya Theory of Knowledge: A critical study of some problems of logic and metaphysics*, Calcutta (II ed.).

Chattopadhyaya, D. (1990) (ed.) *Carvāka / Lokāyata: An anthology of source materials and some recent studies*, Calcutta.

Chu, J. (2006) "On Dignāga's theory of the object of cognition as presented in PS(V)" 1. *Journal of the International Association of Buddhist Studies*, 29.2, pp. 211-253.

Colas, G. (1999) "Critique et transmission des textes de l'Inde classique", *Diogènes*, 186, pp. 37-54.

Colas, G. & Gerschheimer, G. (eds.) (2009) *Écrire et transmettre en Inde classique*, École Française d'Extrême-Orient, Paris.

Cox, C. (1995) *Disputed Dharmas: Early Buddhist theories on existence: An annotated translation of the section on factors dissociated from thought from Saṅghabhadra's Nyāyānusāra*, International Institute for Buddhist Studies, Tokyo.

—— (2004) "From category to ontology: the changing role of dharma in Sarvāstivāda Abhidharma", *Journal of Indian Philosophy*, 32, pp. 543-597.

Dagens, B. (2002) "Architettura, arti e tecnica". In: Torella 2002a (ed.), pp. 896-907.

Dasgupta, S. (1975) *A History of Indian Philosophy*, vol. III, Delhi (I ed. Cambridge 1922).

Deshpande, M.M. (1993) *Sanskrit and Prakrit. Sociolinguistic Issues*. Delhi.

—— (2005) "Ultimate source of validation for the Sanskrit grammatical tradition: Elite usage versus rules of grammar". In: Squarcini 2005 (ed.), pp. 361-387.

Dietz, S. (1984) *Die buddhistische Briefliterature Indiens. Nach dem tibetischen Tanjur herausgegeben*, übersetzt und erläutert, Asiatische Forschungen 84, Wiesbaden.

Dixit, K.K. (1971) *Jaina Ontology*, Ahmedabad.

Dreyfus, G. (1991) "Dharmakīrti's definition of pramāṇa and its interpreters". In: Steinkellner 1991 (ed), pp. 19-38.

D'Sa, F.X (1980) *Śabdaprāmāṇyam in Śabara and Kumārila: Towards a study of the Mīmāṃsā experience of language*, Vienna.

Dundas, P. (1992) *The Jains*, London.

—— (1996a) "Somnolent sūtra: Scriptural commentary in Śvetāmbara Jainism", *Journal of Indian Philosophy*, 24, pp. 73-101.

—— (1996b) "Jain attitudes toward the Sanskrit language". In: Houben, J, (ed.) *Status and Ideology of Sanskrit*, Leiden, pp. 137-156.

Eltschinger, V. (2007) *Penser l'autorité des Écritures: la polémique de Dharmakīrti contre la notion brahmanique ortodoxe d'un Veda sans auteur. Autour de Pramāṇavārttika I.213-268 et Svavṛtti*, Österreichische Akademie der Wissenschaften, Wien.

—— (2009) "On the career and the cognition of yogins". In: Franco 2009 (ed.).

—— (2010a) "On a hitherto neglected text against Buddhism personalism: *Mahāyānasūtrālaṃkāra* 18.92-103 and its Bhāṣya", *Asiatische Studien / Études Asiatiques,* 64. 2, pp. 291-340.

—— (2010b) "Dharmakīrti", *Revue Internationale de Philosophie,* 64, 253, pp. 397-440.

Faddegon, B (1918) *The Vaiśeṣika System, described with the help of the oldest texts*, Amsterdam (repr. Wiesbaden 1969).

Feuerstein, G. (1974) *The Essence of Yoga: A contribution to the psychohistory of Indian civilization*. Delhi.

Franco, E. (1993) "Did Dignāga accept four types of perception?", *Journal of Indian Philosophy,* 21, pp. 205-299.

—— (1994) *Perception, Knowledge and Disbelief: A study of Jayarāśi's Tattvopaplavasiṃha*, Delhi.

—— (1997) *Dharmakīrti on Compassion and Rebirth*, Wiener Studien zur Tibetologie und Buddhismuskunde, Heft 38, Wien.

—— (1999) "Avīta and āvīta", *Asiatische Studien / Études Asiatiques,* 53. 3, pp. 563-577.

—— (2009) "Meditation and metaphysics: On their mutual relationship in South Asian Buddhism". In: Franco, E. (ed.) 2009, pp. 93-132.

—— (ed.) (2009) *Yogic perception, meditation and altered states of consciousness*, Österreichische Akademie der Wissenschaften, Beiträge zur Kultur- und Geistesgeschichte Asiens 65. Wien.

Franco, E. & Preisendanz, K. (1997) (eds.) *Beyond Orientalism: The work of Wilhelm Halbfass and its impact on Indian and cross-cultural studies*, Amsterdam-Atlanta.

Frauwallner, E. (1954) "Die Reihenfolge und Entstehung der Werke Dharmakīrtis". In: *Asiatica. Festschrift Friedrich Weller: zum 65. Geburtstag gewid met von seinen Freunden, Kollegen und Schuler*, herausgegeben von J. Schubert und U. Schneider, Leipzig, pp. 142-54.

—— (1957) "Vasubandhu's *Vādavidhi*", *Wiener Zeitschrift für die Kunde Südasiens*, 1, pp. 104-146.

—— (1959) "Dignāga, sein Werk und seine Entwicklung", *Wiener Zeitschrift für die Kunde Südasiens*, 3, pp. 83-164.

—— (1961) "Landmarks in the History of Indian Logic", *Wiener Zeitschrift für die Kunde Südasiens*, 5, pp. 125-148.

—— (1958) "Zur Erkenntnislehre des classische Sāṃkhya-system", *Wiener Zeitschrift für die Kunde Südasiens*, 2, 1958, pp. 84-139.

—— (1978) *History of Indian philosophy*, vols. I-II, Delhi (Engl. tr. of *Geschichte der indischen Philosophie*, Band 1-2, Salzburg. 1956).

—— (1995) *Studies in Abhidharma literature and the origins of Buddhist philosophical systems*, Albany.

Funayama, T. (1992) "A Study of *Kalpanāpoḍha*: A translation of the *Tattvasaṃgraha* vv. 1212-1263 by Śāntarakṣita and the *Tattvasaṃgrahapañjikā* by Kamalaśīla on the definition of direct perception", *Zinbun : Annals of the Institute for Research in Humanities. Kyoto University*, 27, pp. 33-128.

Ganesan, T. & Barois, Chr. (2003) "À propos des manuscrits de l'Institut Français de Pondichéry", *Bulletin d'Études Indiennes*, 21.1, pp. 255-264.

Garbe, R. (1917) *Die Sāṃkhya-Philosophie: Eine Darstellung des Indischen Rationalismus nach den Quellen*, zweite umgearbeitete Auflage. Leipzig.

Gerschheimer, G. (2007) "Les 'six doctrines de spéculation' (*ṣaṭṭarkī*). Sur la catégorisation variable des systèmes philosophiques dans l'Inde classique". In: Preisendanz 2007 (ed.), pp. 239-258.

Gnoli, R. (1985) *Il Commento di Abhinavagupta alla Parātriṃśikā (Parātriṃśikā-tattva-vivaraṇam)*, traduzione e testo, Serie Orientale Roma LVIII, IsMEO, Roma.

—— (1999) *Abhinavagupta, Luce dei Tantra (Tantrāloka)*, Biblioteca Orientale 4, Milano.

Gonda, J. (1963) *The Vision of the Vedic Poet*, The Hague.

Goodall, D. (1998) *Bhaṭṭarāmakaṇṭhaviracitā Kiraṇavṛttiḥ, vol. I: chapters 1-6*, critical edition and annotated translation, Publications du Départment d'Indologie, 86.1, Institut Français de Pondichéry - École Française d'Extrême-Orient, Pondichéry.

Granoff, Ph. (1978) *Philosophy and Argument in Late Vedānta: Śrī Harṣa's Khaṇḍanakhaṇḍakhādya*, Dordrecht.

—— (1995) "Sarasvatī's sons: Biographies of poets in medieval India", *Asiatische Studien / Études Asiatiques,* 49, pp. 351-368.

Hacker, P. (1958) "Ānvīkṣikī", *Wiener Zeitschrift für die Kunde Südasiens*, 2, pp. 54-83.

Hahn, M. (1999) *Invitation to Enlightenment: Letter to the great king Kaniṣka by Mātṛceta, Letter to a disciple by Candragomin*, Berkeley.

Halbfass, W. (1973) "Hegel on the Philosophy of the Hindus". In: *German Scholars on India*, vol. I, Benares, pp. 107-122.

—— (1979) "Observations on darśana", *Wiener Zeitschrift für die Kunde Südasiens,* 23, pp. 195-203.

—— (1986-1992) "Observations on the relationship between vedic exegesis and philosophical reflection", *Journal of Oriental Research* (Madras), 56-62, pp. 31-40.

—— (1990) *India and Europe: An essay in cultural understanding*, Delhi.

—— (1992) *Tradition and Reflection: Explorations in Indian thought*, Delhi.

—— (1992a) *On Being and What There Is: Classical Vaiśeṣika and the history of Indian ontology*, Albany.

Hardy, F. (1979) "The philosopher as a poet: a study of Vedāntadeśika's Dehalīśastuti", *Journal of Indian Philosophy*, 7, pp. 277-325.

Harikai, K. (1997) "Kumārila's acceptance and modification of the categories of the Vaiśeṣika school". In: Franco & Preisendanz 1997 (eds.), pp. 395-415.

Harrison, P. (1990) *The Samādhi of Direct Encounter with the Buddhas of the Present. An annotated English translation of the Tibetan version of the Pratyutpanna-buddha-sammukhāvasthita-samādhi-sūtra*, Studia Philologica Buddhica 5, Tokyo.

Hattori, M. (1968) *Dignāga. On Perception, being the Pratyakṣa-pariccheda of Dignāga's Pramāṇasamuccaya*, Harvard Oriental Series No. 47, Cambridge (Mss.).

—— (1997) "The Buddhist theory concerning the truth and falsity of cognition". In: Bilimoria, P. & Mohanty, J.N. (eds.) *Relativism, Suffering and Beyond: Essays in memory of Bimal K. Matilal*, Delhi, pp. 361-371.

—— (1999) "On seśvara-sāṃkhya", *Asiatische Studien / Études Asiatiques*, 53.3, pp. 609-618.

Havelock, E.A. (1973), *Cultura orale e civiltà della scrittura da Omero a Platone*, Roma-Bari (Ital. transl. of *Preface to Plato*, Harvard University Press, Cambridge-Mss., 1963).

—— (1982) *The Literate Revolution in Greece and its Cultural Consequences*, Princeton University Press, Princeton.

Hicks, R.D (1966), *Diogenes Laertius, Lives of Eminent Philosophers*, with an English translation by R.D. Hicks, The Loeb Classical Library, London.

von Hinüber, O. (1982) "Pāli as an artificial language", *Indologica Taurinensia*, 10, pp. 133-144.

Houben, J.E.M. (1994) "Liberation and natural philosophy in early Vaiśeṣika: some methodological problems", *Asiatische Studien / Études Asiatiques*, 48, pp. 711-749.

—— (1997) "Bhartṛhari's perspectivism (1): The *Vṛtti* and Bhartṛhari's perspectivism in the first kāṇḍa of the *Vākyapadīya*". In: Franco & Preisendanz 1997 (eds.), pp. 317-358.

—— (1999) "Why did rationality thrive, but hardly survive in Kapila's 'system'? On the *pramāṇas*, rationality and irrationality in Sāṃkhya (part I)", *Asiatische Studien / Études Asiatiques*, 53, 3, pp. 491-512.

Hulin, M. (1979) *Hegel et l'orient*, Paris.

Ingalls, D.H.H. (1988) *Materials for the Study of Navya-nyāya Logic*, Delhi (I ed. Harvard 1951).

Isaacson, H. (1993) "Yogic perception (*yogipratyakṣa*) in early Vaiśeṣika", *Studien zur Indologie und Iranistik*, 18, pp. 139-160.

Iwata, T. (1991) *Sahopalambhaniyama. Struktur und Entwicklung des Schlusses von der Tatsache, dass Erkenntnis und Gegenstand ausschliesslich zusammen wahrgenommen werden, auf deren Nichtverschiedenheit*, Teil I-II, Alt-und Neu-Indische Studien 29, Universität Hamburg. Stuttgart.

—— (2003) "An interpretation of Dharmakīrti's *Svabhāvahetu*", *Journal of Indian Philosophy*, 31, pp. 61-87.

Jacobi, H. (1929) "Ānvīkṣikī und ātmavidyā", *Indologica Pragensia*, 1, pp. 1-8.

Jaini, P.S. (1993) "Fear of food: jaina attitude on eating". In: Smet, R. & Watanabe, K. (eds.), *Jain Studies in Honour of Jozef Deleu*, Tokyo, pp. 339-354.

—— (2000) *Collected Papers on Jaina Studies,* Delhi.

Jha, G. (1964) *Pūrva-Mīmāṃsā in its Sources*, Banaras Hindu University, Varanasi (I ed. Varanasi 1942).

—— (1984) *The Nyāyasūtras of Gautama with the Bhāṣya of Vātsyāyana and the Vārttika of Uddyotakara*, transl. by Ganganath Jha, II ed., Delhi 1984 (I ed. 1912-1919).

Joshi, S.D. (1968) *Patañjali's Vyākaraṇa-Mahābhāṣya: samarthāhnika (P. 2.1.1)*, edited with translation and explanatory notes by ..., University of Poona, Poona.

Kajiyama, Y. (1963) "*Trikapañcakacintā*: Development of the Buddhist theory on the determination of causality". In: *Miscellanea Indologica Kiotensia*, 4-5, pp. 1-15.

—— (1966) "An introduction to Buddhist philosophy. An annotated translation of the *Tarkabhāṣā* of Mokṣākaragupta", *Memoirs of the Faculty of Letters*. Kyoto University,10, pp. 1-173.

—— (1989) "Controversy between the sākāra- and nirākāravādins of the yogācāra school: some materials". In: Id., *Studies in Buddhist Philosophy (Selected Papers)*, Kyoto: 429-418.

—— (1999) *The Antarvyāptisamarthana of Ratnākaraśānti*, Biblioteca Philologica et Philosophica 2, Tokyo.

Kane, P.V, (1974) *History of Dharmaśāstra (Ancient and Medieval Religious and Civil Law),* vol. II, Part I, II ed. (I ed. 1941), Bhandarkar Oriental Research Institute, Poona.

Kano, K. (1991) "On the background of PV II 12ab - The origin of Dharmakīrti's idea of arthakriyā". In: Steinkellner 1991 (ed.), pp. 119-128.

Karttunen, K. (1989) *India in Early Greek Literature*, Finnish Oriental Society, Helsinki.

Katsura, Sh. (1983) "Dignāga on trairūpya", *Journal of Indian and Buddhist Studies*, 32, pp. 15-21.

—— (1984) "Dharmakīrti's theory of truth", *Journal of Indian Philosophy*, 12, pp. 215-235.

—— (1991) "Dignāga and Dharmakīrti on apoha", in Steinkellner 1991 (ed.), pp. 129-146.

—— (1999) (ed.) *Dharmakīrti's Thought and its Impact on Indian Philosophy*, Proceedings of the Third International Dharmakīrti Conference, Hiroshima, November 4-6 1997. Wien.

—— (2000) "Indian logic: deduction, induction or abduction?", ICANAS, Montreal (contribution not published).

Katsura, Sh. & Steinkellner E. (2004) (eds.) *The Role of the Example (dṛṣṭānta) in Classical Indian Logic*, Wiener Studien zur Tibetologie und Buddhismuskunde, Heft 58, Wien.

Kellner, B. (2001) "Negation - failure or success? Remarks on an allegedly characteristic trait of Dharmakīrti's anupalabdhi-theory", *Journal of Indian Philosophy*, 29, pp. 495-517.

—— (2003) "Integrating negative knowledge into pramāṇa theory: The Development of the dṛṣyānupalabdhi Dharmakīrti's earlier works", *Journal of Indian Philosophy*, 31, pp. 121-59.

Krasser, H. (1995) "Dharmottara's theory of knowledge in his *Laghuprāmāṇyaparīkṣā*", *Journal of Indian Philosophy*, 23, pp. 247-271.

—— (2001) "On Dharmakīrti's understanding of pramāṇabhūta and his definition of pramāṇa", *Wiener Zeitschrift für die Kunde Südasiens*, 45, pp. 173-199.

Lang, K., (1986) *Āryadeva's Catuḥśataka: On the bodhisattva's cultivation of merit and knowledge*. Copenhagen.

Larson, J.L. (1979) *Classical Sāṃkhya*, II ed., Delhi.

Larson, J.L. & Bhattacharya R.Sh. (1987) (eds.) *Encyclopedia of Indian Philosophies*, vol. IV: *Sāṃkhya: A Dualist Tradition in Indian Philosophy*, Delhi.

de La Vallée Poussin, L. (1923-1931), *L'Abhidharmakośa de Vasubandhu*, traduit et annoté par ..., vols. I-VI, Société Belge d'Études Orientales. Louvain-Paris.

—— (1928-48), *Vijñaptimātratāsiddhi. La Siddhi de Hiuan-Tsang*, traduite et annotée par ..., tomes I-III, Buddhica: Documents et Travaux pour l'étude du Bouddhisme publiés sous la direction de Jean Przyluski. Paris.

—— (1937) "Le bouddhisme et le yoga de Patañjali", *Mélanges chinois et bouddhiques*, 5, pp. 223-242.

Larivière, R.W. (1989) *The Nāradasmṛti, critically edited with an introduction, annotated translation, and appendices*, 2 vols., Philadelphia.

Lévi, S. (1932) *Matériaux pour l'étude du système Vijñaptimātratā*. Bibliothèque de l'École des Hautes Études, fasc. 260, Paris.

Lindtner, Ch. (1987) *Nāgārjuniana: Studies in the writings and philosophy of Nāgārjuna*, Delhi (I ed. 1982).

—— (1997) "Cittamātra in Indian Mahāyāna until Kamalaśīla", *Wiener Zeitschrift für die Kunde Südasiens*, 41, pp. 159-206.

McCrea, L. (2002) "Novelty of form and novelty of substance in seventeenth century Mīmāṃsā", *Journal of Indian Philosophy*, 30, pp. 481-494.

Malamoud, Ch. (2002) *Le jumeau solaire*, Paris.

Matilal, B.K. (1981) *The Central Philosophy of Jainism (Anekānta-vāda)*, Ahmedabad.

—— (1985) *Logic, Language and Reality: An introduction to Indian philosophical studies*, Delhi.

—— (1986) *Perception. An essay on classical Indian theories of knowledge*. Oxford.

—— (1999) *The Character of Logic in India*, edited by J. Ganeri and H. Tiwari, Albany.

Matilal, B.K. & Evans, R.D. (1986) (eds.) *Buddhist Logic and Epistemology. Studies in the Buddhist analysis of inference and language*, Studies of Classical India 7. Dordrecht.

Mejor, M. (2007) "*Sarvamatasaṃgraha*: an anonymous 'Compendium of all systems'". In: Preisendanz 2007 (ed.), pp. 259-273.

Mikogami, E. (1979) "Some remarks on the concepts of arthakriyā", *Journal of Indian Philosophy*, 7, pp. 79-94.

Mimaki, K. (1976) *La réfutation bouddhique de la permanence des choses (Sthirasiddhiduṣaṇa) et la preuve de la momentanéité des choses (Kṣaṇabhaṅgasiddhi)*, Institut de Civilisation Indienne, Paris.

Mohanty, J.N. (1966) *Gaṅgeśa's Theory of Truth*, Santiniketan.

—— (1992) *Reason and Revelation in Indian Thought*, Oxford.

Motegi, Sh. (1999) "The teachings of Pañcaśikha in the Mokṣa-dharma", *Asiatische Studien / Études Asiatiques*, 53.3, pp. 513-535.

Murthy, R.S.S. (1996) *Introduction to Manuscriptology*, Delhi.

Nagatomi, M. (1967-68) “Arthakriyā”, *Adyar Library Bulletin*, 31-32, pp. 52-72.

Oberhammer, G., Prets, E., Prandstetter J. (1996), *Terminologie der frühen philosophischen Scholastik in Indien*, vol. II, Wien.

Oetke, C (1994), *Studies on the Doctrine of Trairūpya*, Wiener Studien fur Tibetologie und Buddhismuskunde, 38, Wien.

—— (1999a) “The disjunction in the *Pramāṇasiddhi*”. In: Katsura 1999 (ed.), pp. 243-251.

—— (1999b) “Clarifications”, ivi, pp. 261-266.

—— (2003) “Some remarks on theses and philosophical positions in early Mādhyamika”, *Journal of Indian Philosophy*, 31, pp. 449-478.

Padoux, A. (1980) “Contributions à l’étude du mantraśāstra, 2: nyāsa, l’imposition rituelle des mantra”, *Bulletin de l’École Française d’Extrême Orient*, 57, pp. 59-102.

—— (1995) “L’oral et l’écrit: mantra et mantraśāstra”, *Puruṣārtha,* 18, pp. 133-145.

Pandey, K.Ch. (1963) *Abhinavagupta: An Historical and Philosophical Study*, II ed., Chowkhamba Sanskrit Studies 1, Varanasi.

Pind, O.H. (2009) *Dignāga’s Philosophy of Language. Pramāṇasamuccaya V: texts, translation and annotation*. Ph.D. Dissertation, University of Vienna.

Pollock, Sh. (1985) “The theory of practice and the practice of theory in Indian intellectual history”, *Journal of the American Oriental Society*, 105.3, pp. 499-519.

—— (1997) “The ‘revelation’ of ‘tradition’: śruti, smṛti, and the Sanskrit discourse of power”. In: Lienhart, S., Piovano, I. (eds.) *Lex and Litterae. Studies in Honour of Professor Oscar Botto*. Torino, pp. 395-417.

—— (2001) “New intellectuals in seventeenth century India”, *The Indian Economic and Social History Review*, 38.1, pp. 3-31.

—— (2002) "Introduction: Working papers on Sanskrit knowledge-system on the eve of colonialism", *Journal of Indian Philosophy*, 30, pp. 431-439.

Potter, K.H. (1977) *Encyclopedia of Indian Philosophies*, vol. II: *Indian Metaphysics and Epistemology: The tradition of Nyāya-Vaiśeṣika up to Gaṅgeśa*, Delhi.

Preisendanz, K. (2005) "The production of philosophical literature in south Asia during the pre-colonial period (15th to 18th centuries: The case of the Nyāyasūtra commentarial tradition", *Journal of Indian Philosophy*, 33, pp. 55-94.

—— (2007) (ed.) *Expanding and Merging Horizons. Contributions to South Asian and cross-cultural studies in commemoration of Wilhelm Halbfass*, Vienna.

Qvarnström, O. (1989) *Hindu Philosophy in Buddhist Perspective. The Vedāntatattvaviniścaya chapter of Bhavya's Madhyamaka-hṛdayakārikā*, Lund Studies in African and Asian Religions, vol. 4. Lund.

Randle, H.N. (1926), *Fragments from Dignāga*, The Royal Asiatic Society, London.

Rao, S. (1998) *Perceptual Error: The Indian theories*, University of Hawaii Press, Honolulu.

Renou, L. (1941-42) "Les connexions entre le rituel et la grammaire en sanscrit", *Journal Asiatique*, 233, pp. 105-165.

—— (1963) "Sur le genre du sūtra dans la littérature sanscrite", *Journal Asiatique*, 251, pp. 165-216.

Ruben, W. (1928) *Die Nyāyasūtra's. Text, Übersetzung, Erläuterung und Glossar*, Abhandlungen für die Kunde des Morgenlandes 18, 2, Leipzig.

Rukmani, T.S. (2001), *Yogasūtrabhāṣyavivaraṇa of Śaṅkara. Vivaraṇa* text with English translation and critical notes along with text and English translation of Patañjali's *Yogasūtras* and *Vyāsa-bhāṣya*, 2 vols., Delhi.

Sachau, E.C. (1910) *Alberuni's India: An account of the religion, philosophy [...] of India about A.D. 1030, An English edition with notes and indices*, 2 vols., London.

Salomon, R. (1998) *Indian Epigraphy: A guide to the study of inscriptions in Sanskrit, Prakrit, and other Indo-Aryan languages*, University of Texas, Austin.

Sarma, K.V. (1991) "Propagation of written literature in Indian tradition", *Adyar Library Bulletin*, 57, pp. 15-31.

Scherrer-Schaub, C. (1991) *Yuktiṣaṣṭikāvṛtti: Commentaire à la soixantaine sur le raisonnement ou Du vrai enseignement de la causalité par le maître indien Candrakīrti, Mélanges chinois et bouddhiques*, 25. Bruxelles.

Schmithausen, L. (1965) *Maṇḍanamiśra's Vibhramaviveka. Mit einer Studie zur Entwicklung der indischen Irrtumlehre*, Österreichische Akademie der Wissenschaften, Philophisch-Historische Klasse, Philosophisch-Historische Klasse, Sitzungsberichte, 247. Band, 1. Abhandlung. Wien.

—— (1973) "On the problem of the relation of spiritual practice and philosophical theory in Buddhism". In: *German Scholars on India*, vol. I, Benares, pp. 235-250.

—— (1987) *Ālayavijñāna: On the origin and early development of a central concept of Yogācāra philosophy*, Parts I-II, The International Institute for Buddhist Studies. Tokyo.

—— (2005), *On the Problem of the External World in the Ch'eng Wei Shih Lun*, The International Institute for Buddhist Studies, Tokyo.

Seyfort Ruegg, D.S. (1977) "The use of the four positions of the Catuṣkoṭi and the problem of the description of reality in Mahāyana Buddhism", *Journal of Indian Philosophy*, 5, pp. 1-171.

—— (1981) *The Literature of the Madhyamaka School of Philosophy in India* (A History of Indian Literature, ed. J. Gonda, 7,1), Wiesbaden.

—— (1986) "Does the Mādhyamika have a thesis and philosophical position?". In: Matilal & Evans 1986 (eds.), pp. 229-237.

—— (1994) "Pramāṇabhūta, pramāṇa[bhūta]puruṣa, pratyakṣa-dharman and sākṣatkṛtadharman as epithets of the ṛṣi, ācārya and tathāgata in grammatical, epistemological and madhyamaka texts", *Bulletin of the School of Oriental and African Studies*, 57.2, pp. 303-320.

—— (1995) "Validity and authority or cognitive rightness and pragmatic efficacy? On the concepts of pramāṇa, pramāṇabhūta and pramāṇa[bhūta]puruṣa", *Asiatische Studien / Études Asiatiques*, 49, pp. 817-827.

—— (2000), *Three Studies in the History of Indian and Tibetan Madhyamaka Philosophy*, Wiener Studien zur Tibetologie und Buddhismuskunde, Heft 50, Wien.

Shah, N.J. (2000) (ed.) *Jaina Theory of Multiple Facets of Reality and Truth (Anekāntavāda)*. Ahmedabad.

Sharma. H. D. (1933), *The Saṃkhyakārikā, Īśvarakṛṣṇa's Memorable Verses on Sāṃkhya Philosophy with the Commentary by Gauḍapāda*, critically edited with introduction, translation and notes, Poona.

Solomon, E.A. (1976, 1978) *Indian Dialectics: Methods of philosophical discussion*, 2 vols., Ahmedabad.

Squarcini (2005) (ed.) *Boundaries, Dynamics and Construction of Traditions in South Asia*, Firenze University Press, Firenze.

Staal, J.F. (1972) (ed.) *A Reader on the Sanskrit Grammarians*, Delhi.

Stchoupak, N., Renou, L. (1946) *La Kāvyamīmāṃsā de Rājaśekhara*, traduite du sanskrit, Cahiers de la Société Asiatique 8, Paris.

Stcherbatsky, T. (1930-32) *Buddhist Logic*, vols. I-II, Bibliotheca Buddhica XXVI. Leningrad (repr. New York 1962).

Steinkellner, E. (1967) *Dharmakīrti's Hetubindu*, Teil I, Tibetischer Text und rekonstruierter Sanskrit-Text ; Teil II, Übersetzung und Anmerkungen. Österreichische Akademie der Wissenschaften. Wien.

—— (1971) "Wirklichkeit und Begriff bei Dharmakīrti", *Wiener Zeitschrift für die Kunde Südasiens*, 15, pp. 179-211.

—— (1973) *Dharmakīrtis Pramāṇaviniścaya. Zweites Kapitel : Svārthānumānam.* Teil I, Tibetischer Text und Sanskrittexte, Österreichische Akademie der Wissenschaften. Wien.

—— (1974) "On the interpretation of the *svabhāvahetu*", *Wiener Zeitschrift für die Kunde Südasiens*, 18, pp. 117-129.

—— (1979), *Dharmakīrtis Pramāṇaviniścaya. Zweites Kapitel: Svārthānumanam*, Teil II: Übersetzung und Anmerkungen, Wien.

—— (1982) "The spiritual place of the epistemological tradition in Buddhism", *Nanto Bukkyo*, 49, pp. 1-18.

—— (1991) (ed.) *Studies in the Buddhist Epistemological Tradition, Proceedings of the Second International Dharmakīrti Conference*, Vienna, June 11-16, 1989, Österreichische Akademie der Wissenschaften, Philophisch-Historische Klasse, Denkschriften, 222. Band, Beiträge zur Kultur-und Geistesgeschichte Asiens Nr.8. Wien.

—— (1996) "An explanation of Dharmakīrti's svabhavahetu definitions". In: Wilhelm, W. (ed.), *Festschrift Dieter Schlingloff*, Reinbek, pp. 257-68.

—— (1999) "The Ṣaṣṭitantra on perception, a collection of fragments", *Asiatische Studien / Études Asiatiques*, 53.3, pp. 667-677.

—— (2005) "Dignāga's Pramāṇasamuccaya, Chapter I. A hypothetical reconstruction [...]", www.oeaw.ac.at/ias/Mat/dignaga_PS_1.pdf.

Taber, J. (1992) "What did Kumārila Bhaṭṭa mean by svataḥ-prāmāṇya?", *Journal of the American Oriental Society*, 112, pp. 204-221.

—— (1997) "The significance of Kumārila's philosophy". In: Franco & Preisendanz 1997 (eds.), pp. 373-393.

Tillemans, T. (2004) "Inductiveness, deductiveness and examples in Buddhist logic". In: Katsura & Steinkellner 2004 (eds.), pp. 251-275.

—— (2007) "Trying to be fair to Mādhyamika Buddhism". In: Preisendanz 2007 (ed.), pp. 507-523.

Tola, F. & Dragonetti, C. (1982), "Dignāga's *Ālambanaparīkṣāvṛtti*", *Journal of Indian Philosophy*, 10, pp. 105-134.

Torella, R. (1979) "Due capitoli del *Sarvadarṅanasaṃgraha*: Śaivadarśana e Pratyabhijñādarśana", *Rivista degli Studi Orientali*, 53, fasc. III-IV, pp. 361-410.

—— (1987) "Examples of the influence of Sanskrit grammar on Indian philosophy", *East and West*, 37, pp. 151-164.

—— (1992) "The Pratyabhijñā and the Logical-epistemological school of Buddhism". In: Goudriaan, T. *Ritual and Speculation in Early Tantrism: Studies in honor of André Padoux*, Albany 1992, pp. 327-345.

—— (1998) "The kañcukas in the Śaiva and Vaiṣṇava Tantric Tradition: a few considerations between theology and grammar". In: Oberhammer, G. (ed.), *Studies in Hinduism, II, Miscellanea to the Phenomenon of Tantras*, Österreichische Akademie der Wissenschaften, Philosophisch-Historische Klasse, Sitzungsberichte, 662. Band, Wien, pp. 55-86.

—— (1999a) "Sāṃkhya as sāmānyaśāstra", *Asiatische Studien / Études Asiatiques*, 53.3, pp. 553-562.

—— (1999b) *Gli Aforismi di Śiva con il commento di Kṣemarāja (Śivasūtravimarśinī)*. Milano.

—— (1999c) "Devī uvāca, or the theology of the perfect tense", *Journal of Indian Philosophy* (Special issue in Honor of Prof. Kamaleshvar Bhattacharya) 16, pp. 129-138.

—— (2000) "The *Svabodhodayamañjarī*, or how to suppress the mind with no effort". In: Tsuchida, R. & A. Wezler, A. (eds.), *Harānandalaharī. Studies in honour of Prof. Minoru Hara on his Seventieth Birthday*, Reinbek 2000, pp. 387-410.

—— (2001) *The Word in Abhinavagupta's Bṛhadvimarsinī*. In: Torella, R. (ed.), *Le parole e i marmi, Studi in onore di Raniero Gnoli nel suo 70° compleanno*, 2 vols., Serie Orientale Roma XCII 1/2, IsIAO, Roma, pp. 853-874.

—— (2002) *The Īśvarapratyabhijñākārikā of Utpaladeva with the Author's Vṛtti*. Critical edition and annotated translation, Motilal Banarsidass, Delhi (I ed. Serie Orientale Roma LXXI, IsMEO, Roma 1994).

—— (2002a) (ed.) "La scienza indiana", Section of: *Storia della Scienza*, vol. II, Istituto della Enciclopedia Italiana Treccani, Roma, pp. 609-949.

—— (2004) "How is verbal signification possible: understanding Abhinavagupta's reply", *Journal of Indian Philosophy*, 32, pp. 173-188.

—— (2007a) "Studies in Utpaladeva's *Īśvarapratyabhijñā-vivṛti*. Part I. Apoha and anupalabdhi in a Śaiva garb", in: Preisendanz 2007 (ed.), pp. 473-490.

—— (2007b) "Studies in Utpaladeva's *Īśvarapratyabhijñā-vivṛti*. Part II. What is memory", in: *Indica et Tibetica. Festschrift für Michael Hahn zum 65. Geburtstag von Freunden und Schülern überreicht*, herausgegeben von Konrad Klaus und Jens-Uwe Hartmann, Wien, pp. 539-563.

—— (2007c), "Studies in Utpaladeva's *Īśvarapratyabhijñā-vivṛti*. Part III. Can a cognition become the object of another cognition?". In: Goodall, D. & Padoux A. (eds.), *Mélanges tantriques à la mémoire d'Hélène Brunner*, Pondichéry, pp. 475-484.

—— (2007d), "Studies in Utpaladeva's *Īśvarapratyabhijña-vivṛti*. Part IV. Light of the subject-light of the object". In: Kellner, B. et al. (eds.), *Pramāṇakīrtiḥ. Papers dedicated to Ernst Steinkellner on the occasion of his 70th birthday*, Wiener Studien zur Tibetologie und Buddhismuskunde, Heft 70.1-2, Wien, pp. 925-939.

—— (2007e) "Passioni ed emozioni nelle filosofie e religioni dell'India". In: Boccali, G. & Torella, R. (a cura di), *Passioni d'Oriente. Eros ed emozioni in India e in Tibet*, Torino, pp. 22-32.

—— (2007f) "Il Tantrismo hindu e l'invenzione del desiderio". In: Boccali, G. & Torella, R. (a cura di), *Passioni d'Oriente. Eros ed emozioni in India e in Tibet*, Torino, pp. 61-92.

—— (2009) "From an adversary to the main ally: The place of Bhartṛhari in the Kashmirian Śaivādvaita". In: Chaturvedi, M. (ed.), *Bhartṛhari: Language, Thought and Reality*. Delhi, pp. 343-354.

—— (2010) "Variazioni kashmire sul tema della percezione dello yogin (yogipratyakṣa)", *Rivista degli Studi Orientali*, 81, pp. 35-58.

—— (forthcoming a) "Observations on yogipratyakṣa" (to appear in *Prof. Ashok Aklujkar Felicitation Volume*. Kyoto).

—— (forthcoming b) "Studies in Utpaladeva's *Īśvarapratyabhijñā-vivṛti*. Part V: Self awareness and yogic perception", in: *Johannes Bronkhorst Felicitation Volume*, Lausanne.

—— (forthcoming c) "Inherited cognitions: prasiddhi, āgama, pratibhā, śabdana (Bhartṛhari, Utpaladeva, Abhinavagupta, Kumārila and Dharmakīrti in dialogue)". In: Eltschinger, V & Krasser, H (eds.) *Proceedings of the Panel on Āgama and Apologetics, XIV World Sanskrit Conference, Kyoto 2009*, Vienna.

Tucci, G. (1930) *The Nyāyamukha of Dignāga [...] after Chinese and Tibetan Materials*, Heidelberg.

—— (1971) "Linee di una storia del materialismo indiano". In: *Opera Minora*, parte I, Roma 1971, pp. 49-155 (I ed., Roma 1929).

Vergiani, V. (2005), "Dealing with conflicting views within the Pāṇinian tradition: On the derivation of tyadṛś, etc.". In: Squarcini 2005 (ed.), pp. 411-433.

Vetter, T. (1966) *Dharmakīrti's Pramāṇaviniṅcayaḥ: I. Kapitel: Pratyakṣam*, Enleitung, Text der tibetischen Übersetzung, Sanskritfragmente, deutsche Übersetzung. Österreichische Akademie der Wissenschaften. Philosophisch-Historische Klasse, Sitzungsberichte, 250. Band, 3. Abhandlung. Wien.

—— (1964) *Erkenntnissprobleme bei Dharmakīrti*, Österreichische Akademie der Wissenschaften, Wien.

Vidyabhusan, S.Ch. (1920) *A History of Indian Logic (Ancient, Medieval and Modern Schools)*, Calcutta (rist. Delhi 1971).

Vivanti, M.P. (1985) *Il Kiraṇāgama. Testo e traduzione del Vidyāpāda*, Suppl. n.3 agli Annali dell'Istituto Orientale di Napoli, vol. 35, fasc. 2.

Wada, T. (1990) *Invariable Concomitance in Navya-Nyāya*, Delhi.

—— (1998) "Describer (nirūpaka) in Navya-Nyāya", *Annals of Bandharkar Oriental Research Institute*, 69, pp. 183-194.

—— (2001) "The analytical method of Navya-Nyāya", *Journal of Indian Philosophy*, 29, pp. 519-530.

—— (2004) "The origin of Navya-Nyāya and its place within the history of Indian logic". In: Hino, S. & Wada, T (eds.) *Professor Musashi Tachikawa's Felicitation Volume*, Delhi, pp. 439-462.

Westerhoff, J. (2006) "Nāgārjuna's catuṣkoṭi", *Journal of Indian Philosophy*, 34, pp. 367-395.

Wezler, A. (1984) "On the quadruple division of the yogaśāstra, the caturvyūhatva of the cikītsāśāstra and the 'four noble truths' of the Buddha", *Indologica Tauriniensia*, 12, pp. 289-337.

—— (1990) "Sanskrit parīkṣaka, or how ancient Indian philosophers perceived themselves", intervento presentato alla VIII World Sanskrit Conference, Vienna (unpublished).

Williams, P. (1980) "Some aspects of language and construction in the Madhyamaka", *Journal of Indian Philosophy,* 8, pp. 1-45.

—— (1981) "On the Abhidharma ontology", *Journal of Indian Philosophy,* 9, pp. 227-257.

—— (1991) "On the interpretation of Madhyamaka thought", *Journal of Indian Philosophy,* 19, pp. 191-218.

Yao, Z. (2004) "Dignāga and four types of perception". *Journal of Indian Philosophy*, 32, pp. 57-79.

Yoshimizu, Ch. (1999) "The development of *sattvānumāna* from the refutation of a permanent existent in the Sautrāntika tradition", *Wiener Zeitschrift für die Kunde Südasiens*, 43, pp. 231-254.

Yotsuya, K. (1999) *The Critique of Svatantra Reasoning by Candrakīrti and Tsong-kha-pa*, Tibetan and Indo-Tibetan Studies 8, Stuttgart.

Yunis, H. (2003) (ed.) *Written Texts and the Rise of Literate Culture in Ancient Greece*, Cambridge University Press, Cambridge.

Index 1

Concepts and general words

Abhidharma 62, 139-145, 149, 150, 219
absence of self 148
absolutism 20, 125, 133, 167
aesthetic speculation 99, 118, 222
analogy 34, 41, 46, 47, 72, 135, 181
ars politica 122
ascetic 7, 117, 126, 201
astronomy 128
atheism, atheistic 37, 82, 122
atoms 39, 65-69, 71, 74, 98, 99, 131, 147, 220
awakening 213
awareness 21, 84, 85, 88, 94, 95, 119, 120, 135, 161, 164, 165, 186, 209, 218, 223
Āyurveda 95
Bārhaspatyas 121
Bhairava 118
Bhairavatantras 118
Brahmanic 20, 23, 29, 40, 48, 61, 62, 107-109, 117, 118, 120, 121, 124, 126, 127, 130, 142, 145, 157, 158, 161, 168, 198, 202, 204, 205, 207-209
brahmin 19, 126, 129, 136, 197, 199, 207, 208
Buddhism 8, 18-20, 27, 29-31, 36, 53, 57, 58, 95, 97, 104, 107, 109, 110, 114, 118, 119, 121, 122, 126, 127, 129, 130, 134, 137-172, 190, 192, 204, 211
Buddhist 15, 17-20, 30, 31, 37, 38, 40, 42, 43, 46, 47, 49, 51, 61, 62, 65, 78, 89, 94, 96, 97, 100, 104, 107, 110, 114, 116-119, 121, 124, 126-128, 137-150, 153, 154, 157, 162, 163, 168, 170, 171, 176, 183, 185-187, 192, 204, 211, 219
categories 21, 37-41, 44, 59, 63, 64, 66, 73-75, 103, 119, 131, 176, 179
causality 32, 46, 53, 64, 69, 82, 89, 112, 113, 123, 138, 143, 144, 150, 169, 170, 182, 183, 219
causative 215, 216
Cārvākas 121, 123
Cicero 77
cognition 21, 27, 31, 35, 41, 54, 55, 64, 69, 74, 84, 90, 97, 134, 135, 143, 155, 156, 159-161, 164, 165, 170, 184-188, 212, 216-218
commentary 13, 14, 19, 21, 22, 31, 33, 35-37, 40, 44, 58-60, 72, 80-82, 85, 86, 89, 91-93, 96, 106-108, 111, 115, 136, 137, 141, 145, 149-151, 157, 159-161, 166, 169, 170, 173-179, 199, 200, 207, 210, 213
common sense 40, 103, 105, 121, 192
conceptualisation 42, 161
conjunction 60, 66, 69-71, 74, 75, 80, 98
consciousness 14, 77, 88, 94, 95, 97-100, 112, 114, 118, 119, 123,

Index 2

Indian authors and Sanskrit works

INDEX 3

Important Sanskrit words